JUST

" *TAKING STOCK* "

SIXTY YEARS IN SHOWBUSINESS

AN AUTOBIOGRAPHY
OF

CLIVE STOCK

"MR. ARCADIA"

DEDICATED TO

MY DEAREST GWEN

"Walking through life with you dear lady

has been the greatest pleasure"

Just TAKING STOCK

AN AUTOBIOGRAPHY OF

CLIVE STOCK
(MR ARCADIA)
Celebrating
60 YEARS IN SHOW BUSINESS.
As
Actor, Baritone, County Cricketer.
Director Entertainer, Freemason.
Great Grandfather.
including **The Grand Order of Water Rats.**
The Concert Artistes Association.
The Stage Cricket Club
and featuring
NORTH WALES.

First published in 2004.
Derwent Entertainments
42 St. Annes Gradens.
Llandudno, Conwy.
LL30 1SD
Tel:- 01492 573838.

E.Mail:- clivestock42@aol.com

ISBN 0-9546602.-0-X

Copyright   2003
Cover designed by ROY LANCE

Produced by
The Short Run Book Company Ltd.,
St. Stephen's House.
Arthur Road,
Windsor.
Berkshire SL4 1RY

Foreword to "Just Taking Stock", by **Roy Hudd.**

My Brother Water Rat, Clive is a throwback. A throwback to the days of the "Jobsworth". Today the list of names at the end of a film, a television programme show reads like a First World War book of remembrance. Everyone, but <u>everyone</u>, who is connected with the production is credited from the third washer up with the caterers to the highly suspicious "executive", this that and the other. Whatever "executive" means.

Clive is a throwback to the days when often the sole credit was "produced by". It referred to the person who literally produced the finished product out of thin air. He is the throwback to the days when Ivor Novello would write (words and music) direct and star in plays of his own creation. Clive knows because it was the immortal Ivor that began the love affair with the business he has given everything to (and has done every job in) – show business. Unlike todays "one trick ponies", Clive has become a specialist in everything he's tackled- the world of make believe and in real life.

How many can quote that they were a member of the concert party that inspired Peter Nicholls "Privates on Parade" and appeared on live television with Jack Hulbert and Jack Buchanan. Who else while in Australia (playing the lead in "Brigadoon") could take sixty runs off the combined terror that was Ray Lindwall and Keith Miller, appear in "Oklahoma", marry the shows first British leading lady and spend thirty seven years singing with her as half of our most popular vocal double act. Very few can say they produced (literally) a summer show for twelve years, managed and directed productions in thirteen different venues, starred in cabaret on the "Queen Mary" and the "Queen Elizabeth" played county cricket for Caernarvon, managed a top comedian and even organized and hosted Welsh Medieval Banquets——follow that.

Clive is a throwback. A genuine, one hundred per cent, old fashioned enthusiast. A man who has turned his caring hand to whatever is required, be it in entertainment, sport or, most importantly to him, charity. There is one great difference between Clive and all the other "Jack of all trades", Clive is master of them all.

Roy Hudd.

JUST TAKING STOCK...

Tommy Eyton Jones, a talented and popular North Wales journalist, kept on at me to write my autobiography, and when I said "Who would be interested in my exploits". His retort was "Think of all the stars you have worked with, and who have worked for you, and with your wonderful partner, in your well established double act. "Your involvement with star friends. .present and past, like **HOWARD KEEL, KEN DODD, TOM O'CONNOR, FRANKIE HOWARD, IVOR NOVELLO, SEMPRINI, WENDY TOYE, VIVIAN ELLIS, HARRY SECOMBE, FRANKIE VAUGHAN, RUSS CONWAY, LESLIE CROWTHER, JIMMY JAMES, SID FIELD, MARY ELLIS, NORMAN WISDOM, BRIAN REECE, KEN GOODWIN** and many others. Tommy said "What about your bosses in the early days ?". *IVOR NOVELLO, C. B. COCHRAN, GEORGE BLACK, BERNARD DELFONT, and JACK HYLTON* they started your career in the West End. What about your cricket,? with team mates and adversaries...*RAY LINDWALL, KEITH MILLER, ROHAN KANHAI, MIKE DENESS, DENIS COMPTON, ANDY SANDHAM, ALF GOVER, TONY GRIEG,* and many more.... All these people will be of interest to those born in the 30's and 40's. My response to him, was that I would think about it. Every time we met, he would say "Have you started yet ? " Sadly I would say "I have not".

On the evening and early morning, of the 24th and 25th October, 1996, respectively, the depository at Pickfords, Hoole Bridge, Chester, was burned to the ground, everything was gone. There was nothing left but charred remains, twisted metal, bent steel girders, steam rising from the horror for several days. 18 houses were gutted, parked cars melted and rendered a "write off". Over 300 people had lost all their belongings stored for safe keeping. My wife and I had lost all our possessions, every piece of memorabilia, which included seven filing cabinets of music and arrangements, costumes, photographs, press cuttings, recordings of our performances, reference books......*Everything.* On the Friday morning we could not prove that we existed with an established name and standing in show business. Having nothing, it was then I decided to write my autobiography. This should include cricket, freemasonry, local government, our career in the West End theatre, and our life in North Wales.

It came to mind that it was easy for star names to create an interest in their autobiographies, as they would write about fellow stars, and it usually turned out to be a resume of the shows they had appeared in, and their progress in our "business". I thought I would write my book not only about star names, but there should be an emphasis on lesser known performers, who were the backbone of our business, and without them, the "stars" would have no back up or support.

As an impresario, and at one time, being responsible for productions in fifteen different theatres, up and down the country, I felt I had the credentials for knowing my profession and the people in it. All that I have experienced, from playing County cricket, Grade A tennis in Australia, representing England in junior table tennis has given me a very active life, none of this I could have achieved without the support of my darling wife *Gwen Overton* (who was the first British leading lady of "Oklahoma") by my side.

Despite being a mother and home maker, she was the ideal partner to make our established, and successful singing double act, amongst the foremost of duo's.

I left school at the age of 14 and went into *Lloyds* as a junior broker, therefore my education was limited, so I apologize for this not being a great literary work, but it will be a faithful recollection of a most happy life.

Dear Reader,

I hope you enjoy this theatrical journey through nostalgia.

"What's he doing now Mother?"
(With apologies to *Norman Caley*)

Oh, *"JUST TAKING STOCK"*

" *God Bless the family*"   *Bless the Bride.*
Sir Alan Herbert & Vivian Ellis.

In 1926, King George the fifth and Queen Mary were on the
throne, Princess Elizabeth, our present Queen was born. The Great
Houdini died, *George Burns* married *Gracie Allen. Al Capone*
ruled New York and Chicago and all the Speak Easy joints with
the Mafia. The U.S.A. mourned the death of *Rudolph Valentino.*
Irving Berlin eloped with his second wife, causing one of the
biggest scandals of the era. *Monet* died and *Dr Malcolm Sargent*
was conducting the Pier Orchestra in Llandudno. *Stanley Baldwin*
was our Prime Minister. There was a General Strike and in May
Baldwin proclaimed a state of emergency. He organized
volunteers to maintain essential services, and he refused to
negotiate with labour leaders until the strike ended. Amid the
chaos, on the 29th November, I first saw the light of day. I was the
first born to Ernest Harold Stock and Dorothy Grestock. I was
christened *Noel Clive Stock.*

I was, so to speak, born "over the shop". My father was a manager
of the Hatch End branch of W.H. Smith & Sons situated at 13 The
Broadway, Hatch End, Pinner, Middlesex. Although his first name
was Ernest, he was known as Harold, a name that would crop up in
my future life. The family called him "Pop". My father had been
a prisoner of the Germans in the 14-18 war. He spent two years in
a prisoner of war camp. Being a very modest, kind and patient
man, he would never talk about his time as a prisoner. I tried very
hard to extract some of the tales and the suffering he endured, but
we could never find out anything, except the time he was
scheduled to box a German heavyweight champion. The British
boys were all under nourished, a diet of boiled potato peelings did
not give my father very much strength for the fight. On the
morning of the boxing match, Pop cut his hand on a bully beef tin,
so he was not able to fight. He would have been beaten to a pulp.

My mother was not particularly patient, she was well educated, strong and determined, quite adamant at times, and did not suffer fools gladly. Her forthrightness made sure her three children were put on the right road to know the proper way to behave. We owe a great deal to her for our education, and distinguishing right from wrong. Her positive demeanour, assurance and sense of class that came from the Grestock family, made her a "chip of the old block", the old block being her father *Richard Grestock.* He was born in Fitzroy, Melbourne, Australia. He believed that if he eliminated twenty people, he would be the Duke of Norfolk. The line was allegedly, unbroken from the Howards, at the time of King Henry the Eighth, through the Fitzherberts, Fitzallans, to the Greystokes (Tarzans' family") and on to the Grestocks. Richard was a Protestant, and had no time for the Norfolks, who were the leading British Catholic family.

In one of his many intoxicated moments, he wrote a letter to the then Duke, in very strong terms, as to what he could do with his family line. The letter was disrespectful, and after the Duke had read it, it was dispatched back to Australia, where it remained. The letter was kept in Melbourne, by one of my relations, and when I was in Melbourne I saw the letter, but I was not allowed to read it.

Looking at the family, it was uncanny the resemblance of my Uncle Ben (Mother's brother) to the then Duke. It gave credence to my Grandfather Richard's protestations. Richard was a great character, his friendship with Lord Roseberry brought about much drinking and betting on the "Gee Gees". He became one of the first members of the Jockey Club. His gambling at times could be disastrous. He liked his tipple, and on many occasions Pop used to try and keep him quiet, as he used to sing loudly, and in his exuberance he would knock the policemen's helmets off. It would be quite an escapade the journey homeward.

My father would stand him up in doorways to try and keep him out of sight, and save him from falling down...he sometimes failed, so that he would fall, and cut his head. My mother was the only one allowed to bathe his wounds and cuts, to stop the bleeding.

When my mother was born on Friday the thirteenth of May, 1902. all her father could say, with great pride.."Victor Trumper scored a brilliant century today ". He was a cricket nut, and had on occasions played for Surrey. It was also alleged, and has been referred to at numerous matches, that he bowled at W.G Grace, had him LBW, he appealed and when the Umpires finger went up, W.G. went up to the umpire and said the immortal lines "They came here to see me bat, not you bloody well umpire"

In the early days of the tube trains, Richard entered a compartment, where there was only one seat available, and a Chinese gentleman with two large bags of rice, was about to sit down at the same time as Grandfather. There followed great courtesy of "You have the seat, no you have the seat, no you, no you". Richard exasperated picked up the Chinese fellow, and threw him into the seat...the bags burst, and the rice went all over everyone nearby...."Oh calamity, it ought not to be allowed, he ought to be ashamed to look me in the face" as *Robertson Hare* would have said..

Richard's mother Charlotte Roycroft was a disciplinarian, and used to make sure all the boys, (there were six in all) were in bed by 9.30 p.m. The last one in was to blow out the candle by her bed. Richard bribed the maid regularly to blow the candle out for him. I should think he gave his mother great torment. I was brought up on colourful stories about my grandfather. Being young, I thought of him as a romantic type of hero. My grandmother did not have such fond memories of any type of hero.

The Stock dynasty began to grow. In 1929 my dear sister Beryl was born, my brother Brian arrived a year later, we were then known as the B.B.C....Beryl, Brian and Clive. We moved from Hatch End, Pinner to Kenton, Harrow, Middlesex.

My father had the unenviable task of cycling from Kenton to the shop in Hatch End, six days a week. He would cycle on his Hercules with the 28 inch wheels in all weathers. The one redeeming feature was that he did not have to get ready, the morning papers, that was to come later. As a manager of a W.H. Smith & Sons' shop he was responsible for the smooth running, and also the complete stock.

Growing up, was like so many other families, predictable and sometimes to read about it, very boring. It was very obvious that I was not a scholar. Sport took over my interests and activities. At my primary school, I was captain of the Greens, each squad was named by colour. I would always win the egg and spoon, without using the chewing gum under the egg. Having procured the largest sack, I would "run" and win the sack race, and the hundred yards, as it was then, was always mine. My school work was poor. I didn't even pass the matriculation for the secondary school. Apart from sport, my life was mainly spent in Church. The Clergy at St. Leonards, took a great interest in me. I was put through confirmation by the time I was eight years of age. In hindsight, I was far too young. The Fathers were keen to send me to Mirfield to eventually take up Holy Orders. This was not queried by my parents, as they made regular attendance at the church. I joined the cubs and became a Sixer of the Red pack, going on to become Troop Leader with three yellow rings round my arm.

St. Leonards church was to become a church hall, and a brand new church was to be built. After choir practice we caused a lot of trouble playing in the foundations. It was like an obstacle course.

4

Building materials all over the place, dodging night-watch men, trying to manoeuvre the large railway sleepers, and planks over pools of water. We had our own Krypton Factor, with the mass of jungle in the foundations. St. Mary the Virgin, became a spanking new spacious place of worship.

The church and all it stood for, took over my existence. At home in the dining room, my sister and I had our own service. I procured large sheets and draped them in such a way that they looked like priest's vestments. With a tea cosy shaped like a Mitre on my head. My sister Beryl using her skipping rope, which had ball bearings in the handles making a chinking sound, swung the Incense holder. On the wall was a very large picture of a stag (The Monarch of the Glen). We used to genuflect to this picture, and this became our altar. We made up our own prayers and order of service. I suppose the bowing and clothes in church were a prelude to the theatre and costumes in my mind. Singing in the choir, four times Sundays, and choir practice three nights a week, it all became second nature to me. In the choir, we were paid for special services, and always extra for weddings, funerals, and the Easter period. Starched white collars, black cassocks and black bows, Red cassocks and white ruffs for Easter.

The vestments of our clergy at St. Mary's were magnificent. They had special sets for the festivals. The Easter set was superb. Having three Curates and a Vicar, the three sets were in Gold and Crimson velvet, Father Johnson, the Vicar, wore the same colours but a different shape. The overall picture was like the Cathedral scene in Max Reinhardt's "The Miracle" with Massine. Looking at the clergy at Easter impressed me and made a lasting memory for all time.

The only entertainment we had in those days was the wireless. The music was melodious, and we as a family enjoyed to the fill those dance bands. Jack Payne, Carroll Gibbons, Jack Hylton, Ambrose

5

and the master Henry Hall. Even now I remember "This *is* Henry Hall speaking" and the strains of "Its Just The Time For Dancing", and the sign off "Here's To The Next Time". Henry Hall took over the BBC Dance Orchestra in 1932, and this is the year I became a real fan of his programme. Henry Robert Hall learnt his music in the Salvation Army band near Peckham, where he was born. He played cornet and concertina. The public took him to their hearts for over thirty years, through radio and then a huge success in television.

In 1936 I became an avid supporter of the Arsenal Football Club. A support I have given for the whole of my life. I was taken to Highbury by a group of blokes. as a lucky mascot, as for years I had not seen the "Gunners" lose.

Sometime around 1934, Henry Hall and his orchestra came to Kenton to play a cricket match against Kenton Cricket Club. It was well advertised with Henry (who enjoyed his cricket) Dan Donovan, who was his lead singer, George Elrick, (Mrs Elrick's wee son George) who was his drummer, (he latter became our agent), This cricket match I was getting excited about. My favourite game with my favourite orchestra. The day came, all the family were going. The ground was barely five minutes away. In the morning I was obviously in a defiant mood, and I did something contrary to my parents' wishes. My mother said "If you do that again, you will not go to the cricket match". Well, I did do it again and repeated my indiscretion. I was now not going to the match. Tears and tantrums ensued, but no matter how I pleaded, no cricket match, they all went out and left me on my own, the one who was mad about the game, and the band, was left behind.

I was so furious I went upstairs to my parents' bedroom, found some scissors and proceeded very slowly to cut off all my hair in the front of my head. When they all returned full of their enjoyment of the match, they saw me and the mess I had made of my hair. There was hell to pay. Mother commanded that I went and got the stick from the hall stand, and she then proceeded to give six of the best on each hand. Two lessons were learned that day. For my parents...don't leave the boy, on his own again, and for me... don't let mother wield the stick.

We had a nice sized garden big enough for Pop to mark out a badminton court with blanco chalk lines. We had many good games, with the exception of mother who did not like sports of any kind, so she never wanted to be included. At the bottom of the garden there was a patch of clear ground devoid of any grass. It always seemed to be flat and dry. I am sure we had better summers in those days.. I erected two uprights with a bar across the top, like the proscenium of a stage. The day I put sheets up as tabs (curtains) and pulled the chord down so as the tabs drew up to the middle of the crossbar, you would have thought I had invented something new. Of course we three, Beryl, Brian and Clive would enact plays of our own making, and the scripts "what I wrote", always had a religious theme.

It was then that my dormant ambition was kindled. I was definitely egotistical, and always in the forefront of everything that was going on. Captain at games, solo boy in church, troop leader of the cubs. and then patrol leader in the Scouts, Captain of the cricket and football team and so on. I suppose that if I had failed at all the facets of my life at that time, it would have been a very different story. The church was calling and it seemed to be a foregone conclusion that there I should have a career.

My sister Beryl was very forthright and strong, like her mother. We used to fight like all brothers and sisters, although we had great respect for each other. Beryl did very well at all her pursuits. My brother was studious, and found learning a slow business, but he became successful in latter life, through a great deal of hard work.

7

As I mentioned my father, who we called "Pop", was responsible at W.H. Smith & Sons for everything in the shop, and it transpired that stock was going missing, and Pop would have to make up the deficiency. The staff knew the culprit, but could not catch him, this was beginning to pray on my father's mind as the losses were increasing and he could not afford to keep paying out. He eventually resigned. He did not tell us as children what had happened, he carried on as though he was still going to the shop. It must have been a very worrying and painful time for him. Being involved with Newspapers, Books and Stationery he belonged to a monthly publication called "The Bookseller" An advertisement requiring an experienced person to manage one shop and supervise three other venues in the London area, came to my fathers' notice. A Doctor Gainsborough owned the shops, and he knew absolutely nothing about the business. Pop had the arduous task of putting proper systems into each branch, and he would soon have the day to day operations running smoothly, especially in the headquarters shop at West Hampstead, which he was to manage. The shop had living accommodation above, consisting of one room as an Office, three bedrooms, one lounge and utility room and kitchen on the ground floor, and a deep basement. This was to be our living quarters. The family now had to move from a small house in a relatively quiet area, to a busy London suburb. On arriving in this three storied building, we were not too impressed. My sister particularly seemed miserable........no garden.

A suitable church was picked out for us, and our parents took us to a service to see if we all were going to like it. Having experienced the service, they decided it was suitable for us. St. James was the nearest "high" church about a mile away. "We Three ", to quote Harry Korris, went to church without our parents, completely unaccompanied. I being the eldest appointed in charge. We were not keen on the church, probably because we had loved our Kenton church so much, we played truant, as it were.

8

We did this for three Sundays, and then we were rumbled. A customer came into the shop saying, she had seen Pop's nice children playing on the green, Sunday afternoon. Mother was more than displeased, she was raging. When we returned, the cricket bat was taken to my backside. So hard was the stroke, dust flew out of my trousers. Sister Beryl laughed to see the dust arising, so the bat was then taken to her bottom, so from laughter to tears in a very short time. Hampstead with its old fashioned houses set close together, was so much dirtier than Kenton and having no garden for us to play in, was a real tragedy.

Pop got stuck into his task and started to get the shops viable. We three were enrolled into new schools. Beryl and Brian went to Emmanuel School, this belonged to the church nearby, where we all went, although as mother would say "low church". I went to Fleet Central at Gospel Oak, a short train journey on the North London line. This was a London Central school of high standard, with a very successful reputation.

The trains were old and had sliding doors at the end of each carriage. While the train was on the move I would climb out of the carriage through the sliding door, and then I would cross over to the next carriage. It was very dangerous, more so, when going through the tunnels. One day I came quickly in the second carriage, I bumped into a well dressed lady who immediately asked "what school did I go to", not thinking, I gave her my correct school, what a fool I was. Later the headmaster invited my mother to the school to hear about this daring and highly foolish escapade. My mother attended to the office of Headmaster Millward, and I was sent for. I was in a cookery class, as my woodwork was so poor. My drawings were very good, but the practical side was a disaster. My work was always planed down to half the size, so I was foisted on the Domestic Science class...In fear and trembling I was led to the Headmaster's room. As I entered the room in full Chef's hat and apron etc., I struck a pose.

My mother, headmaster and form master all burst into laughter at this poor man's fugitive from "Ready Steady Cook". Needless to say having broken the tense atmosphere with a laugh, I only received a telling off.

There were five Central schools in London, Fleet Central was the nearest for me. My school work began to improve, I knuckled down, studied much harder than ever before. With specialist teachers for specialist subjects, it seemed easier to learn. There was good sport, I liked this school.

It was not long before I became top boy, and did particularly well in French. I couldn't beat the top girl, she was very bright. My form master was the sports master, his speciality was cricket. I tuned into him. His name was Galloway, he was known as "cough". I never knew his first name. I was chosen to go to Lords for coaching. As Neville Cardus said :- *"LORDS the home of cricket, The pavilion seems the Valhalla of the game. the home of heroes of the past. Every cricketer would give years of his life to have the honour of a century at Lords, or of a superb bowling performance"* I didn't get a century there, but managed 91 in the middle in a London boys game, LBW to Trevor Bailey. "Barnacle Bailey, went on to play for Essex and England with great application and success. He played in over 60 Test matches for his country, what a fine ambassador for the game.!
I was sent for a trial to Lords, together with Claude Manning (Bowler) George Samuels (Batsman), I was the all rounder. We were coached by Denis Compton for batting and Laurie Gray for bowling, Denis Compton (1918-1997) was the cavalier of batting, his records are legendary, he was the most charismatic cricketer of all time...playing for Middlesex. He played outside left for the Arsenal, and 11 times for England at football. He would put a sixpenny piece on the off stump, if we hit it, we had the sixpence. I never had a penny.

He taught us well, the fundamentals were paramount, his basis was security at the wicket, but you were not to lose your natural shots. I owe so much to Denis, for I had his teachings in my ears for years to come especially when I eventually played County Cricket. Our duties extended to bowling at the M.C.C members and selling score cards. 1938 was a good year for me, into 1939 my batting was improving considerably, and the bowling developed. I was soon swinging the ball both ways, especially with an old ball, I was very quick between the wickets and like the Stock family of all generations, a very safe pair of hands. It was all going too well. September was drawing nigh, and on the 3rd September, War was declared and hostilities began. Off we went with our little gas masks on shoulders, a case, and the label on our blazer. Our parents were distraught and we were heartbroken at our departure to EVACUATION from the city. The war against Germany had commenced. My brother and sister were sent to Bedford. My sister took charge of my brother, and made sure they were not separated. A Mr & Mrs Cartwright cared for them with great affection and excellent guardianship. They were happy and stayed 18 months. Yours truly was sent to Ashwell, Nr Oakham in Rutand. Six of us were billeted in the rectory, inhabited by the Canon of Peterborough Cathedral, Canon Roberts was a kindly man, and he had a very attractive daughter. "Cough" was with us. We all fancied the daughter, but what chance, we were only twelve years of age, no chance, "Cough" was nearer her age, but he did not get to first base.

These digs were marvellous, the food was first class, we were comfortable, a lovely 20 year old brunette looking after us, how lucky we were. We did not feel that there was a war on at all. After a few weeks of lessons and games, I had a very uneasy feeling about my Grandmother, "Mum" as we called her. She had not been too well before I left home, and I had a strong premonition that she was going to die.

This feeling was very strong and I felt she had not got long. I, without warning to anyone, caught a train from Oakham to London. I was thinking on the journey about all the kindness and help Mum had given me. She tried so hard to teach me to play the piano, one of my great regrets, I always put up excuses. She took me to the Lyceum pantomimes, those great productions with huge casts, transformation scenes, revolving stage with trap doors, 24 rats in "Dick Whittington" A sixpenny programme with all the script and lyrics, photographs of George Jackley, Naughton & Gold, Clarkson Rose, and the Harlequinade at the end, with Charlie Austin. Mum had given me the complete enjoyment of LIVE entertainment. I owed her...the memories of visits to her at 50 Riffel Road, Cricklewood.

The large mirrored side board and inside beautifully bound books. I would open the left hand door. and find a book that intrigued me. in exquisitely bound leather. Inside I was fascinated by the poem:- :-

> **Ben Battle was a soldier bold.**
> **He used to wars and alarms.**
> **A Cannon Ball took off his legs,**
> **And he lay down his arms.**

There was a Hogarth engraving of Ben Battle with the cannon ball taking off his legs. This scared me, but I was always drawn to that page. I would find the book every time I visited. A morbid imagination of death.

When I reached home I found Mum was very ill, within the week she passed away. My premonition was a little scary, although I was only 12 years old, according to my mother, that day I grew up. Amidst the grief I tried to look after all the family who were there, and generally taking a more adult attitude to the very sad occasion. It was a very sombre time, but I loved being home.

The Headmaster was very displeased that I had run away, and ruled that I should have a little more time for my grief, and then return to Ashwell. My grandmother had died on the 3rd October, 1939 and the thought of returning and being away from home once again, filled me with more grief, especially with Christmas not far away. During my stay at home our doctor had discovered that I had Oxalic Crystals. For these symptoms, I was on a very strict diet. No sugar, no eggs, no apples, nothing with acid, and we were on rations at that time. It was misery. I had to return to Rutland,

I was duly dispatched to the station, but this time I took my bicycle with me. My return to Ashwell, was unhappy for me, I realized how much I missed mother and pop. The first night at new digs was unbearable. In the very early morning I said to the lady, who was kindness itself, that I thought she would find it difficult to feed me because of the strict diet for my crystals. I had made up my mind that I was not staying, and I piled on the different types of food I was forbidden to eat. Eventually I was triumphant, and I said I did not want to put her to so much trouble, and I thought it better if I left. I wasted no time, I said goodbye and thanked her for her kindness (I had had a good breakfast) and off I cycled back to Hampstead. It took a lot out of me, as it was a long way. All I thought about, was that I was going home, and this spurred me on.

Mother was not surprised to see me return home, she had felt it all along from my general demeanour, before I left. I was home. There was now going to be the most awful row with the Headmaster, who demanded my return. Mother had other ideas, I would not return. Through the education licensing laws, children had to be educated, so mother found an emergency school. It was Harben Emergency School in Netherwood Street, not a very nice neighbourhood. It was rough and tough. Keep your head down and out of trouble was the order of the day. The education was poor, there was no class and the standards were rock bottom.

One chink of light was the meeting of Arnold Towler. He was like me a boy soprano, or treble as we were called. He was a very fine left handed table tennis player, so he and I spent most of the time on the table tennis table. Because of his very strong left handed forehand delivered at speed to my backhand, I became a very strong backhanded player, so much so that I entered the London Junior championship for the under fifteens. This was in May 1940. Good fortune settled on me, I won. As my name was to the fore with the hierarchy of London table tennis, I was picked as understudy for the National Junior team. It's an ill wind etc., the No 4 was ill, so I played for England. I beat my counterpart in Scotland and Wales, but lost to Northern Ireland.

Mother did not like the Harben School, as I was not learning and I was picking up bad habits, she immediately sent me to Clark's College at Cricklewood. My parents could not afford it, but that was a trifling once mother had made up her mind. The schooling was first class, it was all lessons. A half an hour every morning for spelling, and half an hour for handwriting. No time for sports at all.

Outside school I was still playing table tennis. I would go to the theatre where *Viktor Barna* was appearing with *Alec Brooke,* I would come out of the audience and play *Barna* , who had been world champion more than 14 times. It was fun. we would play up to 11 points, and my backhand flick used to give him trouble, of course I never won. The audience thought it entertaining to see a little boy flying round the table.

When my brother and sister returned from evacuation, we managed to live with the bombs that started to rain down on us at regular intervals. The shop being three storied, had a very deep basement, and we used it as a shelter, we had beds down there to house five of us, and in addition, 2 dogs and 6 cats. Over where the coalhole was, the cats had made a toilet, and the smell of amonia was rife.

The spaniel, although a gun dog, would only bark if a bomb dropped close by. He felt the vibration underneath him. The air raid warning would go, and off we would troop to our shelter in the basement for we hoped would be a good night's sleep. It was seldom that the night went by without incident. There was no pattern to the bombing. The Germans went for the City, and smaller suburbs periodically. There was continued noise from the mobile Beaufort guns. They went round the streets, they seemed right outside our building, but it was not the case, as they were in three or four streets away. The streets were lined with shrapnel, and we all collected this up, until the novelty wore off. Close by in Compayne gardens, *Jack Warner, Albert Sandler and Turner Layton* lived. Turner was the very talented singer and pianist of the double act *Layton & Johnstonne.* Clarence Johnstone ran off with the wife of Albert Sandler, but that's another story.

Turner Layton's house was bombed cleanly, it took the three storied house completely away. All that was left on view, was the bath still hanging to the wall on the second floor. The public came to visit in their hundreds, including myself. Many celebrities lived in our area. Rex Harrison & Lili Palmer, Conrad Veidt, Cyril Stapleton and many others.

Bombing raids were the order of the day, and bombs fell around us all the time. Across the road from our shop, was the large corner house of Dr Alfred Gunasekara, he was a very popular doctor, and he came from Ceylon. He was a very excellent tennis player in his home country, and his brother, Doctor Hector Gunasekara played cricket for the M.C.C. Alfred was married to a tyrannical Irish lady who took him to the cleaners. He would often come across the road to see Pop, and leave money with him so Carmel his wife could not get her hands on it. There were rows galore.

One day after a raid, two ladies were standing outside looking up at a stained glass window of the doctors' house. One said to the other, "look what the shrapnel did last night" there was a rounded protruding swelling of the stain glassed window, the glass was still in tact. Duffy, who was the odd job man for the doctor said "Its the first time I have seen shrapnel come from the inside.", Evidently, Carmel had thrown a tin helmet at the doctor, he ducked and it hit the window.

Alfred would often come over and have a cup of tea, all by himself. Carmel would not know where he was. Doctor Alfred was a popular man, and my mother thought he was the "cat's whiskers". Most of his patients felt sorry for him, they thought he had a hard time, and he did. There were many doctors in the area. There was a Dr. Redhouse who always looked dirty, with a cigarette hanging out of his mouth and crumpled suits. The unanimous opinion, was that he was the cleverest doctor in the neighbourhood. There were characters around, and the sense of humour helped to bring us through the bombing.

On one occasion, there was a stick of thirteen bombs dropped across diagonally, and each one was getting nearer the house. My bedroom was on the top floor, the family were calling for me to come down. When the fourth bomb fell, I was off, and reached the basement by the time the eighth bomb fell. The thirteenth of the stick of bombs hit a block of flats opposite my uncle's basement flat. It was though the block of flats had been hoisted upwards and hurled at my uncle's abode.. We had not the slightest idea of what happened. An hour later there was a knock at the door, and there was my Auntie Nell and Uncle Ben, bedraggled and covered in plaster. My uncle declaimed "We have bbbbeen bbbblown to bbbuggery". He was very agitated as his main worry was the loss of his maroon slipper, he wore as "Othello". He had found one, but the other was missing.

An actor in the family.

I went through to the debris and rummaged around, much to the disdain and disgust of the firemen, and I found the other slipper, I gave it to him, and you would have thought I had given him a million pounds. My Uncle Ben was a very keen amateur actor. Unfortunately, he had a very pronounced stutter. Every time we went to see him, and it was always a Shakespearean play with him in the lead, we would sit and feel a cold sweat coming on in case he would breakdown and stutter. My mother had been worrying ever since she was a girl, the whole family would have to go and see him. Despite the portrayal of long roles, such as "Hamlet" "Richard the Third etc.," he never broke down.

I was now just over thirteen and a half years old and my voice broke. From a strong treble, I was to become a Bass. A medical examination was arranged to see if I should be able to sing straight away. Normally boys should not sing in an adult voice until around 19 years of age. My bits and pieces were all in the proper place. It was suggested I could sing, but not to put too much weight on the voice. Mr. Kyrle-Adkins was allegedly a singing teacher, and he lived at the top of the road. Off I went to have lessons, training on scales and songs. The teaching didn't do much for me, but I did acquire a huge repertoire. One big mistake was to learn the whole of the oratorio "Elijah" at the age of fourteen. The voice was strong, and I thought I was marvellous, but on reflection the quality was "woofy" and uninteresting..

I remember one summer night, I rode my bicycle to the Golders Green Hippodrome, I paid for a seat in the circle to see "The Student Prince" an operetta by Sigmund Romberg. Romberg had written many tuneful musicals including "The Desert Song" "New Moon" and "Blossom Time". Romberg came from Hungary and was educated musically in Vienna. He settled in the U.S.A. in 1909, and was the first to introduce dance bands into restaurants.

I was entranced with the production of the "Prince" and the wonderfully tuneful melodies sung by first class singers. The leading man was outstanding, he outshone everyone else on stage. He had an extremely good singing voice, a fine actor with a rich speaking sound and a high baritone quality par excellence.

His name was *Harry Welchman.* a fine performer and good looks to match. He sang top A flats with ease, whereas most baritones struggled , even if they could reach a top G. The role of "Karl Franz" by this outstanding artist, had such an effect on me, that I was determined to be another Harry Welchman. He had of course been the original "Red Shadow" in "The Desert Song".

Everything about the production was magical, and I came out of the theatre on air, singing those lovely songs. My ambitions were only dreams, and when I told my mother of my aspirations, she very quickly arranged for me to go to Clark's College in Cricklewood, for a proper education. I think the thought of me seriously thinking of a career on stage, was not in her plans for me. The precarious theatre profession, was for others, not for her boy. Learn your lessons and get a proper job. After the memory of the "Prince" had died down, I joined a training organization for young boys, who wanted to go into the Air Force.

The Air Training Corps was becoming very popular in London, so I joined the 48F Squadron. The first 50 Squadrons had an F after their number, to show that they were a founder Squadron. Our unit grew quickly, so we formed a new Squadron No, 2088.. The headquarters was situated at the top of our road, being very convenient. I formed a football team from the unit, and with the exception of beating our old Squadron No 48, we lost every match in 1941. The following year we won the league with the same team. I have never understood the reversal. During this time I was selected to play centre half for the London ATC for a season.

18

Apart from colour charts, aircraft recognition and other Air Force details, we got together (in more ways than one) with the Girls Training Corps. and presented the pantomime "Cinderella". John Redmond, Bill Alexander and Flight/Lt Mark Freeman produced the show. They all had professional experience. Mark Freeman was the manager of the Odeon, Swiss Cottage.

He called Flight/Sgt Clifford Gould to partner me in playing the "Broker's Men". Freeman had a whole routine with patter and business for a very strong spot in the middle of the first half. He rehearsed us night after night at the Odeon, until we had a very polished double. It was quite hilarious. The first time we rehearsed in front of the rest of the cast the night before dress rehearsal, the cast not only creased themselves with laughter, but were completely taken by surprise at the polish and the ability we had for getting laughs, this was due entirely to Mark Freeman. The show played at the Rudolph Steiner Hall in Baker Street, and was an instant success. Cliff and I stole all the notices, and it was then I knew that the stage was for me.

As a contrast, at the age of thirteen and three quarter years, I was engaged by a firm of Lloyds Insurance Brokers, by the name of CHANDLER, HARGREAVES & WHITTALL. My Uncle Ben, who was apt to invent all sorts of odd names, called them "Hothwaite, Widdoshins and Piddle". I was engaged in the Marine Department to begin with. From the observations of my colleagues in 1941, I used to do impressions of all the partners, especially their walks. Mr Johnson, who was the General Manager, had an unusual sombre voice. He would come out of his office and say "There's rather a lot of noise going on out here", then duck back into his office. During that period I was into classical music, and I remember picking up some of the melodies of the symphonies and piano concertos, these I would whistle loudly around the office. His head would come out of his office, and he would say "There's rather a lot of Tchaikovsky going on out here".

"Johnny! As we called him, would then pop back into his den. The main office became the focal point of all the staff, and the clerks and typists would gather to observe me sprawled out over the desks doing the "Death of Nelson", as dear Sid Field would have said "What a performance?"

Hargreaves and Major Whittall were still alive, Chandler had departed this life, without seeing my death of Nelson. Whether it was because I was a little over the top, and therefore I found it my natural bent to get on with people. Major Whittall had me transferred to his department, the Non Marine. He had me join him in the famous Lloyd's underwriting room as a Junior Broker. It was a job of high prestige, and I soon had a good rapport with the underwriters. Major Whittall came to me one day with twenty thousand tons of rum to cover, he had covered already a hundred thousand tons, and he said to me "See if some of those mates you seem to have acquired, can cover the rest of the risk", so off I trotted into the big room where every risk in the world was covered. I begged and coerced, and finally came back triumphant with all the rum covered. It was a very good job, and I liked the rush and bustle. The friendly atmosphere, without any back biting was very pleasant.

One weekend there was a tremendous air raid, and coming into the office on the Monday morning, I turned right into the street where our offices were, and... there was no street, it had been flattened to the ground. New offices had to be found. All the business that had been transacted during the week, would be taken to Ruislip, to our out of town office. On a rota, we took turns in transporting the documents by train. On the return to London we had the benefit of an extra long lunch hour. This enabled us to head for the snooker hall, and play for much longer than the time allowed. Inevitably we were caught, Bill Tamplin had guessed we were playing in the firm's time, and duly arrived and stopped all future games.

Around this time there was a full scale R.A.F. concert presented at the Gaumont State, Kilburn. This theatre, was a 3000 seater, and purported to be the largest theatre in Europe. The cast included the full Central Band of the Royal Air Force, the Squadronaires, a 70 strong choir, with soloists and instrumentalists and yours truly in ATC uniform singing Elgar's "Pomp & Cricumstance No 4." "The Song of Liberty", with Sidney Torch on the Wurlitzer playing for me. It was nerve racking, looking out at the Exit signs, that were all lit up, it looked like a skyscraper. I felt like a Lilliputian on this vast stage. It was great, but the bombs were falling.

My main interest was to present concerts for the Red Cross. They included the appearance of some of the pupils that went to my singing teacher, and with the help of my table tennis friend Arnold Towler, I took on church halls and raised funds for the very worthy cause. At fifteen years of age, an entrepreneurial flair seemed to have entered my character. These presentations were a stimulus, and I was obviously biding my time for a performing career. I didn't have to wait long, as in March 1943 my dear father found an advert in "The Stage Newspaper" wanting singers for the first revival of the great Jerome Kern's "Show Boat" in the West End.

I went along to the Stoll Theatre in the Kingsway at 10.30 a.m. and by 11.30 a.m. I had signed an Esher Standard Contract as a chorister in this lovely melodious show. I sang 16 bars of "The Yeoman of England" and this suited the management, and rehearsals were to start at 2 p.m. There was a problem...How do we inform my insurance firm, that I would not be returning at all. That I had commenced a new career, and I would not be back with the Lloyds of London........My mother wrote one of those letters that only a mother can write about her son, saying that rehearsals started straight away. Most people would say that giving up a secure job in a highly respectable and prestigious firm was rather irresponsible, in favour of a very precarious position.

From the first rehearsal I was mesmerized by the magic of show business. I had now the unique opportunity of proceeding with an exciting profession. I was very aware that I was lucky to have the chance, and that the timing was spot on. It was obvious to me that although the war had curtailed my career as a cricketer, it was fortuitous for me to be in the present situation. At the age of 16 it was very unlikely to go in to a West End musical, but because better singers had been called up for service in the forces, the chance had come my way. The opportunity had arisen for me to make the most of my talents. I was young and a quick study, and I hoped to learn from the performers in the show around me. At rehearsal I applied one hundred per cent attention to my learning of the score of the beautiful music of *Jerome Kern.*

Being wrapped up in the music, I had a few moments of reflection. Was I taking the right road for my future. ?. From security to a complete precarious and unpredictable way of life. "Go for it" I said to myself. The professional career was about to start, I was now ready for.............................

Sixteen years of age

and making my debut

in the West End in

1943.

"Life Upon The Wicked Stage"   *Show Boat.*
Oscar Hammerstein   Jerome Kern.

Show Boat The Stoll Theatre, Kingsway, London, 1943. was
presented by **Prince Littler,** a very busy theatre owner in many
cities in Britain. The show was to be a stop gap, before a new
production to follow. It was thought that two months would be the
maximum run, but even with the heat wave, it ran over five
months.

The show included six Australians in the cast including :-
**Malcolm McEachern, Sylvia & Leslie Kellaway, Lucille
Benstead, Gwyneth Lascelles, & W. S.Percy.** The leading man
was **Bruce Carfax,** a very experienced juvenile lead, with a good
lyric tenor voice, good looks and very wavy hair. Bruce was an
experienced character, his main fetish was on a saturday night, go
to the pub at the top of Kingsway, get drunk and then sing with
Gigli. The landlord put on records of the great tenor singing
operatic arias, while Bruce would try and keep up with the top
notes. I used to worry, that, not only would he fail in reaching the
notes, but that he would strain his voice and not be able to sing on
the following Monday. This did happen once or twice. **Leslie &
Sylvia Kellaway,** were the niece and nephew of **Cecil Kellaway,**
the very lovable Hollywood film actor. They were excellent
dancers and acrobats.
Playing the part of "Julie" was **Pat Taylor.** Pat was one of the
better dance band vocalists and was ideal for the singing of "Bill",
a very popular number. Pat was one of **Jack Hylton's** many girl
friends. Jack had many voluptuous ladies over the years. It was
alleged that Pat was the one who had his baby, and made her future
safe. I used to play cricket on the top of the theatre roof, which
was a large area of bitumen. Pat used to come up to sunbath, we
were enjoying a heat wave, and it was the first time in my life, that
I had seen ladies breasts, Pat loved to be topless. The musical
director was **Reginald Burston,** and the play was produced by an
American, **James Moran.**

We had an orchestra of 35 players, Coloured singers and dancers
both male and female, boasting a cast of just over a hundred, and
this was wartime. The Stoll Theatre was very large, and sported a
very spacious rehearsal room at the top of the theatre. It was built
as an Opera House, by Oscar Hammerstein's Grandfather.

Malcolm McEachern known as "Mr. Jetsam" played the part of
Joe (Originally played by Paul Robeson). He was well known as
"Mr Jetsam" as he partnered **B.C. Hilliam,** in the established
double act of **Flotsam & Jetsam.** They were never off the radio.
You could say they were the original **Flanders & Swann.**

I used to go home after the second show, (It was twice daily, and a
three hour show), with Malcolm. poor old lad, he had to "black up"
for nearly ten hours, and in the heat wave, he was a grease spot, by
the end of the day.. The highlight of the show, was of course, "Ol
Man River", which he sang a third down from the original key. On
the train after the show, we were joined by **Syd Walker,** another
radio favourite of "Mr. Walker wants to know" and I used to listen
to all the stories of their experiences. Malcolm told me many tales
of Oratorio and his duets with the fine baritone, **Harold Williams.**
Recordings of these two, I had in my collection. Malcolm was a
true Basso Profondo.

The singing of "Ol Man River" was a highlight, as it was with
Robeson. Instead of starting the chorus on a bottom G, Malcolm
would commence on a bottom E flat, showing off his wonderful
bass quality. He stopped the show regularly. B.C. Hilliam used to
visit the show while on leave from the RAF, he was a Squadron
Leader, and I would meet him with Malcolm, and I would learn all
about summer show business, he wrote lyrics and sketches for
many famous shows.

I wonder how many reading this account, alive today will
remember their opening :-

We'll tell you our names in case someone forgets em.
I'm Jetsam, I'm Flotsam, He's Flotsam, He's Jetsam.
We want to be recognised by anyone who spotsam.
I'm Flotsam, I'm Jetsam, He's Jetsam, He's Flotsam.
Flotsam and Jetsam as kind pay for lotsam
The songs sung by Jetsam, are written by Flotsam.
I sing all the low notes, You wonder how he getsam,
If the keyboard is Flotsam, so I must be Jetsam.
Yours very sincerely.....Flotsam and Jetsam.

I'm sure dear reader, some will remember the tune.

W.S. Percy, known as Billy, lived a few yards away from me, so
we became good friends, and he gave me many tips on the
problems of the theatre, and the temptations therein. They were
thrust in front of me...Girls.. I was very fond of a girl named
Dorothy Perkins, "Dot" as she was called. She did not give me a
second glance. I suppose a 16 year old boy was so much younger
than a 16 year old girl. I earned the great sum of £6. ten shillings
for 12 shows a week, but this was more than I was earning at
Lloyds, and after all I was living at home...and *single.*

It was an education, and I soon learned that chorus girls in those
days, had much older men as boyfriends. The men were usually on
the plump side and loaded with money. I often wondered how
lovely ladies could go with rich, fat, plain looking men. The
answer of course was simple.....financial security. I also learned
very quickly about homosexuals. In those days they were
called "Queers", and everything about them was said to be "camp"
In "Show Boat" we had only a few of these fellows.
Because of the war, our male singers were a real three pennyworth
of liquorice allsorts. They were all shapes and sizes, varying ages,
and quality of voices.

25

At the end of the show, we had a sextet with "Kim", the daughter of Magnolia and Gaylord Ravenal. We looked a motley crew. In my mind, if you cannot look smart and elegant in white tie and tails, then you will always look untidy. Bert Davenport, was a bass with a very strong voice. As a 16 year old I could not guess his age, but he seemed ancient. He was untidy, dirty, slovenly and scruffy. He put his make up lines on with a match stick, and to see him in his tails was reminiscent of "Almost a Gentleman" **Billy Bennett.** He was a lovely old Music Hall comic, with his tails too big for him, big boots, a big moustache. He would say "It was dirty night and a dirty trick, and his pants came off in the Atlantic". He did the "Boom Boom" type of gags.

Bert with his trousers down over his boots, was bordering on the comical. **Alan Darling** was a tall good looking, smart homosexual, with very little voice. **Don Weston,** my best friend, was six foot two with a fine bass voice, **Couth Griffiths,** a bass baritone of uncertain age, and pleasant countenance. **Lewis Ogden,** a tenor with a thin quality, and a little on the podgy side, roughly 50 years of age, and two others, I don't remember. In hindsight, looking from the audience, the sextet must have seemed an incongruous sight.

Working on a very wide stage with full orchestra for the first time in my life, was thrilling and exciting. Although there were set movements to the number "Dance Away The Night", I found that I was able to perform my own personality on the choreography, and was allowed to get away with it.

In the second half of the show, there was a number called "Dahomey", this was set in a tribal village. All the coloured men were supposed to take part, and the principal dancer was *Mathias Vroom.* Mathias was a real live Zulu, and when he started to rehearse, the routine being a real Zulu tribal dance, the rest of the coloured chorus, not being Zulus, refused to perform.

So Mathias danced the routine as a solo. He was electric. He received an ovation for his talent. He was a fine looking man with a good voice, so it was natural that he understudied Joe, and he didn't have to "Black up". In the lyric of the song, it read "Niggers all work on the Mississippi", so this was changed to "Darkies".

In the chorus was a fine mezzo-soprano named *Anna Pollak.* It was not surprising she became a well known principal at Covent Garden. *Gwyneth Lascelles* played "Magnolia". A very sweet lady with a strong Australian voice. She had played leads in Australia, and had accumulated experience. When the run of the show ended, I went to see her as Principal Boy in pantomime at the Chiswick Empire. Gwyneth invited me to tea after the matinee, and to my surprise *Nellie Wallace* joined us. I began to savour the very warm personality of the Music Hall. Nellie started her career as a clog dancer, and was one of the first female dames in pantomime. She was as funny off stage as she was on. Although with her for just a short time, her prominent teeth and her idiosyncratic way of talking, had me in stitches.

When "Show Boat" came to an end, I was heartbroken, I cried buckets. The whole experience had been so happy with all the people, and I was going to miss them very much. One or two of them, I would surely see again. Reggie Burston was someone who was to play a very important part in my life to come. This was to happen five years later.

I was now out of work and had little idea of what was to come. How do I make things happen. I heard of an audition for a new show at the Phoenix Theatre. Don, Couth and I went along to sing at the audition. When we arrived at the theatre, the pianist was *Harold Purkiss.* "Purky" had been the rehearsal pianist for "Show Boat", so we felt very much at home, although we were very nervous. It was like starting all over again. We had been safe for a few months, and the thought of auditioning for a new management was a little scary. We had the audition and were asked to come back, this had been for the Musical Director, to sort out voices, before the guvnor took the final audition.

Before the second audition, Don, Couth and I, were called to the office of **Bill Watts**, a well known agent, for an interview, we had been suggested for a film. The audition was for **Harry Bidgood,** an orchestra leader. He decided our voices, were good enough to play a quartet of Army privates in a film to star **Vera Lynn.**
The film was called "One Exciting Night". It was about as exciting as watching "Slasher" Mackay bat. It was not a good film. We were called to the studio to learn the harmonies of a song called "Old Times". Vera was standing on the piano in an army canteen, and we were singing a counter harmony in a syncopated style, behind her. When I saw the film in its entirety, I noticed there was a phrase where I was mouthing words, where there was no voice. We recorded the song on tape first, and then mimed as the shots were filmed. Nobody noticed except me, so it just shows you, mistakes are made and can go undetected. It was a terrible film, but apart from the money, it was interesting to see how films were made. During the shooting, I used to play table tennis with **Harry Lewis.** Harry was Vera's husband, and a fine musician. His table tennis was above average, and we used to hold up production, while everyone watched us battle it out.
After the film, I was out of work, and finding the experience of unemployment. I used to attend the Labour Exchange in Edgware Road, which was a little humiliating. It was only made bearable by the sight of a Rolls Royce drawing up outside, and Bill Rowbotham, later known as **Bill Owen**, of "The Last of the Summer Wine", stepping out to collect his dole money. It was twenty five shillings, and this paid for the "Roller".
The second audition, the three of us attended, was for a new musical play. The management was **Tom Arnold.** This was a new show with original music. We had known the music of "Show Boat" before production, but this was a different ball game.

28

We were very excited to be called back for a new show. It all depended on whether we passed the audition. In those days you put on your best suit and tried to look immaculate. I had been to Anello & Davide who made me a full brogue pair of brown suede shoes, with a proper two inch lift, built inside the shoe. This brought me to six foot tall. I realised height was important. When you go for an interview or audition, you don't realise the planning the management have gone through, before they see you. They have types in mind for costumes and the possibility of understudying. A good voice obviously is a requirement, but looks are just as essential.

The theatre was full of singers, dancing hopefuls, and actors all hoping to be engaged for this original production. The ballet boys and girls were all limbering up, in tights, leotards and scarves around their heads. A few singers were humming and doing odd scales to warm up the voice. Actors had a script and were scanning the page. The audition for "Show Boat" was nothing like this. There seemed to be hundreds of people, for few jobs. I realised afterwards *why* there were so many candidates. The stage director started to make a list of those who were going to audition.

Personally I was getting up tight and apprehensive, after all I was only a beginner. Except for Don and Couth, I knew no one, and nobody took any notice of me.

I was called to sing for.............................

IVOR NOVELLO.   *They called him Ivor...*

Chapter Four

The Magic of Ivor Novello.
"France will rise agan"   *Arc de Triomphe.*
Christopher Hassall and Ivor Novello.

He was born David Ivor Davies in Cardiff, son of Clara Novello Davies, he took his mother's middle name for his surname, as a tribute to his beloved mother. The great man was rightly called "The Man of the Theatre". I had read about his stardom in silent films, the many plays he wrote and starred in, and the many films in Hollywood that made him a "Matinee Idol". His musicals were legendary, and I had been privileged to see "The Dancing Years" more than once. Ivor's performance as "Rudi Kleber" was the most charismatic and charming portrayal I had ever seen, and here I was about to go on stage to sing for him. I was doubtful as Ivor was about to hear "The Yeoman of England", and being a Welshman he might have thought it a little cheeky, although he had a hit with "Rose of England".

Luckily I was confident and the voice was steady. He said the usual, "Thank you, please stay". I waited a while, and then I was told he would be pleased for me to be in the new show. "Arc de Triomphe". The three of us all were engaged. The contract was for eight shows a week, and would attract the Equity minimum for the West End. The costumes were gorgeous, there were numerous fittings. My outfit as the boy King, was rather grand, I looked like a young Sir Walter Raleigh. White tights, satin and velvet and gold tunic, with "Raleigh" trunks with pastel blue accessories, and a blonde wig, with black velvet hat.The Phoenix Theatre, Charing Cross Road was a small theatre for a Novello type show, but *Leontine Sagan,* Ivor's German producer and the talents of *Keith Lester,* the choreographer, staged the show to fit perfectly. The leading lady was the superb *Mary Ellis.* Here was a real leading lady, an above average singer, and a consummate actress. Mary had been a leading singer in the Metropolitan Opera House, New York, singing with the great *Caruso and Chaliapin* and all the leading opera stars in the 1918/9 season.

Mary left the Metropolitan to become the title role in "Rose Marie", the most successful Broadway musical of the 1920's. It was produced by Arthur Hammerstein. Mary left the production after a year to concentrate on being a straight actress, but her contract with Hammerstein prevented her from ever performing again as a singer in America.

Ivor saw her in Jerome Kern's "**Music in the Air**" and became enchanted with her. He was determined to write a musical for them both to star in. This was to come to fruition in a most bizarre way. Harry Tennent, who was the management of the Theatre Royal, Drury Lane at the time, had had some failures in succession, and was about to close that famous theatre. He met Ivor in **The Ivy,** one of Ivor's favourite restaurants. Harry sadly informed him that the *"Lane"* as it was affectionately called, was about to close. Things had been financially very bleak, and there was no show on the horizon to recover any former glories. Ivor said that he would write a show for him, he had no idea in mind, but he made up and bluffed his way through inventing a shipwreck and marvellous music with colour and wonderful sets and costumes. Harry Tennent was so impressed he said "Go ahead and do it" and Ivor went back to his flat, and from a blank piece of paper and manuscript, there resulted *"Glamorous Night".* The success of this show, saved the Theatre Royal, Drury Lane. He had written the show he promised, for himself and Mary, who became a real star with the British public, and Ivor went soaring to the top of the British musical theatre.

"Careless Rapture" *"Crest of the Wave"* followed, but Mary did not appear in these two highly successful shows, her next was the lead in *"The Dancing Years",* this success made her the toast of the West End, and her great talent carried the production of *"Arc de Triomphe".* Her role was of "Marie Foret" the opera singer, was one of the longest leading roles in musical plays. She was only off stage for a quick change.

Elizabeth Welch sang two show stopping numbers. *Peter Graves,* son of Lord Graves, played the juvenile lead with light song and dance mood. Peter had a very tuneful and bright duet with Mary, "Easy to live with", this came early in the show. The Honourable Peter was a charming man, with the passing of his father, he became Lord Graves... Peter was a good tennis player, and he and I had a few sets together with close results...Looking back, I seemed to have a bent for climbing. During one performance I went up on to the roof of the Phoenix Theatre, and crawling on all fours, I inadvertently moved a small piece of plaster. The object fell down to the stage, and although it was a small stone, it made a big noise. This was in the middle of quiet dialogue between Mary and Peter before going into the duet. There was hell to pay. I was summoned to the star's dressing room, and Mary Ellis (whom I adored) gave me the biggest and loudest telling off. (And I deserved it, every decibel). She made sure I felt humble and ashamed. She gave me a good lesson in having respect for actors, who were giving their best, and so on.....I never did any climbing again. All part of learning one's craft.

Raymond Lovell had second billing to Mary, he played the heavy, a sort of Svengali type, in competition with Peter Graves for the affections of Mary. Ray was a first class actor, having had many films to his credit. He had a problem with his R's, but this was an attractive part of his delivery. *Elizabeth Welch,* was one of Ivor's favourites. He had written two lovely songs for her in "Glamorous Night", and now gave her two more show stopping numbers. "Dark Music" which was a smooth legato ballad, that Liz excelled in, and the other a point number "Josephine", that she stopped the show every night with, this included her wicked laugh. Liz had a most vulgar sense of humour, which was so infectious. her laugh was her trade mark. What a superb artist. Ivor was very loyal to his artists. Two old queens that had been with him for ten years, were in the show.

They still had very good voices, their names *Harry Fergusson and James Prescott*. These two lovely guys adopted Don and I as their two sons. They spoke to each other, like *Norman Evans*, "Over the garden wall". Harry would say "Do you know what my Don did today ?, he went for a singing lesson with *John McKenna*, and sang, "Great Isis O Osiris". Oh it was so bona". Jimmy not to be outdone would say, "My Clive, played cricket today and scored over fifty". This went on all the time. Among the dancing boys, there were a few "hommie palones", a word for homosexuals, who used to "send up" us heterosexuals, Alan Meredith with full vaselined lips, became *Alan Haynes,* a very excellent "ugly sister" in pantomime, and was in a well established double act, with another female impersonator.

One day during a matinee, and at interval time, one of the boy dancers followed me downstairs underneath the stage. The toilets were there. This dancer came after me and approached me with his arms out to kiss me. I backed off taking long strides until I could go no further. He still advanced in an amorous way, I was panic stricken. Having boxed a bit in the ATC, I gave him a right cross straight on the jaw. He went down and as he did so, he hit his head on the concrete wall and passed out, I trembled and went into shock at the sight of him, not moving. I thought I had killed him. The girls came on the scene and brought him round. He revived, and went to his dressing room. He was alright and was ready to start the second act. I was scared that he might have reported me. He did not. The funny thing was that we became good friends after that incident. The dancer in question, went on to become a very successful West End choreographer. At seventeen years old and with dark curly hair, I seemed to attract the queer fellows. Two tall good looking salesmen, by the name of Tom Burns and Jack Smith were always in the pub where I went after the show. They were very friendly. Tom was immaculate and short on self confidence, and very much a southerner.. Jack, on the other hand was from the North, and a very warm sort of character.

Tom took me out to lunch and bought me gifts, usually gramophone records, and once he had especially made, a pair of brown birdseye trousers for me. I began to think I was in a corner, so I made sure I got out, so to speak. Tom and Jack had both met my parents, they had no idea of their sexuality. As my father was having a bad time, these two lads kindly fixed him up with a travelling job around South London, but this did not work out. To my annoyance, "Purky", who knew my family quite well, told my mother that Tom was after me, and this caused a lot of intrigue and unpleasantness. It transpired that "Purky" wanted me for himself. This was not only embarrassing, but difficult because he had a son, Fred, who had a book shop in St. Martins Lane. Fred had been in the Marines and he and I played some super games of table tennis, he had been a champion of his unit. Of course it turned out that Fred was not "Purky's" son, but his boyfriend. "Arc de Triomphe" struggled manfully against the buzz bombs. The business in the West End suffered. Ivor had a feeling that France would soon be liberated, so he wrote a new scene ready for the victory in France. Ivor came to the theatre to see and hear us rehearsing the new song titled "The Mayor of Pepignon". This song was later put into "King's Rhapsody". During rehearsal a very official looking man complete with Black jacket, striped trousers, black bowler, rolled umbrella and briefcase, arrived. He approached the great man with the words "You've let us down, we haven't received your composition". It transpired that the members of the British Composers Association had promised to write a march for a competition. The winner would have the piece recorded and performed in the Royal Albert Hall, then it would be sent to the underground movement in France, to be used as a signature tune. At the end of the rehearsal, Ivor went to the piano and started to pencil on manuscript paper, he did not play a note. He gave it to the official gentleman, who departed a happy chappie. We asked Ivor "How did it go?", another said "What did you write?". Ivor said, "I'm not sure, but I know it was the first sixteen bars of *"Keep the home fires burning"* backwards.

He won the competition, *Olive Gilbert,* sang the song in the Albert Hall with full chorus, and then it was taken to France. The underground people used to whistle the march regularly.

Among the cast of "Arc" were some very warm and kindly people. *Maidie Andrews* had a very strong comedy role, and she played it to the hilt. She had a tremendous sense of humour, and was responsible for most of the comedy in the show. Maidie was the sister of *Robert Andrews. Bobbie* was Ivor's constant companion, he appeared in many of Ivor's plays. It was a friendship that lasted to the end of Ivor's life. *Vicki Bruce* a very friendly lady used to cuddle and kiss me. She didn't have any children of her own, and I suppose a young boy was a good substitute. I felt her affection was genuine and very enjoyable. It came to pass that Vicki was having a liaison with *Carroll Gibbons.* He would meet her at the stage door on regular occasions. Carroll Gibbons and his Orchestra, had the most prestigious engagement in the band world.....The Savoy Hotel. It transpired that an agent had seen him in America, together with *Rudy Vallee.* The agent cabled the news to the Savoy, with the merits of these two musicians. He received the succinct reply "Bring Vallee, Not Gibbons". The hotel bosses thought that the Saxophone of Rudy Vallee, would add glamour to the band, as there was a preponderance of talented piano players in London. Carroll eventually got the job, and made a name for himself as the man with the piano. In 1927 Carroll was offered the baton and never looked back. He died at the early age of fifty one. A well known music author wrote :- "All who have been entertained by his music for so long, felt they had lost a friend". During the run of "Arc" there was to be some very sad tidings, shared by the company's of both "The Dancing Years" and "Arc de Triomphe. You can imagine that having the same guvnor, we were close friends, and we shared parties and get togethers. I learnt how performers had a bond with each other, and had a love that they shared with kindred spirits. So we were all heartbroken, when.......

On the 16th May,. Ivor was sent to prison for four weeks, for a petrol offence, He had a red Rolls Royce, and it was difficult to get petrol. He had tried to get extra petrol through the Transport Office, but to no avail. A very loyal fan, Miss Dora Constable was to be secretary in a firm near Reading, the car was registered and insured by the firm, it was claimed that it was necessary for war work. The permit was arranged and for a while all things went well. It was alleged that someone, who was a competitor, who was not friendly toward the popular idol, tipped off the Transport Office, and a check up ensued. It was found that Miss Constable was only a filing clerk, and the firm knew nothing of the Rolls Royce. Ivor was summoned to Bow Street court. Unfortunately and foolishly, Ivor pannicked and blamed Miss Constable, she was fined £50 and left the court weeping. Ivor was fined £100, but the judge realising that this would be no punishment to him, sentenced him to eight weeks imprisonment. An appeal was made and through character references from *Lewis Casson & Sybil Thorndike* and other celebrities, the sentence was reduced to four weeks. Prison was terrible for him, but working in the library made his term a little more bearable. The inmates enjoyed his playing with piano recitals.

When he returned he was apprehensive as to the reception he would receive on resuming his role in "The Dancing Years". That night there were queues all the way to Nelson's column. He need not have worried. As he walked on stage, he received the longest and loudest ovation of his outstanding career. We were all ecstatic and the tears were shed in litres that day.

My gratitude to Ivor was boundless. On the first weeks of the show, I had said to *Leontine Sagan,* the producer, I wanted to understudy *Harcourt Williams,*who played the professor. "Billy" Williams, who had been a director of the Old Vic, was a very accomplished actor, and had been a tremendous influence on *John Gielgud,* the great classical actor, who was the first to admit a debt of gratitude to this lovely man, who gave him confidence.

Billy Williams was very elderly, or so it seemed to me, was a class performer. "Leo" mentioned my aspirations to Ivor, and it was arranged that I should meet him in the theatre one morning. I was told to come on stage, so that Ivor could have a good look at me under lights. Ivor sat in the stalls. Leo said "Ivor this young man wants to understudy Harcourt Williams. "Does he" said Ivor, "Bless his little heart". He said to me, "How do you think you can understudy the part ?, " Mr. Williams is around sixty five years old, and you are only seventeen ?". Being seventeen, I had no inhibitions, and where ignorance is bliss etc., Quite assertive, I said, "If I could have a few minutes, I would put on a make up and show you.". This was perfectly alright. I think Ivor thought it was all a bit light hearted and relaxed.

I went to my dressing room, and with false bits and an old trick of putting white Meltonian cleaner on my hair, and then combing it through, it gave the appearance of a grey haired old fellow. I came back to the stage and did a complete impersonation of the professor. We all started as mimics. Ivor liked this and I was put down as an understudy, which attracted extra weekly pay to cover Paul Merrimer, as the part was called.

I had no real acting experience, so Ivor had given me a chance. "Arc de Triomphe" was a tremendous learning ground for me. The finale of the show was a "final act of Jeanne D'Arc. The singing was operatic, Mary a hard vocal role with *Eric Starling* as the mad Dauphin. *Olive Gilbert* opened for the first few weeks, and then went back to "The Dancing Years", *Edgar Elmes,* who had sung the original "Rose of England" in *"Crest of the Wave"* sang the part of De Beaudricourt. The full company with "France Will Rise Again" ended the performance to an ovation every night. The quality of the music was more classical and operatic than Ivor had ever written. The critics went mad about it, saying that Novello should really write a full opera, but he had other shows in mind...like, *"Perchance to Dream" "King's Rhapsody" & "Gay's the Word".*

The Green Room Club was exclusive to actors. and boasted many big star members. Each year they had a Green Room Rag, and a member was responsible for arranging a show given by the Green Room. The member chosen to do this, was called the. Ragpicker". Ivor took his turn as the rag picker and he asked us to do the finale, and sing the rousing "France Will Rise Again".

The Rag was in the London Hippodrome on a Sunday night. Wendy Toye was the chorographer, and she appeared in a super ballet to the music of *George Gershwin. Sybil Thorndike and Lewis Casson* did an amusing double act. *John Gielgud* transfixed us all with a moving Soliloquy. *Sid Field* convulsed everyone with the famous "Golfing". During the rehearsal I was sitting watching, when Ivor came down the centre aisle. I was three feet away when he met Sid. The magic of the meeting of these two giants was electric. You would have thought Sid would be in awe of the great composer, but the opposite was true. Ivor was so thrilled to meet Sid Field. Being in close proximity of this momentous meeting, I became quite emotional. The Green Room Rag was a complete "sell out", and the theatrical charities were the winner.

During the run of "Arc de Triomphe" my friend Don was called up to the Royal Navy, I was so sorry to see him go, but I knew we would meet again. As if he wasn't busy enough, Ivor performed in some of his plays for the troops on a Sunday. It was interesting seeing "I Lived With You" "Full House" and "Fresh Fields".. Ivor had to re-learn some of his old parts, and this was while playing "The Dancing Years" at the Adelphi Theatre. He had tremendous drive for the live theatre, but then the stage was his life, he had no other real hobbies.

As Mary Ellis wrote in her autobiography, I came to see her to say Goodbye. I said to her "Its a good job the show is closing tonight Miss, the cat's pissed on my wig". and so ended a very important part of my life,...so far. Now out of work again, seventeen years old...... What next ????????

"Come boys, lets all be "Gay" boys"   The Student Prince.
Dorothy Donnelly.   Sigmund Romberg.
It was ironic recalling **Harry Welchman** in "The Student Prince"
that I should pass an audition to become a "Student". I go back to
the Stoll Theatre for this Romberg classic. Starring **Bruce Trent**
(who became a good friend right up until his death). Bruce was a
Bass Baritone and had the musical score put down for him. He
was ideal as "Karl Franz". We boys had a lot to do in this show.
Frank Adey produced. **Bernard Delfont** presented "The Student
Prince", and I was set to enjoy the Harry Welchman memory.
Bernard Delfont was born in Russia, and while his brothers Lew
and Leslie made the Grade, the surname they adopted, he took his
name from his first dancing partnership, "The Delfont Boys". He
helped to establish such stars as **Norman Wisdom, Harry
Secombe, Morecambe & Wise, Bruce Forsyth, Freddie Starr and
Frankie Vaughan.** and many others. He was responsible for many
famous musicals. Frank Adey was a down to earth producer with
no frills, he was keen on sports, so we jelled. He was a specialist
in lighting. I always said he could light a cardboard box. During
the run the bombs were beginning to reduce in their intensity,
although we still had to do fire watching. Little bedrooms were
made at the top of the building in that huge rehearsal room. My fire
watching partner was **Bryan Johnson.** Brian was a serious actor,
he had been with **Donald Wolfit**, touring Shakespeare the year
before, he also possessed a fine baritone voice, he understudied
"Dr. Engel" and played the part many times, singing the lovely
"Golden Days". You will remember, dear reader, that he went on
to win the Eurovision Song Contest with "Singing High High
High." He was great fun.
With the name of Shakespeare, in mind, it reminded that one
afternoon, during the run, I had a call from **Denis Arundel.** His
voice was easily recognizable, as he was on the radio all the time.
He played sinister parts mainly, apart from these roles he was a
stage actor and producer, and directed opera now and again. He
wanted to know if I would go to lunch with him the next day.

I agreed. I met this unusual man. He had piercing eyes, smartly dressed, with a plummy quality of voice. I asked him how he had procured my telephone number, he told me he was an Equity Councillor, and had access to telephone numbers. In the course of conversation, he said he was impressed with my comedy in the second act of "The Prince", we the students were slightly drunk, and I invented some comedy mime business, that always received laughs, comedy was hard to find in operetta. Denis said he liked my style for one so youthful, and he would like to take me on tour in the "Scottish play" as Banquo and Fleance.. I like Shakespeare, but I was not fluent with these two characters. The way he looked at me told me that I didn't want to tour with him or Shakespeare, that I was a musical comedy chap and not a real thespian. I didn't enjoy my lunch as I wanted to escape as soon as possible.

It was slightly ironical that on the end of that evening performance, a very smart WAAF was waiting for me at the stage door after the show. Her name was Edith, she was very dark and attractive. I knew her, as she lived about three hundred and fifty yards from me, she reminded me of *Maria Montez* We had a drink and then went home together. Whether she thought that stage folk were easy or not, I don't know, but we held hands and kissed, and she went to great lengths to tell me her parents were out, and she had the house to herself. Would I come in for coffee.?. What with Denis Arundel for lunch and now this offer at night, I thought I have to lose my virginity sometime...but this was not the time....so I left her and went home. Walking home I thought well, coffee keeps me awake anyway, so I went home to bed, I think I was right..............was I ?

While out of work, I did my best to see productions in the West End. How lucky I was to see the great Olivier and Richardson season at the New Theatre (Now the Albery). The company presented a repertory of plays, the two stars would alternate. *Laurence Olivier* would play "Richard the Third", and then *Ralph Richardson* would play "Peer Gynt", and Olivier a small cameo.

I remember the company was full of great actors...***Peggy Ashcroft, Joyce Redman, Nicholas Hannan*** and many more. In retrospect, I realised that I witnessed one of the outstanding seasons of productions ever seen on the West End stage. ***Ralph Richardson*** was one of the giants of the acting profession. He kept a ferret named "Harry". He would ride on his motor bike to the veterinary surgery, where my sister Beryl, was employed. My sister had to clip the claws, "de flea" him, and wash this ferret in Lux soap flakes, and clean his eyes. The actor was devoted to this unusual pet.

Ralph Richardson was playing at the Richmond Theatre, Sir Ralph suffered from Parkinson's Disease, and in the middle of the second act one night, he stepped forward and pleaded the immortal phrase, "Is there a doctor in the house ?", amidst a mumbling of concern, a man in the balcony stood up and said "Yes Sir Ralph I am", to which the great Actor Knight replied :- "Isn't this a bloody terrible play ?".

Laurence Olivier & ***Ralph Richardson*** were knighted for their services to the theatre and charity. Ralph and John Gielgud were friends, but Olivier and Gielgud were never soul mates, but even so they both acknowledged the talent of Johnny G, so much so, that they both went to see ***Winston Churchill*** to persuade him to put Gielgud on the honours list, from which he had been excluded so far, because he was a homosexual. Churchill did not acquiesce., it was later that John Gielgud was eventually knighted. It impressed me to think, how generous the two great actors were in trying to see that a colleague should have the same honour, when they believed it was merited. It shows the loyalty that was apparent in the legitimate theatre.

During this time, I went to see a wonderful production of "The Merry Widow" presented by Jack Hylton, starring ***Cyril Ritchard & Madge Elliott, George Graves, Leo Franklyn,*** directed by ***William Mollison.***

"The Widow" was probably the best of the *Franz Lehar'* operettas. The music was melodious and catchy. Among the world of operetta lovers, it was a classic. There had been many productions of this popular show, and of course two wonderful films, one with *Maurice Chevalier,* and the M.G.M. version starring *Lana Turner.* A beautiful lady to look at, it was a pity she couldn't sing the songs. Her voice was dubbed. I loved the music.

It was surprising to learn that the Government had an arrangement with the London Theatre Managers, that all shows should play to the troops under the auspices of E.N.S.A. (Every night something awful) for six weeks, and "The Widow" was to commence a tour. I went to see Jack Hylton, to sing for him. He informed me that I should wear a two and a half inch collar because my neck was too long, (It was even longer than *Nat Jackley).* This would be the first show I toured, and left home and the West End for.

Hylton was a well known band leader. He had risen from being a partner with *Tommy Handley* in "Two entertainers and a piano", to a premier orchestra of the 30's. *Peter Yorke, Billy Ternent,* were two of the names who perfected their conducting skills with the Hylton set up. *Jack Jackson, Paul Fenoulhet, Woolf Phillips* graduated from the brass section to lead their own bands, and *Cyril Stapleton* violinist, *Bruce Trent* was his vocalist and double bass player. Jack was responsible for presenting "Call Me Madam" "Kiss Me Kate" "Pal Joey" "Kismet" and "Paint Your Wagon". One of his last shows was "Camelot", so he had a good track record. . I duly joined the cast, and rehearsed this famous show.

The rehearsals were fragmented, as many of the performers had already played the show. It was a new experience to have, what I would call "bitty" shots at the score and action of the piece, but I soon settled in with these excellent people.

"Oh the women, oh the women"   *The Merry Widow.*
Adrian Ross.   *Franz Lehar.*

The stars Cyril and Madge, were wonderful. **Malcolm Goddard**
and I became Cyril and Madie's sons. They were like a mother and
father to us, having no children of their own, we became their
family. Malcolm was to progress to being one of the most
successful choreographers in television, and specializing in
pantomime. We shared a room at most of the digs. Theatrical digs
and Landladies were a very important factor in the life of an actor.
Variety Acts and Repertory actors had lists of popular and
acceptable lodgings. Usually the Visitor's book was signed with
code words, intimating the talents of the landlady.

The stories of landladies were legendary. They were often
addressed as "Ma". The front parlour would have heavy lace
curtains, antimacassars on horsehair sofas, and usually a big
picture of Landseer's "Monarch of the Glen" or some other well
known portrait. There was an aspidistra covered in red velvet, wax
flowers, and photographs of the famous who had stayed there, and
the essential object, the cruet. Many landladies put in their
advertisements..."Use of cruet". A famous story, that had many
versions, was the young actor, who was being pursued by the
landlady, he managed to keep out of her way, was on his way to
rehearsal, he had gone some way, when he realised he had left his
script in the digs. He went back for it, and going through the
kitchen, there lying on the kitchen table was the landlady
completely naked, doing what comes naturally with another actor.
She turned her head, smiled coyly and said "Ooooh Mr
Terence...you must think me a dreadful flirt".

Malcolm and I were very lucky with our digs. He was a strong
dancer himself, and his choreography was forceful and dominant.
He had a great sense of humour, unlike some West End dancers
and choreographers, I have known.

All The Ladies are Lovely.
"Ladies of the town, Ladies of the town.   ***Bitter Sweet.***
Noel Coward.

Cyril Ritchard being an Australian, was a good tennis player, and he and I would play a lot during the tour, while, Madge "Madie" would bring a chair, and knit while watching. The troops loved the show, and it was amazing how they placed the sets on some of the small stages.

The tour began at the Devonshire Park Theatre, Eastbourne with a tremendous reception. Playing to the troops was an education. They proved that if a show was of good quality, high standard of performance, and melodious, they were discerning and very responsive. The music of ***Franz Lehar*** was completely captivating.

Playing the part of "Cascada" was a short man with a cherubic countenance. He was always pleasant to me, and one day, he said to me, "Stock is an uncommon name, the only other Stock I ever met, was with me in the choir in Wealdstone, Harrow.". Of course, that choir boy was my father. I often heard Pop talk of ***Frank Tickle,*** and this was he. A lovely chap and a good performer.

In the show were four matured ladies. Anybody over twenty was matured to me. There were two Betty's, one was tall, thin and sultry, she was the mistress of Raymond Lovell. The other one was slightly shorter and rounded. I got attached to this one, she was cuddly and I found her very attractive, with a sense of good fun. We used to go to the cinema together, and we became very close. It was difficult with Malcolm sharing a room, but it was inevitable. One night I lost my virginity on the bathroom floor, and I was never the same after that. Betty and I formed a good friendship, and I saw her regularly, when on leave from the RAF, before going overseas.

44

In the chorus were two Australian tenors, who were very friendly, *Freddie Angles & Ray Carey.* Ray was to go on to a great career in teaching, more about him later. Freddie was a silvered wavy haired old "Queen", with a wicked sense of humour. He and Ray used to laugh incessantly all the time. When the six weeks were over, I returned home. It was now September 1944. I was thinking that call up was not far away. I went to the Air Ministry in Kingsway and managed to get an appointment with *Squadron Leader Ralph Reader.* He was in charge of running the famous "Gang Shows". He told me to do my first six weeks "Square bashing" and then apply to him, as I was a professional with West End experience, it should be plain sailing. At the end of the month, I went for an audition for *George Black* at the London Hippodrome.

London was being bombed all the time, but now Hitler veered away from conventional bombing, and the "Buzz Bombs" were the order of the day. The V1 and V2 were playing havoc with the London people. These devastating weapons were universally known as "Doodle Bugs". You could see the bombs flying across the skies with no pilot, they had been fired from Germany, and as *Ted Ray* said..."They were big fat cigars with wings, with their arse on fire". The flames at the deriere of the bomb were considerable, and the system for the deadly weapons of destruction, were that at a point the engine would cut out, and then a few seconds later, the bomb would hurtle to the ground and destroy anything in its path. They were easy to spot at night, but not quite as identifiable during the day. One day I was walking down Shaftesbury Avenue toward Piccadilly, when I heard the drone of the doodle bug. Looking into the sky, there was the object. It went across the Piccadilly area, and then the dreaded cut out of the engine. The explosion was fearsome, I hurled myself into the doorway of a shop, and as I did, broken glass came sailing up the street. If I had not darted into the entrance of the shop, I would have been cut to ribbons.

There is little chance I would have survived. It pulled me up with
a start, and I shook with fear. After getting myself together, I
carried on to Piccadilly.
The business in the West End at that time was abysmal, but despite
this, new shows were produced, and although the runs were
shorter, the theatre going public consistently attended the live
shows to cheer their spirits up. I thrived on the shows I saw. All the
time I was learning about production and publicity, and generally
appreciating a wide style and content of different tastes of plays
and musicals.

During the very short breaks I had between each West End show, ,
I was a regular visitor to see as many shows as I could. How lucky
I was to see The Olivier-Richardson season, The Lisbon Story, The
Merry Widow, The Lilac Domino (one of the most melodious
shows I ever saw) and many straight plays. The finest revue I saw
seven times, was "Strike a New Note" starring the superb *Sid
Field.* Sid had been around in the provinces, for many years. Sid's
agent *Len Barry,* had tried to get the big managements to see him,
and they never bothered, even when he was playing in smaller
theatres around London. In the show, Sid had teamed up with a
fantastic feed, *Jerry Desmonde.* They were perfectly suited to each
other, absolutely sympatico. Sid became the talk of the town, and
Len was receiving calls from all the managements asking him,
"Where had he been ?, Why didn't you tell me about him ?", Len
(who was our agent for a time) told them, "Why didn't you come
to see him at :Penge when I asked you ?". They had all missed the
boat. It took *George Black* to give Sid a break. The great
character of *"Slasher Green"* the loveable cockney barrow boy,
The Campanologist, with bells, the confused golfer, the camp
photographer, "I haven't been the same since my last operation"
Brushwork, the aspiring painter, these beautifully honed sketches
became classics. The public adored him, and all the comics set
him up as the zenith, one to aspire to.

It was a coincidence that *Morecambe & Wise and Billy Dainty* were in the show, in the chorus. They very obviously learnt a lot during this record breaking show. Sid unfortunately lived to 1950 and was only 45 years old when he died.

Watching Sid Field regularly made me a devoted fan and completely besotted by this man's talent. There will never be another *Sid Field.* Many comedians copied him and used some of his material, including *Yours Truly".*

Sid Field, went on to appear in "Strike It Again" and "Piccadilly Hayride" all huge successes at the Prince of Wales Theatre. He made two films ;- "London Town" and the "Cardboard Cavalier", and then he starred in the play about the rabbit, "Harvey". "London Town" would have been a big success if only they had filmed an audience for the comedy reaction, but it fell a little flat.

The West End theatre was a hive of industry, and the number of productions entertaining the theatre going public was prolific.
In wartime the number of star performers giving enjoyment to our overseas visitors, on stage, was magical.

There was a repertory of Opera outside of Covent Garden, and the standard of production was very high. How lucky we all were to see the best, when there was a war, and the blackout resticted the movement of people intent of having a good time.

"My wish was born on a summer's morn" Jenny Jones.
Harold Purcell.. Harry Parr Davies.
On the 2nd October, 1944, I opened at the London Hippodrome in a new musical *"Jenny Jones"*, lyrics by Harold Purcell and music by *Harry Parr Davies.* This gifted composer was a shy young self taught prodigy from Briton Ferry, in Glamorgan. They called him the childhood genius. His shows included *"Black Velvet"* *"Gangway"* with *Tommy Trinder, "Dear Miss Phoebe"* and the long running *"Lisbon Story"*, which we followed. Parr Davies had a hit with "Wish me luck As you wave me goodbye", written for *Gracie Fields,* for whom he became her accompanist, all over Africa and America.

The play was produced by *Hugh Miller*, a talented actor, and the choreography was by *Wendy Toye.* The show was about a Welsh miner with 18 children and he wanted to make it 21. The idea was to bring the straight and the musical theatre together.

Mary Waterman and Ronald Millar were the main love interest for the legitimate theatre, and *Carole Lynne and Robert Sydney* were the singing leads. The comedy was in the hands of a great vaudevillian..*Jimmy James.* The role of the apothecary went to *Baliol Holloway,* he had played "Hamlet" in one of *Sir Henry Irving's* companies. Jimmy was the real star of the show, with his well tried "Chipchopper" and the hilarious, "What have you got in the box". During rehearsals *George Black* said to Jimmy about his number "Why Worry". You sing a chorus, and then you dance three quarters of the second chorus, and sing the last eight bars. Jimmy with a quizzical look said "What's with this dancing ?, I don't dance". George said "Oh yes you do, I remember those tap dancing steps you used to do, years ago, where you used to click your toes together". Black was a real impresario, who always went round the Country seeing all the acts, and he never forgot. Jimmy duly obliged with the toe clicking bit, with great success. *Wendy Toye's* "St.Ceiriog" ballet was sensational. I played a Lord in this, once again in tights.

The principal dancer was *Tommy Linden,* he was the juggler that had no gifts for the Madonna, but he could only juggle the coloured balls. The mime and dance was very emotional, and Tommy extracted every ounce of sadness with his outstanding talent. He wept every performance.

Wendy had dancers who were very close to her, apart from Tommy, there was *Beryl Kaye, Paddy Stone and Irving Davies.* I felt very privileged to sometime join in with them on the social side. The artist who captivated the audience each evening, was the cherub faced *Malcolm Thomas,* a twelve year old Welsh lad who had one of the hit songs "My Wish". It was an exceptional voice, not a treble, but a pure tenor quality. His voice did not break, He went through the years without any change. Malcolm sang as a tenor for the rest of his career, he later took the name of Malcolm Vaughan, and formed a highly well known successful double act, *"Malcolm Vaughan & Kenneth Earle".* *Malcolm* had many individual hits with recordings. We all have to start somewhere, and playing a small part was *Keith Beckett.* A superb comedy dancer and when he became the popular Television director, his comedy talents were to enrich his skills as a T.V. Producer and Director.

Ronald Millar, was the juvenile lead. He was tall with blonde hair and an athletic figure. He had been in the Royal Navy, and had been invalided out. He became an actor, at a time when handsome actors were in short supply. In 1946 he wrote the play "Frieda", which was later filmed. It proved an instant success. He followed with other plays, and also wrote a musical version of "The Barretts of Wimpole Street" entitled "Robert & Elizabeth". He was drawn into politics and was soon writing speeches for *Margaret Thatcher.* He was Knighted, and in 1998 he died at the age of 78. I liked him, and we had many drinks and talks together. My circle of actor friends was widening and I was absorbing so many facets of our business.

The London Hippodrome.

Vincent Tildsley's Choral Group "The Mastersingers" who had a monster hit with "Pedro the Fisherman" from "The Lisbon Story" the show we followed into the London Hippodrome, were with us in "Jenny Jones". The eight singers were Welsh in the majority, and Stebbie the leading bass was big, tall and had an outstanding voice. Unfortunately, he and the lads got me into bad habits. After the show each night, we would go out of the stage door, and straight across the road into the hostelry, for a pint. I started off with a couple of pints of mild ale. Each night they would entice me to consume another pint and then another, and so on, and in the end, I was drinking eleven pints. Luckily the tube was close by the theatre, and I could doze on the way home. Mother used to listen to me going upstairs to bed, if she heard a trip, which I did regularly, she would pass remarks the next morning. It taught me a lesson, as to this day, I very seldom drink beer, my bladder will not hold a large capacity.

I was particularly partial to the girls in the company, they were all very attractive, and the more mild ale I consumed, the more attractive they seemed to get. *Claudine Goodfellow, Diana Dell, and Diana Beall* were very desirable. *Diana King* had a small part, but she was deifinitely destined for very good work in the future.

"Jenny Jones", didn't open in the West End straight from rehearsal. We played a week at the Hippodrome, Brighton to iron out any problems with the show, before opening in the West End. During the week "Flare Path" was playing at the Theatre Royal. Starring *Bryan Forbes.* We had parties with the company, and with the legitimate actors in our company, it was a very happy time. It was obvious that Bryan was going to ascend to great heights in our business, and I am sure dear reader, you will have followed his career on stage, and in films, ending up as a premier director with *Richard Attenborough.*

50

We had a further week's rehearsal on returning to London to polish and bed in the whole production. During this time, *Cyril Ritchard,* telephoned me to say that the "Merry Widow" was now at the Coliseum, the fellow who had taken my part, was off, and would I pop on for that night's performance. I told him I was rehearsing prior to opening, and I would not be allowed. Cyril telephoned George Black asking for permission for me to appear that night, and release me from rehearsal. George Black kindly gave his consent, and I appeared at the Coliseum.. Cyril had not told me that the whole production was on a revolving stage. You can imagine my hesitancy for getting on and off the revolve. It was fightening, my balance was all over the place. It was a good thing it was only one performance.

We were still on rationing, and coupons for sweet foods had to be cut out of the ration books, I did this when I helped pop in the shop, it was a daily operation. My eighteenth birthday was approaching and the company arranged a party for me. They went to an Italian patisserie nearby and ordered special gateau type cakes and pastries. I never was told how they found the coupons, but they did. On the 29th November, 1944 my 18th birthday, at the party *Carole Lynne* (who later became Lady Delfont) had a long chat with me, she was very certain that I would not be called to serve in the forces, but that I would last the show out. NEXT DAY I received my calling up papers.

I was to report to the Royal Air Force at Cardington, Bedfordshire to commence my six weeks training, commonly known as "Square Bashing". It was a terrible shock, to leave home and the theatre I loved, a real heartbreaking feeling.

Trotting off to see Sqdn Leader *Ralph Reader* at the Air Ministry, I was to re-affirm that I would be in the "Gang Show" after the initial six weeks training. He confirmed the procedure of applying after the extensive exercise.

51

It was a friendly discourse, and another Officer by the name of Cracknell, was in attendance. Between them they showed me photographs of various companies that made up the RAF Gangshows. They had the latest picture of the new show that was in France. The subject of "Queers" was mentioned, and like a fool, I said that I could always tell a homosexual. A big mistake I guess. They intimated that there was only one gay airman in the picture. The photograph was well scrutinized. There were three rows of RAF personnel, they were all normal looking fellows, but in the right hand side of the middle row was a thickset "Butch" looking chap, and his eyes gave him away. I said to the two officers, "Thats the one", I was hurried out of the officer very quickly. I know dear reader you are saying, "How can you tell by the eyes". This is something that is quite unexplainable, it is not their movements or their voice, it's the eyes. I will leave it at that.

It was a little disconcerting to have had such interest in my career so far, by homosexuals. They were delightful people, and with the exception of the "Purky" incident, I was always happy with them. I suppose I was always a man's man because of my involvement with teams in cricket and football. I was always with the lads, and I could never be called a "Ladies Man". It was obvious to me that I had artistic tendencies, but sexually, it was the female of the species I felt for. Nice faces and jovial personalities attracted me, and throughout my life I knew through a form of radio waves, and general tuning in, I was "sympatico" with either sex.

Because I was leaving home to go into the Air Force, my parents were not very happy. I wasn't either. The only plus was that I would go into the Royal Air Force. the service of my choice. All A.T.C. boys automatically went into the Air Force, and their number would start with numeral three, my number was 3055055. A number you never forget, as all service personnel will tell you. The "Doodlebugs" bombs were still falling, there were restrictions, and rationing was still in force.

They do say that the rationing contributed to a fitter Nati
we are today. We had not starved, and the diet was obvic
balanced and nourishing.

After my birthday party, as I went home on the tube, I was
thinking.....Cricket at Lords, London Table tennis junior champion
and England International. Centre Half for the London A.T.C. at
football, junior broker in the world famous Lloyds of London. Five
West End musicals..(Two original, three revivals) The Magic of
Ivor Novello...Mary Ellis, Jimmy James, and the friendship of
Cyril Ritchard and Madge Elliott, the lovely Wendy Toye.....not
bad for a newsagents' son and a 18 year old.

The last twenty months had been glorious, and the theatre had
really been well and truly indoctrinated into my demeanour, and
had cemented my vocation for the future. The question was that
after my time in the service of my Country, would I get back into
the profession.........only time will tell.

The unit I was about to join in the Royal Air Force, Cardington/

"Give me some men who are stout hearted men".   New Moon.
Oscar Hammerstein.   Sigmund Romberg.

On the 4th December, 1944,   I set out with other stout hearted men
to sign on for the Royal Air Force. Reporting to RAF Cardington
in Bedfordshire, I registered, received my Air Force number
3055055 together with all the kit. Two pairs of boots (one drill and
one walking out) tunics, shirts, socks, sheets, three blankets, great
coat, forage cap, badge, rifle, sten gun and many other bits and
pieces. Allocated to a hut, and No. 5 Flight.

It was a sparse looking hut, with beds either side, and a coal fire in
the middle of the room, There were 24 men in each billet, twelve a
side. I was number five from the door, adjacent to the fire. I was
very glad of this as it was bitterly cold, and first thing in the
morning, the dying embers still permeated a little heat to yours
truly. I was very unhappy, and shed a few tears during my first
night. It was not pleasant being away from home. The square
bashing, drill, obstacle courses, rifle drill and intelligence tests and
rifle shooting started. I thought I was fit, but this concentrated
routine without a break was exhausting. Coping with it all fairly
well, the one trial I found very painful, was at the end of the day
we had to stand to attention in full pack, then drill with rifle and
stand at attention, stock still, for at least half an hour.

There was a competition each week, to see which was the cleanest
and smartest hut in the whole flight. There were ten huts. We had a
Corporal Edwards and Corporal Cockcroft, from the RAF
Regiment to order us to do everything. I soon learned if it moves,
salute it, if it is stationary, paint it. As a squad we became very
smart, the two sheets were folded just so, so that the blankets went
in between and were squared off, from the front. We even put
shaped pieces of cardboard in behind, to make everything at right
angles. The lino floor was polished so you really could see your
face in it, and if it was not up to scratch, Corporal Edwards would
make you do it again.

Because we won the best hut the first week, we got the bug to make sure our hut won, with the exception of the fourth week, we won the prize every week, we had great pride in this achievement.. Before the end of the six weeks, we were able to go home for Christmas. to be home with all the family was wonderful, I knew how much I missed them all, but I never realized how important they were to me.

Returning after Christmas, to the "Square bashing". I was lined up for a boxing match. RAF Cardington were to box an army unit from Bedford. I had some experience of boxing in the ATC. I was now fitter than I had ever been, I was 11 stone 7lbs of pure muscle. The RAF training had been successful. My bout was against a highly rated army boxer, and I was not too optimistic about my chances.

We started very evenly matched, and the points score was pretty well drawn, and although I was scoring with left jabs, he was beginning to get on top. When we came to the last round, I knew I would have to hurt him. I hit him very hard with a right cross to the jaw, and as he was going down, to make sure, I threw a big left handed punch, this gave me excruciating pain.; I had over reached and my arm had come out of its socket, and was up my back. The fight was stopped and awarded to my opponent. Apart from being upset and disappointed, I kept thinking I would have rheumatism or arthritis in the shoulder in the future. Luckily this did not happen.

After the six weeks, we had as very comprehensive test, practical and written. Immediately I got on to **Ralph Reader** at Air Ministry, only to be told I had passed out with eighty two per cent, this made me classified as a tradesman...Clerk General Duties, with Release Scheme qualifications was my designation, this would be so, after I had taken the proper course.

I was very down and annoyed to think that Ralph Reader had not told me about grading, he more or less inferred I should have failed, so that I would have no trade. It was not my way of thinking to ever do less than my best, so the situation was accepted, and whatever the future may bring. It was obvious that entertainment was not going to figure in my duties. There was a passing out parade, and then on the notice board, we received our orders. Many of us were going to be posted overseas to India.

Embarkation leave, and then report to Warrington, after two weeks at home. The ship was going to leave from Liverpool. We were issued with a complete new kit, for the hot climate.
Two weeks of bliss, at home.
As soon as I was home, it was off to see shows. I saw *Sid Field* in "Strike It Again" as usual he was exceptional with some very strong material, which I absorbed completely.

There was a highlight, I went to see Ivor Novello in *"Perchance to Dream"* at my old home, The London Hippodrome. Naturally I went to see him afterwards in uniform, he gave me a warm welcome, and was more than interested in my experiences so far. I knew most of the cast, so the reunion was a feel good factor. The only downside was that I felt more miserable at leaving the theatre. The only redeeming feature, was to see the show, and enjoy the music, and the performance of the "guvnor".

"Dear Ivor"

MAN OF THE
THEATRE

IVOR NOVELLO.

A respite from the Royal Air Force.
"There's No People, Like Show People" *Annie Get Your Gun.* Irving Berlin.

"Perchance to Dream" was a very musical show in three parts, as usual Ivor's melodies were superb. The sheet music sales of "We'll Gather Lilacs" eclipsed the sales of "Waltz of my Heart". The gorgeous melody of "Lilacs" was sung by **Muriel Barron & Olive Gilbert,** clearly the hit of the show. Ivor, as the Regency buck commanded his usual huge public following. This was one of the only shows that Ivor wrote both lyrics and music.

"Gay Rosalinda" was playing at the Palace Theatre, starring my good friend **Cyril Ritchard.** The show was based on Johann Strauss' "Die Fledermaus". It was a beautiful show in every respect. Cyril had made a tremendous hit, and the press, were more than generous to him. The part of "Eisenstein" suited him totally. Off to see him afterwards, brought about an emotional reunion, what a welcome !, .as stated before, he was like a second father. We were talking away and reminiscing about our time in "The Widow", when there was a knock at the door. Cyril said "Come" and in walked **Bernard Delfont ,** followed by **Richard Tauber,** who was conducting the show. "Bernie" recognized me, as I had been in the "Student Prince" for him, we smiled, shook hands, and then I was introduced to Tauber, quite an honour. The two of them had obviously come to see Cyril, so I said "Shall I leave?" Cyril said very quickly, "No you stay". He obviously knew the reason for their visit.

I was to witness dialogue I had never seen or heard before. It was doubtful I would ever see this type of meeting again. Bernard Delfont and Richard Tauber were imploring Cyril to stay with the show. Cyril had received an offer for New York. He was very versatile, and apart from starring with **Mary Martin** in "Peter Pan", playing Captain Hook. he directed opera, in New York..

57

Anyway, back to the plot. These two giants of entertainment, were all but on their knees, to make Cyril stay with the show, for his performance was the talk of London, and he was creating very good results at the box office. No matter how they pleaded and coerced, Cyril was adamant he was going, and so the two impresarios took their leave. This persuasion scene stayed in my memory for years. I said farewell to Cyril, and I to, departed.

My next visit was to see a prestigious variety bill, with the king of the "Stand Up" comics, *Max Miller.* Here was a magical personality, who held an audience in his hands, so that they laughed, until he had wrung every chuckle out of them, he was intimate with his style, and his timing was exemplary. I studied him carefully, and a lot of his patter seemed to stay with me.

Off to Warrington for what we thought was embarkation from Liverpool. During this time we had a chance to travel. A fellow airman came with me for a day trip to Morecambe. The first visit, , was to see a matinee of "The Dollar Princess" starring *Michael Cole.* It was a sugary type of musical of the old school, I have never seen it since, and I never hear the music. Stan came with me, and he loved it, although he was not at all "showbiz". It was very tuneful, and the sets were good and the costumes were sumptuous. Musical comedy was definitely......me.

So we are now getting ready to pack for going off to India, everything was labelled, and we were on our way...but as *Danny Kaye* would say: But no..." There were problems and we were sent home again on three weeks leave. I played some football this time, to keep my hand with old buddies. I couldn't miss the opportunity to visit the West End, I saw some shows that former colleagues were appearing in. After this happy period, back to reality.

It was now time to go back to Warrington to get ready for the voyage that was to come. The U-boats were sinking our shipping, and caution was taken to insure our departure from Liverpool, was at the minimum of risk. We sailed from Liverpool, on the ....

"We're riding along on the crest of the wave"   *Gang Show.*
Ralph Reader.

"Mauretania". This grand ship was so fast, we went on our own with no convoy, the U-boats could not catch us. It was now adventure time, on a ship with hammocks and greasy food. Most of the lads were sick, but I was lucky, my stomach was strong, I would finish up the pork and rice pudding. On deck there were chaps "throwing up" over the side, I said to one bloke, "You must have a weak stomach ?" he said indignantly " I'm throwing as far as the others", he was not amused.

On the ship we had the Cruiser weight champion of the world, *Freddie Mills.* A very good accordion player...*Tito Burns.* I made friends with both these characters, but my favourite was *Charles Chilton.* Charlie was an authority on the history of cowboy songs, he was a virtuoso on the guitar, and when we arranged some concerts on board, Charlie and Tito supplied the music. After the services, Tito played with several orchestras, and formed his own group, and later became an important agent and impresario, representing many star names. Charlie was a regular broadcaster with his songs and detailed history programmes.

Freddie Mills carried on boxing. As World Cruiser Weight champion there were no challengers, so he went up a weight to heavy weight. This was not very successful. He opened a chinese restaurant in London, but he was mixing with the wrong types. In a book published in 2002, it was alleged that he took secrets to the grave, inasmuch that he was involved with a vicious serial killer, responsible for brutal deaths, the bodies being found between 1959 and 1965. On the 26th July, 1965 Freddie was found shot in the head. Whatever Freddie was, or did, I liked him, he was friendly and was a great help to me on the "Mauretania", when together, we did little gags.

The job of getting a show together on board, was very difficult, you had no idea if any of the personnel could do anything, the music was taken care of. There was Charlie and his cowboy ditties, and I found an actor *George Spenton Foster,* who did the golf sketch with me, and between us we wrote a play. It passed the time for the lads. Unwittingly, our play was like the "Monkey's Paw". I had no idea of the play, but what is it "Great Minds". ????

The voyage was very enjoyable except for sleeping arrangements, and the crowded accommodation, there were several thousand RAF personnel aboard. Arriving in Bombay in one piece, we were greeted with the smell of the East. The stench permeated through our nostrils. It was pretty awful. The aroma of India was absolutely unique and unlike any other odour, you could experience.

We were transported to RAF Worli, just outside Bombay, a perfectly planned transit camp. We were soon into our billets, all under canvas. There was warning to us on arrival, we must be vigilant, as there were thieves about, called, "Loose Wallahs" they were completely naked and greased all over, so that anyone catching them, would not hold them through slipping. It sounded a tall story, but on our first night at three a.m. in the morning, it happened. A loose wallah was in the camp, like "grease" lightning he sped through our sleeping quarters. He stole one or two items like watches and wallets, he was pursued, and slipped through the hands of his pursuers, needless to say, he was not caught.

Our lightweight khaki tunics and shorts were a godsend in the excessive heat. The Aussie style hats helped to keep the sun of our necks, but I still managed to sunbathe. The next journey was to Secunderabad by train. Well dear reader, if you have ever been on a Indian train in the forties, the experience was terrifying.

Now the study in Secunderabad.

Our seats were reserved, but otherwise the whole train was packed.
The Indians hung out of the windows, they were on the roof,
holding on by their finger nails. How they faired through the
tunnels, I can only hazard a guess, remembering my boyhood
memories of going from one carriage to another. It was hot and
smelly, and very uncomfortable.

The town of Secunderabad was in the Province of Hyderabad. Our
unit came under the umbrella of the H.Q. of the 229 Group in
Bangalore. Some of our lads went to Bangalore, while we started a
thirteen week course in Secunderabad. We trained hard to learn all
the administration and system of clerking and pen pushing. It was
very comprehensive. The filing and titling of policy documents
was quite intricate, but once you had learned the procedure, it
became second nature. We learnt to touch type.
The normal working day was from 9 a.m. to 1 p.m. Then tiffin
followed by an enforced siesta, this was on the premise that it was
far too hot to work, so you should lie down and rest. Most of the
lads were only too pleased to "bash the charpoy", this was a
wooden frame with legs, and rope criss-crossed to make a platted
base for the blanket, and then the sheet. This was all that was
needed. Rightly or wrongly, I could not lie down in the afternoon,
I was outside playing football with the Indians, who were our
bearers, all of us in bare feet. The Indians were excellent at
Hockey, and we would often have matches against them, also
without boots. It may sound a bit bizarre, but I am sure that is why
I have always had good feet.. Like my father.

During my time there I was still homesick, especially when I was
sent to a film unit in Madras, to host a series of interviews for the
services parents, this was to let them see how we were, and to give
them a warm greeting. Madras was the first place, where I sampled
proper Madras Curry. The journey on the train was still dreadful.

When back at the unit, I used to write home to Mother and Pop, Mother wrote regularly, but Pop running the business, had little time, he wrote spasmodically. To have a letter from him was a highlight. He always had excellent handwriting, and the ability to be newsy.

Dear reader, I don't want you to think I was a mother's boy, or that I was "mamby pamby", but I did miss them both terribly. Conversely, I had many tough and rough times, that I was pleased to forget, I took many challenges in my stride, although at times there was loneliness. Being on guard duty with a loaded rifle for the whole night by yourself, was a little nerve racking, guarding 3 ton and 15 cwt lorries, knowing that a "loose wallah" could easily cause some damage. I used to sing all my old ballads, partly in fright, and partly to remember the lyrics. It did keep the voice in a good spot. Passing out at the end of the course with good marks, qualified me to do the Release course, this resulted in giving me the rank of a substantive sergeant. Paid in full, I kept part and sent the rest home.

Now, a fully fledged N.C.O. I was ready for the next posting, which came very promptly. Off we went to Ceylon, now named Sri Lanka. Once more on the crest of the wave, from the southern tip of India to Colombo. On the way, an Indian threw himself overboard, the Captain slowed down and we circled round and round, and finally picked up the poor wretch. He had tried to commit suicide, and when he came aboard, he was in a terrible state, covered in excrement, and although of very dark skin, he had turned white.
Eventually we arrived in Colombo. This was a very much cleaner place, and the inhabitants were kindly and friendly. A few days in a transit camp, gave us some swimming time at Mount Lavinia, and then on our way to Kandy, the headquarters of Air Command South East Asia.

The A.O.C. was Air Chief Marshall, Sir Keith Park, who put us to work straight away in Cyphers, this entailed sorting out codes and sending them to appropriate departments. The touch typing I had learned in Secunderabad came in for a lot of practice in this job. It was shift work, and quite often we would be on night duty, this entailed sleeping through the day, my time clock was all over the place. I was picked for the Command football team, and this meant quite often, loss of regular sleep. There was to be an important match against the Army, and we were training very hard. All of a sudden we were whisked into the Medical unit and were inoculated with a Cholera and Yellow fever vacine, normally this would be given in two jabs, making up 1.25 in strength, but we had the whole lot in one go. When I told the Medical Officer I was playing football the next day, he smiled, and said "Sergeant you will be in bed for 48 hours" and we were. It was impossible to think of football, when in a coma.

When we could comprehend, we were off to Singapore, for the surrender of the Japanese on this great Island. On to another ship. Singapore, a free port, was founded by **Thomas Stamford Bingley Raffles,** around 1819. The nucleus of the modern city of Singapore, is still as **Raffles** planned it. He knew it would develop and become a place of magnitude and importance. It was inhabited mainly by the Straits Chinese. When we arrived, the Island was amassed with Japanese. Our job was to control these little, strong, muscular, thick set people. They were the opposite of the Straits Chinese, who were small and thin, very clean and charming people, who befriended us immediately.

There were many nasty incidents during our command of the prisoners. Some of the servicemen, who had had brothers, cousins and close friends tortured and killed by the occupiers for the last three and half years, went berserk. In some cases they would knife the Japs with bayonets and any other weapons close at hand, they would never forget the atrocities dealt out by the enemy.

When the Japanese were rounded up, and transported back to their own Country, it was amazing how rapidly the change back to the peaceful idyllic spot, that was formerly Singapore. Air Command was set up at Changi. This unfriendly building, where the British and Australian prisoners were incarcerated for the last three and half years. In no time at all, the offices and billets were set up, and running. My function was in charge of the Orderly Room, with special management of Welfare. The other units at Seleter, Kallang, and Tengah, were soon in operation. Nee Soon, an army transit camp, and other smaller camps were gradually formed with a compliment of personnel, fully posted.

Being in charge of Welfare, gave me an inroad to the main units on the island, and their Officers. I formed my own show with four others, and sold it to each welfare department. The show was called "Clive's Cabaret" with Vic Gregory on the piano, Ernie Tomlinson. accordion, A mime act and a soprano by the name of Mavis Coppledick. I could only bill her as "Mavis", the troops would have made up their own name for her. With a driver, who doubled as stage management, we were a unit of six. The unit covered the whole island, and was very lucrative. Ernie Tomlinson was a good musician, and sixteen years later, we met up again in North Wales, where he was a piano tuner. For years I had him tuning the pianos in the Arcadia and Pier Pavilion theatres.

The other members of the cabaret I lost touch with, and have never heard anything about them since. We had some very happy times, and the shows were a change from the ordinary duties. Wherever these lovely people are, I hope they used their respective talent to advantage.

A new beginning to entertainment.
"Theres No Business Like Show Business" **Annie Get Your Gun.** *IRVING BERLIN*
.Life was pleasant, the climate suited me. I was issued with a tin of fifty cigarettes per week, and as I didn't smoke, I sold them to augment the income. Among my pleasures, I made friends with ERIC TAYLOR, the manager of the Cathay Building, the largest building in the city at that time. Eric had been an actor and was very "stagey", I remember the taste of the lemonade, he used to serve me, even now.

There was a big change in the entertainment scene for the troops. E.N.S.A. (Every Night Something Accidental) had now been replaced by Combined Services Entertainment. The Royal Air Force, were in command of the enterprise in India, and the Army controlled Singapore and South East Asia. The fact that I had been a professional before entering the Services, seemed to open doors for me, plus the reputation of my cabaret show. I was instructed to see the Commanding Officer. He asked me if I would like to go to the new entertainment unit, he explained that there would be only two RAF men in the unit, as the whole operation was to be administered by the Army. Try and stop me I thought. My reply was in the affirmative. The C.O. made comment that I would be upholding the good name of the RAF, and I should set a good example. I arrived at Nee Soon, the transit camp. This was fitted with a proper theatre. The other airman was Flt.Lt *Albert Arlen.* His claim to fame was that he composed the "El Alamein Concerto". Albert was a good pianist and artistic. He was soft and had a face like a spaniel, (No insult to the breed I loved) and a homosexual. We got on well to start with, ordinary variety shows were all we presented in the early days, until an influx of army personnel came for auditions. It had been quite a ruse with the lads in the infantry units, that this entertainment lark was a good scam. Get into doing a "turn" and you would miss all the ordinary duties. The Officers, such as they were, brought me in for the auditions. Can you imagine the different types, trying to get out of their units.

There was a wonderful surprise waiting. With the poor standard generally, there were four that were like a breath of fresh air. The talented four were *Kenneth Williams, Stanley Baxter, Peter Nicholls, John Scheslinger.* Can you imagine Kenneth Williams in the Army. "Could you kill a man ? " "Umm..Yes.Eventually". Ken was exactly the same in 1946 as he was when starring in the "Carry On" films. His impression of *Felix Aylmer* was brilliant, it was this character voice that he based all his voices on for the future. *Stanley Baxter* was the most versatile comedian of all, he was so adaptable and always found the common touch, though he at times, was very subtle. *John Scheslinger,* was a good actor, and *Peter Nicholls* an actor, and a useful writer. Among the personnel was *Morris Aza,* a very fine photographer. Morris was the son of two very popular agents, *Lillian & Bert Aza,* his job was to take photographs of all the productions. All the lads were made acting sergeants so that they could go into the Sgts mess after a show. This was fine but they were still paid at the private's rate.

Combined Services Entertainment felt that they should present something more of dramatic and historical importance. It was decided to present a dramatic reading of John Hersey's *Hiroshima"* the story of the obliteration of a city by an atomic bomb. *John Hersey* wrote for the first time, not a description of scientific triumph, of intricate machines, new elements and mathematical formulas, BUT an account of what the bomb does - seen through the eyes of some of those to whom it affected. The readers included *Stanley Baxter, Peter Nichols, Bill Ewart and Yours truly.* We took the parts of the different characters affected by those who endured the catastrophic experiences, AND LIVED. The reading was preceded by Paramount's film "The First Atomic Bomb Test" and during the reading we had back projection of the actual aftermath of the devastation.

The whole presentation was a triumph, and with all the technical back up, it created an outstanding success, and this was 1946, with service personnel starting from scratch. Our cast was first rate, the calibre of these performers was incredible. From these beginnings you could see Stanley Baxter growing with talent, and Peter Nichols accumulating ideas for characters that would manifest themselves in his clever plays to come later in his career.

Albert Arlen called a few of us together, to plan a new revue called "High and Low", to star *Babette O'Deal,* and myself. Babette would fly out from London. Being a prepared "pro" I had a load of music with me, and more than three quarters of the revue I supplied. As we were getting down to the running order and the content of the show, a cable arrived to say that Babette was held up, and we could not start rehearsals for at least six weeks. The new revue was shelved. Albert Arlen the overall producer of the unit, had arranged that six professional actors were to come out from London, to rehearse and present the Melodramatic Farce "Seven Keys to Baldpate" by George M Cohan, of Yankee Doodle fame. When the first rehearsal was called, it was discovered that the cast was eight handed, so two servicemen were to be added. The two parts were big and important to the plot, such as it was. The part of "Hayden" the arch villain who instigated the robbery and the murder, and the Detective Sergeant, who has the third act to unravel the crime, rather like an Agatha Christie.

Kenneth Williams was cast as the Detective Sergeant, and I had the plum part of the arch crook. This entailed my old wheeze with the Meltonian grey hair, and grey pieces, moustache etc., The rehearsals went along quite smoothly, the leading man was effeminate, and really should have been butch, but Albert had looked after some of his old cronies. *James Viccars,* who was not camp, was my sidekick, who carried out all my dirty work. The general opinion was that Ken and I more than held our own. I was bugged by the fact that Ken and I were not billed on the posters, this really upset me, especially being a "pro".

Then for once in my life so far, I did something unethical. Nearing the dress rehearsal, I went to the officers, and stated, that unless I was included in the billing, I would not go on. I knew that it was un-forgiveable, but I felt so strongly, the powers that be, could not move me. Consequently I was billed in the same size print as the civilian actors. I was upset about the whole incident, and even more so because Ken was not billed. Anyway the show went on. I know that Albert was enraged, so much so, that I thought he would get his own back at a later date.

"Seven Keys to Baldpate" opened on the 12th September, 1946 at the Victoria Theatre for a week, and then played all the camps on the Island. I particularly remember Seleter, as they appreciated plays, this was because **Leslie Randall** played in, and produced many plays regularly for the servicemen at that camp. On to Tengah, Kallang, and Johore Bahru. The piece was not really the servicemen's cup of tea, but we had some fun. When the tour finished I went back to Nee Soon. I was very lucky to have a real friend waiting for me. **Morris Weintraub** was RAF and was a great fellow, great was the size of his heart and personality, but he was small with tight curly auburn hair, he had a centre parting with tight waves spreading from the middle outwards. He used to write to his wife every day, he never missed, this impressed me. I called him "Morry", what a wonderful human being, we jelled from the start. Eventually we shared a billet, it was like a two up and two down. We spent most of our time playing table tennis, snooker, and going off to Ciros for a mixed grill, and then on to Eric Taylor at the Cathay building for drinks etc., Eric would often telephone Morry and I for swimming at Johore, then lunch at Raffles, a film at the Cathay, supper at the Jubilee and then back to camp for 11 p.m.. Eric paid for the lot, such a kindly man. Well dear reader, your probably thinking if was the life of " old Reilly", this was a good time, when not rehearsing.

Babette O'Deal was about to arrive from London, Albert called a meeting of the cast of "High & Low". I can picture the room even now.

Albert sat at a desk, with a large pile of music (mainly mine) in front of him. We were all sitting like being in the school classroom. Albert then read the running order and the content of the show. The whole programme had now changed. I personally was now only in two items, his revenge had started. You can imagine I was seething. It was then that I could see that he had not anticipated my positive reaction, knowing that the lads did not want to be returned to their units at any price, he was not prepared for my demonstration. I stood up and saluted, and said "Flight Lt Arlen, in the original run out of the show, I had more than two items. Came the reply, "What are you going to do about it, *Sgt. Stock ?* ", his jowls were now wobbling more than ever. All the lads were looking at me, there was a complete hush. In my strongest Actor's voice, I said..."I am not going to do it". Arlen said "You know what that means, don't you ?", I said "Yes...and I shall return to my unit, and before I go, I will have my music" Slowly, I walked to the desk, the lads had frozen. I took my music, it was easy to identify as my service number was stamped on the front page of each copy. After taking the music, (The pile on the desk had dwindled), I walked slowly out of the room, the atmosphere was electric, as I left, the lads were murmuring and mumbling, there were sounds of disbelief, that someone could defy the hierarchy, with the return to the unit.

I strolled into the Orderly room, music under arm, to get my transit voucher for the journey back to Changi. Captain Peter Ohm asked me where I thought I was going. Peter changed his name to Vaughan, and is now the *Peter Vaughan* that fine actor you see on your television screens. He plays great "Baddies". When I told them all I was going back to my unit, there was pandemonium....It had never happened before, threatened, yes, but never carried out.

I was quite happy to be on my way, the only regret was that I would miss my good friend Morry, the island being small, I was sure we would meet up again.

Welcomed back to my unit by Sqdn. Leader Jim Bonner, I was back in the old routine immediately, the welfare officers were contacted straight away, and *"Clives' Cabaret"* had bookings at the units all over the Island. once again. It was good to be doing my own show, and earning some dollars.

On the island was *Freddie Trinder,* brother of *Tommy Trinder.* Fred had been an electrician at the Liverpool Empire, and was a real character. Fred and I between us, used a lot of Tommy's material. Fred, naturally could remember more than I did. Tommy was about to arrive in Singapore with *Dan Draper, Jeffrey Piddock, Peggy Wilding and Diane Glover (*Tom's girl friend) Tommy had caused a lot of trouble with the troop ship that brought him out, and with the Port Authority. He had complained about his treatment, his cabin, his lack of comfort. This did not go down well with the troops that sailed with him, and what with Fred and I using his material, he was not a "happy bunny", when his reception was poor, and the laughs did not come. He was so annoyed with everything, he left and went to Australia, where he bought a lot of property, and became very successful. Fred and I patted each other on the back for helping him to financial success.

The cabaret was still successful and giving me great experience, for I could now go on stage, for at least 20-25 minutes, not knowing a set routine, it was mostly ad-lib to suit the type of audience, get to a definite gag for the pianist, and then lead into my impressions of Jolson, Sinatra, Nelson Eddy, finishing with Richard Tauber, this was always a show stopper, no good for today, but in 1946/7 it was mustard.

70

Booked for a solo performance at Raffles Hotel, I was about to do my act, when I was told someone important was in front. They couldn't tell me who the V.I.P. was. I went through the act with careful timing, and received a wonderful reception. I thought that it was a good outing for who ever the important person was attending that night.

While away from CSE, Albert Arlen was in his element. He designed costumes with an expensive shop called Doris Geddes. The price of materials alone was exorbitant. Still the army was paying for all the costumes, and some rackets were abounding. The unit had grown and many more servicemen had joined the unit. Albert devised a show titled "At Your Service" a strong cast including **Kenneth Williams, Stanley Baxter, Rae Hammond and Les Wilson.** The shows were of very good quality, coupled with the couture of Doris Geddes.

Out of the blue, a cable was sent to CSE Nee Soon from the G.O.C. of South East Asia, Maj. General. Stopford V.C. stating that Sgt Clive Stock RAF should be entertaining with CSE. Action immediately. Yours truly, was back to CSE, to find that Maj. General Stopford was the VIP at the Raffles Hotel that night. He of course had no idea that I had been with the Entertainment unit at the very beginning, and left.

The Officers acted very quickly on the orders from the boss man, and I was returned to my friends and fellow performers, especially my dear Morry. Albert Arlen was furious, and he made sure he kept out of my way. I remember vividly, the first Sunday back. Kenneth and Stanley had just returned from a tour with "At Your Service", and I joined them with a spontaneous comedy hour. The three of us adlibbed, feeding off each other, it was magic. We did this get together each time we were all back from our individual tours. These impromptu performances for getting laughs in any situation, proved a wonderful exercise for the future.

In the unit we had characters, there was pianist, **Royston Tandy** by name. He was a composer and had a playing style all of his own, rather like the great **Charlie Kunz,** You knew immediately who was playing. His music was distinctive and was ideal for dinner music. Roy had a saying that we all copied. Anything you asked him, he would reply, "It's all rather funny really", we used this expression regularly. Another character was **Johnny Brown,** a trumpeter of rare quality. He went on to become one of the foremost session musicians with **Don Lusher,** and a big band regular together with **Ken Rimmer** a fine Sax player. Capt **Bill Ewart** was a bass player, who put ST in front of his name, and on return to the U.K. will be remembered as **William Stewart,** television producer. Not to be confused with William G. Stewart, of "Fifteen to One", Bill married **Anthea Askey.**

As I wanted to start work straight away, I devised a revue called "Thru the Hoop". The company was very talented. **Norman Compton and Johnny Glass** were a superb double act, who had joined while I was on my banishment. There was an excellent soprano **Agnes Smith** from the ATS. Two dancers **Joanne Findlay and Norah Lyons** from the WAAF, **Dave Perton** a real Jack of all trades...Singer...pianist...dancer. **Bill Baterip** a loveable cockney, who played small parts and stage managed. He was always pulling my leg. The whole show was brilliantly accompanied by **Benny Kleinman.** The dancing was choreographed by **Johnny McKenna,** a professional. I borrowed Norman Compton to feed me in two Sid Field pieces, Slasher Green and Brushwork. I had made for me a great coat for "Slasher Green", from this time the name of Slasher Green followed me around all the time. Norman Compton was marvellous, and I shall always be indebted to Johnny for letting me use him. Johnny was a brilliant solo performer, everything fitted in perfectly. We became the No 1 revue in South East Asia. At that time the only service show to have girls. Our first tour was to Ceylon. (Sri Lanka).

We opened at the Garrison Theatre, in Colombo. During the time there I did a broadcast on Radio SEAC. This was a Forces radio station for all the troops. The station was run by **David Jacobs, Desmond Carrington and Josh Mink.** These talented people produced a show I had written about Ivor Novello, I interpolated some relevant songs. I also recorded the sketch "Brushwork" and at the end they gave me recordings of the broadcasts. They were recorded on 14 inch shellac discs. I kept them for years until they disintegrated. Our tour was from Colombo to Trincomalee, Kandy, Koggala, Kurunigala, Katukurunda and finishing at the rest camp in Diyatalawa. We stayed for rest for two weeks. During this time the crew of the Aircraft Carrier "H.M.S. Glory" came in for a break. They arranged a cricket match. I was included. I was over the moon, when one of the officers turned out to be my old pal from the ATC... *Cliff Gould,* who played the other brokers man with me in the first pantomime, in 1942. What a reunion ?!! Good cricket, batting I badly needed, and then Cliff was off. A real highlight.

One night in the moonlight with the silhouette of the trees all around the camp, I was sitting with Agnes Smith talking about the pure air of the place, and the effect of the moonlight. Agnes, not a bad looking girl, looked into my eyes, and said most seriously "What do you think of trees ?", I came back at her with "They're all rather funny really". I couldn't help myself, Royston Tandy was there in spirit. Agnes was not really sure of me. I could not cuddle or kiss her, as her boyfriend *Bryan Neely* was back in Singapore with another show. Bryan was a Cambridge blue for athletics. One day a loose wallah came into the camp at Nee Soon, and stole some money out of a billet, and then bolted. Bryan who was in the shower, came running out after him with just a towel around his waist, and nothing else. He sprinted after the thief, and needless to say, he caught him, but had lost his towel. The money was returned to the rightful owner. Everyone gave him a long round of applause.

Sorry I digress. Bryan Neely at a later date did all the swimming and diving for **Donald Houston** in the "Blue Lagoon" with **Jean Simmons.** The first film version of the **Henry de Vere Stacpoole** novel, written in 1909.

The show went on to Malaya and then back to Singapore. by now many well established artists were coming out to join our unit. **Reg Varney, Johnny Law, George Clarkson & Gail Leslie, Barri Chat & others.** .

Barri Chat was a female impersonator, who was a tremendous character. He always got involved with the wrong type of people, while he was with us, he ended up in jail. Being a homosexual with a tremendous sense of humour,.while in prison, he had all the inmates in hysterics. There were numerous unusual characters in the unit. There was a Sgt/Major. Hank Marriott. He lived in Singapore, and was involved with one or two rackets. He was mixed up with taxi-cabs, girls, drugs and dealings of a shady nature. He became so embroiled in intrigue and tension, that he committed suicide in the billet one day, in front of several other ranks, that happened to be with him at the time.

It was a very versatile unit.

One of the greatest accolades you can give any performer, is to call them a "real pro". I met one in **Reg Varney.** Here was a consummate artist. In a show at Nee Soon, he presented his famous ventriloquist doll on top of the accordion, which he played exceedingly well. His performance through the show earned him a standing ovation. One night the piano accompanist was brought down with Malaria. We had special mepecrine pills to make us immune. They sent your eyes yellow, but made your tan a golden colour. There was no way the pianist could appear. There was no other musician that could take on the evening. **Reg Varney** went into the pit and played for the whole show, and did his own spots into the bargain. What a "Pro"

A good "pro" was **Bert Bullimore,** a comedian in the style of **Bud Flanagan,** he even looked like Bud. He and I were the two main stand up comics on the island. Bert had a very popular double act with a good vocalist...I was a single act, mainly because I pattered and could sing. One time we were both asked to open a new theatre, I was a little apprehensive, Bert was a visual and broad performer, the double between us would have to be spontaneous, and would have to make sure we didn't talk across each other, as there was no rehearsal. We entered at this new venue to a tremendous reception, there were minutes before there was hush for us to talk. I think we were both scared, as we had no idea of the other ones grasp of the situation. We both said "Well whose going to start ?", you, no you, so I took the **Bull**imore, by the horns, and said "Good Evening ! What a wonderful theatre this is, and how delighted, I am, to be working with the second best comic in Singapore.". well ! Bert's face dropped, this remark had blown him away, the wind had gone out of his sails, every time he did a bit of business, he would mutter under his breath..."Second best comic" this worried him all the evening. Poor Bert, he never got over that remark. and the following week he fell off a stage and broke his leg, and was in plaster for a long time. A great fellow, and a great comic.

"Thru the Hoop" had played very successfully all over South East Asia and it was getting near the time for the return to the U.K. We had one more tour to do and this was to Burma...Mandalay, Meiktila and finish in Rangoon. There was a lot trouble in Burma with Dakots, Terrorists and civil unrest. We were about to leave to go back to Singapore, when a terrorist by the name of Usaw went into the Council chamber and shot Usong the President and six other councillors. A curfew was put on the city immediately. Our thoughts turned to the possibility of not catching the ship, and not going back to "Blighty". Our hearts were in our mouths and the tension was unbearable.

Luckily it all calmed down and we were released to get the boat. A few more "one nighters" for me in Singapore, for about three weeks before getting the ship back home.

Before I left, it was cricket time, I was selected to play for the RAF against the Army on the 24th August, 1947. During this time I became involved with a soprano by the name of Heather Leas, she was very attractive, I seemed to be drawn to sopranos. Heather said she would meet me on the Sunday, the match started at 11.30 a.m. As opening bat, for the RAF. I went in first, we won the toss. Fortunately I was still there at lunch 58 not out. When we were leaving the square, Heather arrived in furious mood, and looking like the wrath of a frustrated soul. In front of everyone and in a very loud voice, she bellowed "What do you want, me or cricket ?". This was very embarrassing in front of all the players, so in an equally loud voice I said "CRICKET"...game set and match. After lunch I continued my innings, I was caught at Square Leg for my highest score of 133. Morry wrote in his diary "Clive scored a brilliant 133 in two hours with 16 boundaries." It was a great stimulus, as I had not played an important match since Lords in 1938.

It was a command that I should go to the Medical Orderly room to receive clearance for all medical matters before leaving for the U.K.
I was sitting awaiting my turn, when a large bloke wedged himself in the doorway. This giant of a man wore a green beret, a huge Commando. He was six foot four inches, also having a check up for going home. He espied me with the words "You're him, your that fellow" he proceeded to do "Spivlike antics" "You know your'e....er..Slasher Green I saw you at the theatre the other night, you did all that...It was hilarious, it was great, it gave me an idea. You see you and I could wrestle", I said "I beg your pardon" he said "Well you see...*Con Balasis,* the World Light Heavy Weight champion is coming to the theatre next Wednesday.

He will fight the Heavy Weight Champion of the Royal
Navy...*Kid Callon,* and I thought we could give an exhibition in
the middle of the bill".. I said "I don't think so, I have built up a
good reputation here on the Island, and there is no way I mean to
sacrifice that for a gamble and risky appearance" "He said "It
wouldn't be risky. I would teach you all the wrestling holds and
counters, and you doing the Slasher Green bit, it would be
marvellous" I said. "I don't think so".

This big man was known as Flash Hammond, the Masked Marvel
and was the middle weight champion of Malaya. His real name
was *Ritchie Hammond,* he had been taught by *Jack Pye,* one of
the famous Pye brothers, of Blackpool.. He was very persistent and
said "You come with me to the theatre, and I will teach you
various holds and effective throws, and you see what you think
about it" Like a fool I agreed and I went to the theatre, and sure
enough he explained the wrestling techniques. He was a very
heavy man, but I threw him yards across the stage. His elevation
was tremendous, I got him into half Nelsons, and he showed me
the counter to each hold. I was quite excited, and he talked me into
the biggest gamble I had ever made, and this without any idea of
how the rounds were going to plan out.....No rehearsal. The show
was to be two bouts followed by us, another bout and then the top
of the bill. Flash fought as a masked man, the idea being that if you
won the match, you took his mask off. I was learning about these
things. It would all appear to be spontaneous. Morry would be my
second., all four foot ten of him.

There was absolutely no time to discuss how we would plan the
rounds, and with the exception of the proper holds he taught me, it
was going to be a "Make your mind up time, as you think fit" To
say the whole idea was "dodgy" is an understatement.

This was to be the biggest gamble of my life so far, and I was not
looking forward to it.

"Stand up and fight, until you hear the bell"   *Carmen Jones*
Oscar Hammerstein. Richard Rodgers.   BIZET.
The night came, all the wrestlers around me were very large and
fat. They ignored me completely. I was in a corner, with my props,
shivering with nerves and fright. My thoughts were of all the
successful shows I had performed over the months, and now this. I
said to myself, it's your own fault, you should have said "No" to
this gamble.

The first bout went on, and the audience started to boo and jeer. I
thought these are real wrestlers, what chance have I got. The
crowd were quite hostile. Evidently their whole performance was
contrived, and looked a fake. I expect, dear reader, you have seen it
on television.. The second bout received more attention, it was a
little better. The general criticism was that it didn't ring true.. My
palms were wet with fear, I was trembling and shivering.

There are times, in this life, when someone or something comes to
your rescue, and are with you. I sincerely hoped that this was one
of those moments. My religious childhood was now upper most in
my mind, I talked to my maker, and prayed fervently that I should
come through this ordeal with success. I always used to say a
prayer of thanks when I reached fifty while batting. I stood behind
the curtain before my entrance, to hear the M.C. say.........in a
stentorian voice.........

"Adies and Hentlemen, the next bout of the evening is a three
round challenge between the *"Masked Marvel"* the middle weight
champion of Malaya, Flash then entered to jeering and booing. He
went to his corner knelt on the mat, as if in prayer. (I was behind
the curtain hoping the ground would open up, and hoping the one I
had prayed to was listening) M.C...."And here we have the
challenger, all the way from the Elephant & Castle...SLASH.....
ERrrrrrrr GREEN .

I walked through the crowd to deafening cheering, clapping, the crowd went wild. I hadn't realized so many people had come to say "Goodbye". It had leaked out that I was going to leave the following week. They had all been so loyal over the time I had been there. While they were cheering, I managed to get to the middle of the ring. I went to Flash, still kneeling, felt his muscles and then felt mine, then knelt and prayed on the mat with him. This cheering had made me full of "emulsion" and my adrenaline was really flowing. Quickly into the middle of the ring, standing with my trilby on, the long black coat down to the ankles, the huge padded shoulders, that I had worn for the last year and a half, and my little thin moustache. Still the audience was clapping. I took off my coat, and underneath I had a large golden dressing gown with the words "Slasher Green" on the back. Slowly I slid the dressing gown off, and all the shirts, towels, pyjamas and padding, fell to the deck. There I was looking like a pipe cleaner, I was only 10st 2lbs. Round my waist I had the middle weight champion's belt with knives forks, hammers and chisels tucked in the top. During all this, laughs were in abundance, the last thing I took off was the trilby. This was the cue for the first round bell. I cannot remember blow for blow what happened, but the crowd was in disbelief, as the holds he had taught me looked more authentic than the former wrestlers. Having him in an armlock, I threw him nine rows of seats, into the punters. His elevation was fantastic, he was marvellous. he came running at me and in no time I had him in an Indian whip, that sent him somersaulting around the ring. I would stop and say "Want another one ?" he would say "Yes" and I would continue whirling him around. In between rounds I would be gargling and sending the water all over the officers, this was very popular, a few bars of "Largo al Factotum" brought extra applause, the ad libs were continuous. Flash would run at me as if to kick me in the face, and I would side step, and he would land on his front, I would side step, and pat his bottom with a camp gesture, suddenly he was up to his six foot four inches.

Morry would then run in to protect me, this would increase the laughter, as he was so small. Finally we finished with me standing on his chest, my arm raised in triumph, and then I unmasked him. The audience went wild. It was a personal success for me, but the real star was Ritchie Hammond, the masked marvel was superb.

An anti-climax followed. I felt sorry for the world light heavy weight champion as the high had been reached, and *Con Balasis* was in no mood to give an exhibition, he was going for real, he nearly killed *Kid Callon,* the Royal Navy champion, he was vicious and brutal. They just managed three rounds.

My thanks went to Flash, and to the one I pray to. I was truly helped to give one of my best performances of my life so far. Morry my dearest friend, gave me support when I was down and so nervous as to how it would all end in such a gamble. My well being and health owed so much to my friend, who shared an artificial sort of existence in a foreign country.
I was leaving Singapore with my reputation enhanced, my memories were golden, and I tried so hard to bring back the wonderful "Slasher Green" coat, but CSE would not let it go. The black tin box, that had been with me throughout my tours in the Far East, was full of suit lengths, poplin shirt material and many other goodies, and was now packed for the voyage home. We were sent to the Tebrau Transit camp in Johore Bahru, just over the bridge across the causeway from the mainland. The day before boarding the ship, I had a night in Singapore with Morry, a farewell meal and drinking session. The duty Sgt who would drive me back to Tebrau was dead drunk in bed, so we woke up Jerry Clynes and persuaded him to get Major Woodings' staff car and drive us. On the way the car kept stopping. I was asleep in the back, so I didn't know too much about it. Eventually I was delivered.

Morry and I said farewell to each other, in an emotional and grateful embrace. They left me to go back to the mainland. Jerry fell asleep, so Morry took over. I learned after that they finally got back at 4 o clock in the morning..

The next morning, the Major wanted his car, and when the engine was started there was a terrific noise. The fan belt was loose and the fan tore straight through the radiator. What a good job it didn't happen the night before, we would have all gone to prison.

On reflection, my time in Singapore was fantastic, the cricket, football and above all the many different types of showbusiness was edifying and a tremendous joy. The time in the service was a life of enjoyment, and an education for the future.

Before I boarded the ship, I thought of the wonderful performers, our unit had produced in its short life. I recaptured all the friends I had made, the laughter that had greeted me, there is nothing like the sound of hearty laughter on the tag line of a gag. Those magical and talented blokes flooded into my memory...........
It was pure enjoyment to recall the wonderful personalities in my unit......To think we had the following performers in our tiny camp in Nee Soon, Singapore...

KENNETH WILLIAMS, a very talented performer who had a cynical and brittle outlook on life. He did not suffer fools gladly, he was a snob and highly intellectual. He looked down his nose at the majority of us, and did not exude any warmth in his life with us. He was to become the most famous and popular name out of all of us. His comedy films and his reputation in the "Carry On's", was outstanding. He was not a happy man. He suffered from Melancholia, but a tremendous talent. Many of us forget his legitimate success as the Dauphin in "St. Joan", this being a highlight of his career.

*STANLEY BAXTER unlike Kenneth, had the ability, to cut
across class, race and age barriers. He had a tremendous and
sharp observation of people. He had an uncanny portrayal of
women, and his television success in the eighties, proved to be
without equal at that time. His ratings routinely nudged around
the 20 million mark. It was wonderful to see Stanley's great
impression of Kenneth Williams. Although he was a very nervous
man, he was a warm human being, and was one of my favourites.*

*PETER NICHOLS, did not show his true skill and talent with us,
he was confined to acting parts in revue, it was not apparent the
huge brilliance of his writing capabilities. His plays were West
End successes. In 1966 he was co-writer of the film "Georgy
Girl", this was followed by "A Day in the Death of Joe Egg". His
plays were produced by the National Theatre at the Old Vic. His
musical "Privates on Parade" written in 1977 was based on our
unit in CSE. In 2001, Peter had three plays presented in the
West End, at the same time..*

*JOHN SCHLESINGER appeared with me in John Hersey's
"Hiroshima" this was a treasured memory. He was a very
intelligent performer, and was a leading member of the Stage
Club playing a variety of different roles. He had a good grasp of
the perplexities of life. These attributes stood him in good stead
for his ultimate triumph as a film director. I have spoken to
actors, who say he had an unusual and definitive skill in
handling people in all circumstances, and getting the best out of
them. We can take a real feeling of pride that he was in our unit,
and became one of Britain's finest film directors.*

*John Schlesinger won an Oscar for "Midnight Cowboy". He was
a Londoner and studied at Oxford. He created more than 20
films, which included "Billy Liar" "Sunday Bloody Sunday" and
"Marathon Man". Michael Winner said his contribution to
British Cinema in the 60's was supreme.*

82

PETER VAUGHAN one of the most talented television and film actors of our time. His portrayals of sinister and dark characters are now legendary. He has many television series to his name. Part of his acting expertise, was a command of many different accents. He was a good friend to us all, and his rank of Captain did not make any difference to his genial persona.

ALBERT ARLEN, was a person that I would forget easily, I did not hear anything of him as I believe he went to Australia, and married a contralto. He was a talented man, inhibited with jealousy and a very large amount of bias.

PAT WOODINGS disappeared into oblivion. He was a stage director in the West End Theatre at one time, before the Services.

LES WILSON a most versatile of comedians. At home whether as stand up, character, summer show principal, pantomime star, his versatility is tremendous. His comedy talent had some good slots in television..."New Faces" "Seaside Special" "The Ronnie Corbett Special" and then his acclaimed performance in "Muck & Brass" with Mel Smith. A notable farce actor in Ray Cooney's "Out of Order" and "Two into One". His other claim to fame, is that he is the only artist to beat me at tennis.

Morris Aza followed his parents, and became an agent, his great success was managing ROY HUDD, a great performer.

I am still in touch with Les and his lovely wife Joan, but I have not seen many of the old Singapore gang. We are all much older now, and if a reunion was envisaged, it could be down to single figures attending..

I am so glad that my dearest friend "Morry" is still in touch after all these years.

The old troopship the "Empress of Scotland was to take us home to the U.K. *Ritchie Hammond and Morris Aza* came back on the ship, and with Flash being there it prompted many impromptu sessions. For no reason at all, I would pick a fight with Flash, and with all the expertise I had acquired during our famous wrestling exhibition, it once again looked real, and the skirmishes were quite frequent. Being a troopship all the lads entered into the spirit of the fights.

Morris Aza had proved himself an excellent photographer with CSE and he was not sure what he was going to do in "Civvy Street", we used to have long discussions on board. Neither of us knew that he would take all the photographs for my wedding three years later. He set up a photography firm Mobile Photos, this did very well, but later being the son of two very well established agents, he went in to agency and steered the career of *Roy Hudd,* and many other star names.

Ritchie Hammond was going back to Blackpool, where he would start his old wrestling career again. He did very well, because wrestling was popular, centres and theatres were promoting this "Sport" all over the U.K. Wrestling enjoyed every success, because television had not yet started the pseudo presentations. The advent of *"Big Daddy, Giant Haystacks* and the like, had not manifested.

The thought of returning to the theatre to earn my living seemed daunting. It had been marvellous being a stand up comic with impressions and vocal bits and pieces. I had been the star of all my shows and now I would go back to starting afresh.

Singing was the trade I had been trained for, and the forthcoming period could be very difficult, for I was not sure what course I should take. In hindsight you learn about patience and the thought of inevitability, but I was still very young for prophesy and clairvoyance.

Crossing my bridges, I was putting up all the barriers, and anticipation before knowing the whole situation. The profession would be overcrowded, all the actors and singers would have returned from the forces, ninety per cent of the Equity membership would be out of work.

This percentage has always been consistent for as long as British Actors Equity Association has been in existence. I was putting up all the obstacles. "All rather silly really"

Thinking of all the actors that had returned home long before me, I was thinking how best to start again. What had happened to my contacts, there were self doubts entering into the equation, and the uncertainty of my ability to start from scratch.

I had left a stolid straight singer, and over the past years the singing had taken a back seat, and I had ventured into comedy, I was starting to have little panic attacks. Never mind the ship was on its way...........HOME.

My highest score.....133 for the RAF, Singapore.

"Mother's there expecting me, Father's waiting too" New World.
Fisher   Anton Dvorak.

The homecoming was very emotional, I was back with my family after two and half years. I still had a few months to serve, but now I was going to enjoy two months leave. The first port of call was Lords. Middlesex were playing Somerset. Robertson and Brown were the openers. Sid Brown had been a paper boy for my father in the early days. Robertson went fairly cheaply, Bill Edrich joined Brown, a good stand followed until Sid was out, Edrich was then sixty something, Denis Compton came in, I have never seen such fast scoring in my life. Arthur Wellard, who was the main bowler, publicly stated that he wanted to go home, he didn't want to bowl anymore. At stumps **Bill Edrich** was 168, and **Denis Compton** was 252,, both were not out., we had heard overseas that the Middlesex terrible twins were having a great season. Compton scored 3,816 in all games at an average of 90.85 which is the all time record still standing. What a wonderful start to my leave.

On a visit to the Marquis of Granby in St. martins Lane, I met **Henry Oscar,** a well known actor who always played villains and sly characters, who was married to the sister of the doctor's wife, as aforementioned He had just come from a meeting of the Stage Cricket Club, Henry was a Vice-President, and we started talking cricket, he was quite impressed with my past playing. The rest of the committee came in for a drink, and I was introduced to **Garry Marsh,** a busy film actor. I was asked to audition the following week-end at Richmond Cricket Club in the nets. Garry lived at Richmond and the Stage had a game there on the Saturday. I bowled rather quickly for the batsmen there. I was comfortable with the batting, and I caught a few awkward balls, so I passed the audition and played that day. It was joy to become a member of the Stage Cricket Club in 1947.

I shall write a full chapter on this very unusual but talented cricket club, where actors only talk about the noble game, and not shop, which is very unusual among thespians. I was starting to meet local girls, no special one in particular, but they were all very nice. When they started wanting to take me home to meet mother, I was off.

My leave was coming to an end, and my posting came through to report to Maintenance Command at Andover in Hampshire. To see on my arrival, groups of airmen, 3 ton lorries and Officers all walking about looking official, it was not a sight that I thought I would enjoy, even less when I discovered with one other, we were the only two conscript Sergeants in the Mess. All the other N.C.O's were regulars. We were ostracized. The situation was not conducive to harmony, especially as I had been in a free and easy entertainment unit. Within two weeks I had to be in charge of a flight on the parade ground. Luckily I remembered most of the commands and bluffed my way through the early morning of the Squadrons' early morning inspection.

The Station Warrant Officer was a swine to me, because I was not a regular. Some of the regulars had served 25 years, and this is the reason they were taciturn. Very shortly, my demobilization number, would be coming up, it was 64. All things being equal, I should be released at the end of the year. Christmas was coming, and it would be my first Christmas at home for two and half years. Would you believe it, ? the SWO put me on duty over the festive four days. It was inconceivable that anyone could be so petty and paltry. I quickly arranged with my fellow conscript sergeant that I would pay him to do cover my duty. He agreed. On Christmas Eve I had travelled to Andover Junction station, sitting and waiting for my train. An announcement came over the tannoy :- "Would Sgt Stock report back to his unit, the matter was urgent"

I was very distraught, and when I returned the SWO met me "You are on duty Sgt Stock, and you cannot swop duties". My disappointment was obvious for all to see. I suffered through the Christmas, but on New Year's Eve, there was to be a concert.

I was asked to appear, my first reaction was to refuse, but I thought better of it, as I had a plan. My act was at the end of the show, and it was slanted against all Officers in general, and the SWO in particular. I had the lads on my side, and I pulverized the Officers, especially my nasty type, the SWO. Lots of little gags and "throw aways", were scoring, especially talking to the Officers, little gags like "Ill be alright, I'm going back to my old job, you'll be back on your milk round". The SWO would never forgive me, I didn't care, but the objectionable little man, put me on Duty Sgt on the 1st January, 1948, the day I was demobbed. I ran up the Union Jack for the last time, I saluted the SWO (not supposed to), not with two fingers.

In Padgate, we were demobbed, issued with a dark blue suit, with a chalk stripe, brown shoes (I ask yer), I was taught you never wear brown shoes with a blue suit, one white shirt. A Raglan sleeve overcoat, trilby hat, red tie, I looked like a hospital case. The thought of home obliterated any feeling of discontent with this free outfit.

Happy and free and whistling, I received my travel warrant, on to the train, and home to 83 Mill Lane, West Hampstead, London.

Back we hope, to a normal life once more, with the family.

I was feeling so happy.

RICHARD GRESTOCK
Maternal Grandfather
1864-1930

FLORENCE GRESTOCK
"Mum" Grandmother
1870-1939

ERNEST HAROLD STOCK
"Pop" Father
1897-1974

DOROTHY STOCK
Mother
1902-1989

Right: *Pop and I above the shop.*
2 months old, 1927

Below:
The BBC, Beryl Brian & Clive.
Kenton, 1932.

Yours truly with the Afghan Hound "Baa Baa" 1938.

An "Erk" in the Royal Air Force. Cardington, 1944.

My closest friend,
"Morry".
Singapore, 1946.

As "Valentine"
in "Tough at the Top.
Adelphi, 1949.

Above: *Our Wedding.*
Emmanuel Church Hampstead,
1949

Left: *Gwen as "Laurey",*
Oklahoma, Drury Lane, 1949

Our first "Guvnor"
SANDY POWELL, 1953.

Gwen as "Fiona", Brigadoon.
Australia & NZ, 1951

Our Family.
Gwen and I with Richard
& Duke, 1966

Two lovely Scottish "Freens"
George & Gail, 1958

"All men must be free" **Pomp and Curcumstance, Number Four.** **Sir Alan Herbert.** **Sir Edward Elgar.**

Arriving home was wonderful, mother displayed great happiness in having her boy home, she was not given to emotion. Pop, his usual quiet way said "Its good to have you home" It took a little while to adjust, I remember when I came back from the east, I would give the clothes brush to Pop expecting him to brush me down. I made sure I didn't do that again. Home was wonderful, I got to know my sister and brother, they were young teenagers when I left.

How I came to meet a Jewish lady called Razelle Lapin, I don't know or remember, but she was keen to help me, she wasn't a well known agent, but she had some good contacts, and she was a keen operator. A big film of "Caesar & Cleopatra" starring **Claude Rains,** was about to go into production. Miss Lapin arranged an interview with **Gabriel Pascall and Brian Desmond Hurst.** While I was waiting to be ushered into the inner sanctum for the interview, a man was waiting to see the same two men..

Standing with his back to me was the wonderful **Claude Rains.** He was very friendly, and we talked about the British film industry. I listened intently, I was in awe. Claude Rains was a very good friend of John Gielgud, he taught the classical actor, through his encouragement, to lose his self consciousness. A lovely moment went all too quickly, as I was called into the office to meet these two giants. **Pascall** was brusque, and was not very popular, but **Desmond Hurst** was amiable. Gabriel Pascall in his broken English accent said "Your neck, she is too long, You want big centimetre collar", needless to say, I didn't have anything in the film. I was a little disappointed, as I usually walked into engagements, but not this time. I went for an interview with **Clive Brook** for a part in Frederick Lonsdale's "On Approval", as soon as I said my name, the face changed from affability to a stern countenance. No job there, but my friend Don Weston landed a nice bit in the film.

Miss Lapin suggested I write to **Michael Powell,** as he was Producing and Directing "The Small Back Room" by **Nigel Balchin.** Receiving a reply and an appointment with the famous man, I met this very successful director of the Archers film company. The interview was very formal, he took down a few particulars, and thanked me for coming to see him. I thought its one of those "Don't call us, we'll call you", But no.....I was called for four days work. In those days I hadn't a car, so I had to ferret out buses and trains to get me to the studio for a 4.30 a.m. call. I was made up and dressed in a very smart suit. I was a young civil servant. The set for the scene was a replica of the room that **Winston Churchill** conducted his meetings in, with the boffins, the inventors of special bombs used during the war. The large board meeting table was the focal point. Around were seated the actors ready for the meeting.

Next to me was **Patrick McNee,** then **John Stratton, Hamlyn Benson, James Dale, Leslie Banks, Walter Fitzgerald, Elwyn Brooke-Jones, David Farrar** and **Jack Hawkins.** Can you imagine how I was feeling in the company of these illustrious actors. A positive star studded set, with a nervous twenty two year old singer. Various shots were taken, and I learned that if they managed to get two minutes of film in the can in a day, that was success. That was in 1948, they do better than that these days. It now came to my close-up. I had a line to be delivered in to the ear of Pat McNee. . Michael Powell lined up the shot and told me where to aim my line. He said "Action" I did the line, and Powell said "Cut, its not right, try again, so it was "Take 2" and I thought it was alright, but he was not satisfied. One more try, and he was now red in the face, by this time, and I was a bundle of nerves. To flame my embarrassment, he asked Pat to do the line, that was no good, then John tried, then Hamlyn. Powell was not at all satisfied. He asked me to do it again, I did, he said "Cut and Print" they then killed all the lights. I sat there in a form of mesmerized paralysis.

Jack Hawkins the saviour.

Jack Hawkins came across to Powell and said "How dare you do that ?. Don't you ever do that to an actor again." Powell looked vacant. Jack continued "You have undermined and taken it out on a young actor, because you were in a bad mood through our disagreement this morning". Jack and Powell had a contretemps first thing. Evidently there had been a stormy row between the two men, and Michael Powell had taken it out on me. Everybody was kind to me and I felt a lot better, having been cleared of a possible mistake. Film making is a specialized art form, I was quite impressed with all the setting up and especially the lighting. It was a Black & White film, and to have all those stars in one scene, and to be part of it, was an experience I could not buy, so now what next ?..

Richard Stone, a well known impresario, telephoned me to see if I would do a variety show at Woolwich. This I was pleased to do, as I had an audition for Vivian Van Dam at the Windmill Theatre, but I was not the right type for that, and they said "Thank you very much". I then, appeared as a Coast Guard in "True as a Turtle" a film starring ***John Gregson*** and directed by my dear ***Wendy Toye.***

It was going to be a very lean time, with nothing coming in. Walking up Endell Street near Drury Lane, I met my old friend ***Reginal Burston,*** who had been the conductor in my first show "Show Boat". We were pleased to see each other, and I told him all about my experiences in Singapore. "What are you going to do now ?, " he said, my reply "I have nothing in mind, and no job at the moment.", Reggie smiled, "They are wanting 2nd tenors in "Oklahoma", and there is an audition next week " I'm not a second tenor " he said "I remember you used to hit a few top G's. You come along on Tuesday at 10 a.m". "I'll be there", I said..
When I arrived for the audition, I learned that Reggie was Musical Director and Conductor.

Thank you old friend.

It was quite an ordeal to sing on the empty stage in this wonderful theatre, for an American producer, who I was told, his moods were controlled by the condition of his Gout. I think being young, I had age on my side, for they wanted young cowboys. I sang well with strong voice, and put a couple of top notes in for good measure, and I was accepted. I was started on the pay roll straight away. I was given a musical score of the show, and was told to attend performances, and stand at the back, as each performance was sold out, and learn the show musically and see the choreography of the musical numbers. This I did.

I was told that the usual auditions for "Oklahoma" required the stage to be covered with singers, and the producer would go around and tap those on the shoulder, that he thought the right type. One day there were only six, he wanted. The others were all dismissed. He would hear those chosen, and then might not even employ any of them. I was quite proud I had been engaged, not only in the smash hit show, but at this very prestigious theatre.

The stage at the "Lane" was vast, I remember that the largest set in "Oklahoma" could be accommodated another twice, and at the back was a huge moving frame for the designers and artists to paint on canvas.

In 1947, "Oklahoma" along with "Annie Get Your Gun" were the most successful and financially rewarding productions in London. The Americans came in great numbers to see, whether or not the Broadway productions were superior. The jury is out on that one.

The finest theatre, I know.

"Welcome to the theatre, to this business we call show"

Applause. Betty Comden, Adolph Green, Charles Strouse

The Theatre Royal Drury Lane was the fourth on the site, and opened in 1812. The original theatre was built in 1660 and the Giant names of the acting profession were leading players at this legendary venue. *David Garrick, Mrs Siddons, Richard Brinsley Sheridan, John Philip Kemble, Edmund Kean,* the list is extensive. *Ivor Novello* had his great successes there between 1932 and 1939. I was caught up in all the history and the inspiring atmosphere of the "Lane" . The famous ghost was the man in grey, supposed to be *David Garrick.* If you saw the ghost of *Dan Leno,* in the Dress Circle during the dress rehearsal, the show was to be a hit. Of course many say they saw this happy ghost on the dress rehearsal, that is why "Oklahoma" was such a resounding success. The history of this great theatre is like the history of our nation. Sir Augustus Harris, whose bust is outside the theatre, led Drury Lane through a great success, with pantomime alternating with melodrama through the late nineteenth century. His idiosyncrasies were well published, especially the time when he snored throughout a first night of Sir Henry Irving. Another Knight of the realm.....Sir Cameron Mackintosh worked backstage during the *Loewe and Lerner's,* musical "Camelot", he can now boast that his show "Miss Saigon" has the record for the longest run of over ten years.

It was a very theatrical moment, in 1916, when Frank Benson appearing in "Julius Caesar" was knighted by King George V in the Royal box at the end of the performance. Being a cricket nut reminds me that Sir Frank Benson had his own cricket team, especially when he was touring in the summer. He once sent a telegram to a leading London agent, saying :- *Send up a left arm spin bowler, to play Laertes"*

Anyway, back to the chase...........

93

Within a few days I had learned all the harmonies, and I had tried very hard to absorb all the movements and the choreography. The producer gave me a scant rehearsal with the male singers, and then one run through with the whole ensemble, and then I was in. The first performance was nerve racking, I am sure that nobody noticed me, with so much going on.

I was now in the most successful show that had ever been in Drury Lane since its inception. "Oklahoma" played 1,375 performances in the "Lane" and then did 6 months at the Stoll Theatre to finish. *Richard Rodgers* had two partners, *Lorenz Hart and Oscar Hammerstein, Oscar Hammerstein* had four partners:- *Jerome Kern, Rudolph Friml. Sigmund Romberg and Richard Rodgers*. If you were to list all the successes these collaborations presented, then you would have the most outstanding material ever written in the musical theatre.

The ruling by British Actor's Equity and the Government, was that the Americans could only work in the show for six months. Some of them seemed to have wangled a longer stay. *Harold Keel* had been in the show since it first opened in Manchester in 1947. He told me personally, that he didn't know why he stayed on for a further twelve months, as the pay was not very good and he had income tax in two countries. He added that he was broke when he returned to the U.S.A. that didn't last long. I was glad he was still in the show, when I started. Harry, as he was affectionately called, later became *Howard Keel.* He made a British film with *Valerie Hobson* called "The Small Voice". In the film he played the part of an American crook. The M.G.M people came to see him, already knowing how well he sang, they signed him up for the film of "Annie Get Your Gun" with *Betty Hutton,* and as they say "The rest is history". Harry was a real star. He had taken London by storm, and gave a scintillating performance every show.

It is hard for the younger performers in our business, to comprehend that we did nine performances a week, with a 37 piece orchestra, and not one microphone in the theatre. We used the diaphragm to project the voice to the back of the theatre. "Harry" gave full voice every show, and even in the encores of the Oklahoma chorus, when he could have eased up, he was still pounding away. the company was super and I was getting bonded with them. The show was presented by the Theatre Guild of America in association with H.M. Tennent, under the direction of *Hugh (Binkie) Beaumont.* "Binkie" was a very successful impresario. In 1954 he had 15 shows running simultaneously in the West End. Even the recent Knights Lloyd Webber and Mackintosh never had such a prolific output. "Binkie" put on "My Fair Lady" first, and it ran for eight and half years, it was the first show to have microphones. So good were the acoustics of Drury Lane, that even *Mary Martin,* didn't have a microphone in "South Pacific". Binkie Beaumont was described by *John Gale,* president of the Society of West End Theatre Managers as "The greatest impresario of our time. a giant". I found him a very kindly man. He was "Class"

The Americans in the show were charming people, who loved London and the British. *Howard Keel,* was very grateful to our Country, as he believed that *we* were responsible for his success. There were some lovely girls in the show, and my eyes fell on one special lady. Not only did my eyes fall, but I fell for *Gwen Overton.* I was besotted with her. For three weeks, she did not notice me or talk to me, just a smile, but no contact. I had made up my mind, that she was the one for me. One Monday night during the show she said, :- "Were you playing cricket at Denham on Sunday ?, as I was flying with my boyfriend, in his plane over a cricket match, and I said to Harry I wonder if that Clive Stock is playing there", (Everybody knew I was a committed cricketer) I said "No, I was playing at, somewhere in Surrey" Where many of our fixtures were played.

I meet the OVERTONS.
"Your hand feels so grand in mine"   Oklahoma.
Oscar Hammerstein and Richard Rodgers.

We gradually became very close, and although Gwen had had a millionaire friend complete with "Roller" and Harry with his own plane, it was obviously meant to be. On the 23rd December 1948 (Gwen's birthday) we were engaged. The press printed a nice photograph with us in our Western costumes.

My mother was not very keen on my engagement. It was not Gwen, it was the fact that I had been overseas and away for so long, she thought it all a bit too soon. A source of aggravation was that Gwen spoke with this western Oklahoma accent all the time. Harry Keel had been coaching her, as she was the understudy for "Laurey", the leading lady in the show, and she was determined to be perfect for the part.

It was time for me to meet her family. Her mother and father were gems, especially her father. He was a jovial and open man with love for everybody. He loved his sport, which suited me. He loved music and was a professional violinist. His mother, Grandma Overton, was an old performer, she had done everything from silent films, to melodrama. She and Grandpa were in the "The Miracle". Marie Munro Overton was in the variety theatre, when you could book your act well ahead. Her act was titled "Dare Ring" it was a quick change act. Grandma played all the parts, and Grandfather was the detective in the office. Marie , as she was called, tied some cotton on her finger, to prove she played all the parts. If anyone could disprove this, she would give them a hundred pounds, which in those days was a fortune. needless to say, nobody could prove that she didn't play all the nine characters in the piece. They travelled their own set and had three dressers, and the act was booked three and a half years ahead. They were a real "pro" family. Gwen had a younger sister, Yvonne. she was nine years younger.

Under sufferance at first, Gwen came to cricket matches with me, and gradually accepted that this was my only vice. The members of the club took her to their hearts, and it became another family. The Stage Cricket Club gave us so many happy times, more about the club later.

As I was earning a regular salary, I needed to have some singing lessons, and I found my old friend from the "Merry Widow" *Ray Carey.* He was an Australian, and his teaching at Weekes Studios, Hanover Street, near Oxford Street was becoming very famous. Dame Eva Turner sent all promising young voices to him. I started lessons, and felt an improvement straight away. He taught in a uncomplicated style, with a natural production, and placing the voice well forward. My singing was required for an audition for a new *C.B. Cochran show.* This show was to follow *"Bless The Bride"* which was such a success, and still running. The general Manager for Cochran was *Fred Wilby.* He told me what to sing. He tipped me off to sing a song to show of the voice, and then a fast cockney song. For the straight romantic song, I sang "Song of Songs" which was legato, and then an old music hall song "Down The Road", it must have sounded like an operatic *Max Miller.* There were two parts in the new show of equal importance. *Cochran, Vivian Ellis and Sir Alan Herbert,* wanted me, and "Cocky" wrote to me to say that whatever happened I would be in the new show. This new musical, was yet without title. To have this letter a year before the show was produced, made me feel like walking on air. I thought, I have only been back five minutes from the services, and here I am in a great show, in love and engaged to a wonderful lady, and now in demand for a show for the great Cochran, that will come to fruition in the future,.all this, and I am getting lots of runs and wickets in the sporting side of me. During the run, the senior executives of the Theatre Guild of America, Theresa Helburn and Lawrence Langner came over to check on their production, and to meet the company.

97

We had a big party, and I got together with a few of the cast and put together a skit on the show, using the proper costumes. The hit of the show was *Lulu Dukes. Lulu* was the daughter of *Madame Rambert and Ashley Dukes*. In the show she played the "Fall Down Girl". The show in Drury Lane straight after the war, before "Oklahoma" was "Pacific 1860" by Noel Coward. Lulu went for an audition for *Noel Coward,* her dancing was perfect "The Master" was impressed. He said "Delightful, would you sing for me ?", Lulu said "Oh I don't sing" Coward retorted, "of course you do, everybody sings" Lulu nervously, spluttered "I don't", from the great man came "Well sing me a scale" The pianist struck a chord, and Lulu went into the most awful discordant sequence of notes, that was hardly recognizable. Coward froze in disbelief, and in his famous clipped delivery, paused and said "Try it again in A flat". There is no good trying to disguise it, Lulu could not sing. So you can imagine the tremendous reception she received, when I cast her as Curley. The tunes of Richard Rodgers were wailed into oblivion. The photographs of this "send up" were featured in the popular publication "The Illustrated" With the exception of myself, as the "Pedlar", all the blokes played the female roles. The guests of honour were very suitably impressed. The bon hommie in the company was never more apparent, than on a night like that.

Another night for the company to get together, was the 6th January of each year for the twelfth night cutting of the Baddeley Cake. Richard Baddeley left money so that whatever company was appearing at the "Lane" on twelfth night, would have a special cake to cut for the whole company, this was a very enjoyable ceremony.

And so the show gaily progressed from week to week, playing to packed houses. Every night we had to sing the "Oklahoma chorus" again and again. I think the record was seven encores, it was so exhilarating.

Cochran contacted me to come to the office at Old Bond Street. I arrived, and went to the studio at the top of the building, to find *"Cockie", Vivian Ellis and Sir Alan Herbert* waiting for me, Vivian sat at the piano, and asked me to sing a varied selection of songs. He chose songs that I knew the lyrics of, they ranged from "Annie Get Your Gun" to their current show "Bless The Bride". I had no idea, why this was happening. They thanked me very much, and hoped all would continue to go well in "Oklahoma". My dear friend *Fred Wilby,* told me that they were thinking of me to take over from *Edmund Goffron,* who had succeeded *George Guetary* in the lead role. I was very surprised, it was not a role I thought they would have had me in mind for. I was too young. However, I forgot all about it. Later I learned, Cockie had got in touch with Binkie, asking if he would release me to play the part of Tommy Trout in "Bless The Bride" for a month, while *Brian Reece* went on holiday. He also mentioned he hoped I would be released for the new show. Binkie wisely said, that if it was to take over the part he would happily agree, but for a month, he refused. He would release me for the new show, and that was that. I was rather flattered that they should think I was good enough to play for Brian, who became a close friend. We were now well into 1949 and Cochran notified me that the new show was to start rehearsals, and so I duly gave notice, and *Ivor Emmanuel* came in to take my place, another baritone.

The new show was to open at the Adelphi Theatre in the Strand, where "BlessThe Bride", had such a long run. Well before the show was produced, I went along to the Adelphi Theatre, to see "Bless The Bride" and I stood at the back of the stalls, there also watching was Wendy Toye, we talked and recalled memories of "Jenny Jones". In a slightly boastful way, I told her that Cochran had signed me for the next show, (I didn't know that Wendy was to produce it) Wendy looked at me, with a "Nobody told me" sort of expression.

After a lot of wrangling between *Cochran, Vivian Ellis, Alan Herbert* and *Lord Anthony Vivian* (Cochran's Partner), The new show was titled "Tough at the Top", the majority wanted the new show to be called "A Kiss In The Ring" but Cochran was adamant, that it should be "Tough at the Top". The show was about a Champion Boxer who falls in love with a Princess, and "Cockie" wanted to prove that it was tough at the top of whatever profession you were involved in. He of course had been a boxing and wrestling promoter, as well as an impresario for musicals. He had staged *Max Reinhardt's spectacle "The Miracle" at the Olympia, choreography by Massine, 1,500 people in the cast including 500 in the chorus and a 200 piece orchestra,* he was well known for promoting :- tennis exhibitions, circuses, rodeos, as well as *Diaghilev's Ballets.* This man was the complete impresario and pioneer of live entertainment. Many ladies became big stars, having been in *Cochran's Young Ladies. Jessie Mathews, Evelyn Laye and Anna Neagle* to name but a few. "Cockie" got his way, and the show was called *"Tough at the Top".* incongruous with "Bless The Bride". The title did not appeal to the elderly ladies who kept the "Bride" going for nearly three years. The Princess was played by *Maria D'Attili,* and the Heavyweight boxing champion, by *George Tozzi. George* was an American Italian with a gorgeous voice. He was principal bass at the the Metropolitan opera in New York, and he dubbed the singing voice for Rossano Brazzi, in the film of "South Pacific". *Brian Reece* had the comedy role as the Count Victor, *Eddie Byrne* as the Irish trainer. There were three professional boxers in the cast for the boxing scenes, and they also taught George how to box. There was a lot of fun in that show. *Wendy Toye* directed the whole show with great skill. Here was a brilliant lady of the theatre. It was a joy to see her handling the whole cast. She had bits of business for all the company, and she treated the chorus as individuals. The chorus master was the BBC's brilliant *John Clements.*

"This is not the end, this is only the beginning". Tough at the
       Sir Alan Herbert.   Vivian Ellis.   Top.

The rehearsals for "Tough" were tough. The main role for me was
"Valentine" *The secretary to the Court.* It was showy, and my
morning suit was specially made by Morris Angel, the complete
definition of sartorial elegance. To show my authority I would
look down stage, especially when *Brian Reece* had a scene with
me. I would take a step upstage, and Brian would either have to
speak up stage or he would get in line with me. He said once "If
you want to act this scene on the backcloth, I will be there with
you "

Playing the Prime Minister was *Geoffrey Bayldon,* known to most
people as "Catweazle" and of course the "Crowman" in "Worzel
Gummidge". He and I became very good friends and we had quite
a lot of dialogue together. My operatic *Max Miller,* was as a
cockney tipster in the Derby scene. Vivian Ellis had written very
tuneful music and it was a pleasure to sing these very melodious
songs. The part of the German General was played by *Felix Kent.*
He was German, and he shared the dressing room with Geoffrey
and I. One of the most moving interpretations of *Shakespeare* I
have ever heard, was Felix, in German, portraying the famous
"Soliloquy" from "Hamlet". Geoffrey and I were spellbound.

George Tozzi and Maria D'Atilli had outstanding voices. They
made the lilting melodies pure operetta. George had to train hard,
and the boxers choreographed some very authentic bouts.
The show was Ruritania in concept, and told the story of a World
Champion boxer who falls in love with a Princess, and with all the
sub plots, proves that they will never be happy together because of
their positions in life, and therefore proves that it's "Tough at the
Top"

The show was described as "A LIGHT OPERA" the book and the lyrics were by *A.P. Herbert.*

Sir Alan Herbert was an Independent Member of Parliament. for Oxford University from 1935-1950. With versatility and wit, he wrote for the satirical magazine, "Punch" for many years. He campaigned for changes in the Divorce laws, and improving authors' rights. He wrote many books, and his best seller was "The Water Gypsies". He was a true English gent. His lyrics for "Big Ben" and "Bless the Bride" were the most charming.
Vivian Ellis created more than sixty musicals, and wrote single compositions for such programmes as the BBC serial "Paul Temple", the tune was the famous "Coronation Scot". While still only twenty five, his smash hit "Mr Cinders" established him as a forefront show composer,. The hit song "Spread a Little Happiness" made the pop charts, sixty years after it was first sung by *Bobby Howes and Binnie Hale,* in 1929. He was a dedicated President of The Performing Rights Society, and a Vivian Ellis prize was created annually for stage musical writers.
Oliver Messel designed the show, his costumes were gorgeous, although very extravagant. They must have cost "Cockie" an arm and a leg.
Michael Collins, brother of *Harold Collins,* conducted the *Louis Levy Theatre Orchestra.* with orchestrations by *Phil Cardew and Leighton Lucas. Chappell,* were the publishers. *Tommy Linden, Keith Beckett and Beryl Kaye,* were principal dancers. Cochran acknowledged in the programme, the advice and assistance received from *Tom Webster,* for his help in the Derby scene.

As the show seemed successful, and had settled down, after two months, I said to Gwen that we should get married.

"This is my lovely day"   **Bless the Bride.**
Sir Alan Herbert.   *Vivian Ellis.*

And so on the 23rd September, 1949 we were married. We chose
that date because it was my Grandmother's (Mum's) birthday. It
was a wonderful day, but the only drawback was that we went to
different theatres at night, Gwen to Drury Lane, I, to the Adelphi. I
had asked Cochran if I could have time off for a honeymoon, but
he wrote to me explaining that if I was off, three actors had to go
on, and he did not want to lose my performance so early in the
piece. He finished by writing :-
*"You are a young man with a great talent, and I have my eye on
you"* signed *Charles B. Cochran.*

The wedding was the happiest affair, as you can imagine. Gwen's
mother and father were pretty wonderful in supporting and
financing a gathering of many. Just under 200 people attended.
Apart from family, there were members of both the "Oklahoma"
and "Tough at the Top" companies. My dear friend *Don Weston,*
was my best man, and how efficient he was.
Everything went like clockwork, and the success of the day was
largely due to him. Wendy Toye and her mother came, *Garry
Marsh, Abraham Sofaer, Russell Napier,* and a full compliment
of the Stage Cricket Club. The members did say, if I was not there
with the best man for the ceremony, throw a cricket ball down the
aisle, and I would be there in a thrice.
 The Cochran office had (without me knowing) organised press
photographers. Gwen looked radiant and just how a bride should
be, I was allowed to wear my morning suit, made especially for
"Tough at the Top"

When we came out of Emmanuel Church, there were cameras
everywhere. They took their pictures and ran off to catch the
evening papers, leaving our photographer all by himself. The
reception was followed by spontaneous entertainment.

Reggie Burston was on the piano. **William Thorburn,** who went on to play "Mr Snow" in "Carousel" in full Scottish highland costume, sang "Bonnie Mary of Argyll" other party pieces were performed, and the lovely crowd pulled Gwen and I on to the rostron to sing "This is my lovely day". My poor father had to leave early to open up the shop, as he arrived on the doorstep, there were the evening papers with a super photograph on the front page of the Evening News, Standard and Star.

The picture was of two year old Christopher Thorburn, son of Bill, presenting us with a Lucky horsehoe. It certainly was lucky.

We managed to get away for the weekend at an Hotel in Petersfield, Hampshire, but we were both back promptly to go to our respective theatres for the Monday night show. "Oklahoma" was packed for the nine shows a week, and we were doing quite well, although not sold out. Soon it started to lose money and Cochran took it off before it lost any serious money. The show lasted five months. It was sad that a show with so much melody and with some of the finest lyrics, A.P.H. ever wrote, should comparatively fail. The charm of "I Wish I Could Sing" "This is not the End" "I don't want to marry anybody very much" and the lyric that goes :-

England is a lovely place   You should see what I have seen.
Honey suckle in the hedges,   Cricket on the village green.
Children on the high hay-waggon, Ploughman with a god like

grace

Old men at the "George and Dragon.England is a lovely place.
England is a lovely place, there are daffodils in the wood.
Silver bells across the valleys, whisper peace and brotherhood.
When the sunny soft day closes, lovers in the lane embrace.
All the country smells of roses, England is a lovely place
England is a jolly place, there is joy in all they do.
They go mad about the Derby and they have a boat race too.
England is a band of brothers, There's a smile upon her face.
Like the smile of sweet old mothers, England is a lovely place.

The melody to this lyric was beautiful, and the harmonies were so attractive. It was the one time when I wish I was back in the chorus, to sing the effective music. With a lyric like that, it proved that Sir Alan Herbert, was the quintessential Englishman.

It was a very kind gesture from **Brian Reece.** He gave us his house on the Thames at Kew for a month, so that Gwen and I had some time together. It was at Strand on the Green, Kew.

Brian had just finished a very successful radio series of P.C.49, and he wanted to go up to Yorkshire for a much deserved rest. He said you have the house while I'm away, so it will not only be aired, but will deter burglars. It was an idyllic spot, although we had one catastrophic experience. Gwen went off to Drury Lane from Kew one night, and the fog was a real "pea souper". I was left on my own being now out of work. Kew station was a few yards from the house, so it was close by for Gwen to get the train to London for the show. Off she went and I said goodbye, although the fog was bad, with the speed of the trains it was reasonable to think that she would get to Drury Lane on time. One and half hours later, Gwen rang the bell and there she was in a real state, she shouted at me, and called me for all the names under the sun. It transpired that she had arrived at the station, and the fog was so bad, all trains were cancelled. On the way back well over an hour later, she had slipped down a manhole that had its cover left off, and stuck at her hips. Nobody about, no vision. She levered herself out of the manhole, after quite a while, and in shock, had finally reached me in tears. The only show she had ever missed, she blamed me for it all.

"Tough" coming off in November, made it a difficult time for getting another engagement. A stroke of luck manifested itself, in that **Kenneth Milne Buckley** was producing a television pantomime, to star **Jack Hulbert.** Ken Buckley played cricket with me in the Stage Cricket Club, he was the son of May Buckley, who was our very faithful scorer.

Ken was married to *Sylvia Peters,* the well known T.V. announcer at that time. *Wallas Eaton, Eunice Gayson, Abrahan Sofaer* as the Sultan, and myself as the "Pasha" were featured. The whole production was "LIVE" at the Alexandra Palace. The "Ally Pally" as it was known, had broadcasts, live from August 1936. It had two studios, Studio A operated on the Marconi EMI television system, and Studio B on the Baird system. In 1937 the Marconi system was judged to be superior, so the Baird system was scrapped.

Can you imagine having to have all the sets staged in a very small space, and then have an orchestra included with all their music stands. It seems absurd that the whole of the BBC once planned, shot and transmitted from a small complex, scarcely bigger than a modern studio. Anyway...Cheapside, Fitzwarrens' store, the ship, the Sultan's palace and the Guildhall were all erected, and we had to squeeze into the sets with a chorus as well. Being live, we had to make sure we remembered our lines, as well as the difficult camera angles and positions in the tiny space . It was quite an ordeal but luckily a success.

It was not long before I was back again at the Ally Pally. I was engaged to appear in the Television version of "Gay Rosalinda", a commercial production of "Die Fledermaus". This was a very prestigious television programme. It was to star *Jack Buchanan.* The conductor was the young American *Charles Mackerras.* A reunion with *Peter Graves,* as he was cast as Prince Orlovsky. The singing was very important, and we all learned a lot from this exceptional conductor. Rehearsals were always on a cliffhanger, as the longer we rehearsed the more everyone was wondering whether Jack would know his lines. He found the role of Eisenstein hard to commit to memory. Nearing dress rehearsal the tension was mounting, it was painful to see this great star in difficulty. Imagine the situation trying to get a quart into a pint pot, the sets were squashed in the tiny studio.

The ballroom was the largest set, and on camera, looked palatial. On the dress rehearsal Jack just walked off, saying he couldn't do it. We all wondered if he would be there for transmission, he was, idiot boards everywhere. The press next day, said that "*Jack Buchanan* had the greatest triumph of his career"............It was wonderful.

At the end of 1949, it was rumoured that *Isabel Bigley* was going to leave "Oklahoma" and that a new leading lady was to take over. There were two understudies for Isabel, Gwen was one and *Brenda Barker,* was the other. It was decided that both girls should play a matinee each, and from that a decision would be made as to who should take over the role. I went along to see each matinee, and in my unbiased opinion there was no contest. I sat in the Grand Circle with Gwen's father, who disappeared to the toilet every five minutes with nerves. It was a superb performance and she was chosen. This 19 year old had now got to sustain nine performances a week. *"Binkie",* wise man that he was, arranged and paid for extra singing lessons to strengthen her voice. Gwen was now going to my singing teacher, and Ray soon had her well up to strength. At the end of February, Gwen took over the role of "Laurey" and created the record of being the first BRITISH leading lady of "Oklahoma" at Drury Lane at the age of nineteen. The coaching by *Howard Keel,* had truly paid off, plus her exceptional singing voice.

During the month of March, the "Lane" hosted auditions for a Rodgers and Hammerstein show. "Carousel". I have never seen so many singers lined up for auditions. The queue went from the stage, both sides, right through the theatre and into the road outside. It was a real shock to see so many after so few jobs. 90% of the Equity membership was still out of work, it will never alter, as I have said before..

The great show was now into its fourth year. On the 29th May, the whole production of "Oklahoma" transferred to the Stoll Theatre. I very fortuitously, got my old job, back in the show, this was the third time I had been at the Stoll Theatre. Playing the part of "Ado Annie" was *Billie Love,* the second British performer to take over a principal role. Gwen and I became good friends with Billie. and her sister *Helga Stone*, Helga was an impressionist, her mother *Josie Bradly* and father, *Mark Stone,* they were known on radio as the *Murgatroyd Family.* The parents became known as *Joe Murgatroyd and Poppet. Billie* played the tour of "Oklahoma" but we did not. After the tour of "Oklahoma", Billie found a new niche in life by becoming a superb photographer. She set up her own studio, and was known as *Amanda.* Many stars, including ourselves, used her photographs for publicity with great success. Helga was married to *Len Barry,* who was the agent for *Sid Field. Len* took us over and worked for us for a number of years.

Gwen and I had decided that we would not go on the tour, as an audition for Gwen came along. Being the leading lady of "Oklahoma" opened doors, and she was interviewed for the lead in "Brigadoon", for the original production in Australia and New Zealand. I sang for the management J.C. Williamson Theatres. There were five brothers named TAIT. There were known very irreverently as HESIITAIT, COGITAIT, AGITAIT,MILITAIT, and MEDITAIT. Frank was the Managing Director in Melbourne, Nevin Tait, did the casting overseas. Gwen was engaged as "Fiona", I was to understudy the leading man, and play the part of "Frank" a nice part in the last act. We were to sail from Tilbury on the flagship of the P.& O. "The Strathaird", this was to leave in January 1951. for Melbourne, the voyage would take 5 weeks. Gwen and I finished with "Oklahoma" at the end of November.

Dear Faithful Fred.

Fred Wilby, our dear friend from Cochran's office, started his own firm and put on a pantomime. He invited us to play the principal roles for a few weeks leading up to embarking on the ship, this was very convenient. The pantomime was in the London area, so we were at home.

We signed our contracts and were instructed to see "Brigadoon", while it was on at Her Majesty's Theatre. We had seen it before, but neither of us were particularly enamoured with the show. Now we were going to play this *Loewe and Lerner* tuneful musical, we took more notice of the production, and the parts we were going to play. *Alan Jay Lerner* had written the book and the lyrics. *Frederick Loewe* the music. Amazing, two Americans wrote about Scotland, based on a German fairy story.

Before sailing we had to learn a pantomime. We had never played together in this type of show, and Fred had gone to a lot of trouble to see that we had good parts and we were happy. It was most enjoyable, and a great experience. It played three different theatres. Although we played number two theatres it filled in a gap, and gave us a taste of shows, other than the West End. *Clifford Hensley* was the principal comic, very experienced, he knew all the comic wheezes and as you watched him, you saw the wisdom in his track record. It was good for me, having to feed him with dialogue and comedy business, and I found it a good piece for learning. The general public, were used to seeing the big pantomimes in the cities, but there are many No 2 managements who present the many subjects, like Aladdin, Cinderella etc., in smaller theatres, giving the children the chance to see live artists. The Fred Wilby pantomime was very much the basic story, with small sets and cut outs, and produced on a shoe string budget, we were lucky with Fred, as he took a week off the run, so that we could catch the ship for Australia.

With few in the cast, it meant we all had a lot to do, especially with the comedy. The main ingredient was laughter with funny lines and plenty of slapstick. The kitchen scene was full of "slosh", the dame with the undressing scene was very visual. Each dame had a very extensive personal wardrobe, and all the comedy bits of business were featured year in and year out.

During the show we began to start our next task, to get packed and ready for Australia. It was not like packing to go on a tour in Britain, we had to prepare for a long journey by sea, and then a long time away in another country.

We were both sad at the thought of leaving our families, we were indeed fortunate, that we had loving parents and a close knit family. I thought to myself, this is history repeating itself, the memories of leaving for India during the war, came flooding back.

Before we left, my hero, *Sir Charles Blake Cochran* died from a terrible tragedy. the scalding hot tap in his bath. He went to Middlesex hospital, but with great courage, he passed on. He was cremated at Golders Green. *Wrestlers, Boxers, Cochran's Young Ladies, Authors, Composers, Actors and Actresses* came to the funeral, to say "Goodbye". With the passing of "Cockie", the theatre had lost its taste, glamour, enterprise, individualism, and a superb entertaining culture.

I recall the tribute to the great showman made by *Sir Alan Herbert :-*

Sir Alan Herbert's tribute to Sir Charles Cochran.

"For fifty years with pleasures grave and gay,
You have invited all the world inside
To see the playhouse in its right array.
A thing of beauty and a place of pride.
And what a fine mixed feast you had to show
Ibsen and Coward, Shakespeare, Shaw and all,
Ballet and boxing, Robey and Rodeo,
Cowboy and circus / and the Albert Hall.
Reinhardt and Hackenschmidt were one to you ;
Carpentier, Bernhardt, Duse did your will;
Helen of Troy and Jessie of Revue,
Barrie and Pirandello, filled a bill.

Nothing was done because it was "the thing"
Nothing was done in avarice or haste.
Beauty was Queen, Efficiency was King,
And over all there ruled the god of taste.
How much you spent on that young lady's shoe
Was not a worry....if the show was right :
How much you made...or lost....you hardly knew
If only London loved it on "the night"
Alas, how little can the actor keep
Of all the joy he lavishly distils /
Some faded programmes in the scrap-book sleep------

A few old photographs....and many bills.
"Who was the man in that delightful play ?
"Who was the girl who took the leading part?
Well, never mind. For she has had her day,
and lives in lodgings with a broken heart.

To men like you we pay no living wage,
And all their work is swept away like snow.
You have left your footprints on the stage;
The world is richer for the "Cochran Show"

111

Melbourne, Australia here we come.

"When the wind and the weather blow your dreams sky high."
"SAIL AWAY"   Noel Coward.

We sailed from Tilbury, it was quite rough. Gwen didn't care for it to start with, but she soon settled down. It was wonderful for me, as I had always been a good sailor, the sea brought back memories of the "Mauretania". Having left Britain, with all the rationing and shortages, to have seven course meals, was a dream. There was food and drink in abundance, I found I was going through the card quite often, and of course I was putting on a little weight. We had a very "camp" steward, who we called the "Silver Queen" and what a time we had with her/ him. *Lionel Baker* a tenor, was with us in "Oklahoma", had been signed to play "Charlie Cameron" in "Brigadoon", so he sailed with us. He was a strong lad, and he found his weight started to increase. We played as many deck games as we could fit in, we tuned in to some Australians, who were going back to their homes, after a visit to the "Old Country", as they called Britain. This was our belated honeymoon, we were very happy. I wanted to have a cricket match between England and Australia, so I approached the Pursers Office, The pitch was netted in, and lines were marked across, to show the number of runs scored, once the ball had passed. The ball was made of a special substance and had to be soaked in water, and then left to dry. I was told that we could not have the game, as it involved insurance and security arrangements. I was a little peeved to say the least. We were on our way through the Mediterranean to Port Said, the usual boats came out to meet us, with all the so called bargains. I remember India and all the bartering that went on. Gwen saw a lovely pair of real skin shoes, that she really wanted. They were three pounds. Remembering my experience in India, I bartered the Egyptian boatman down, he came reduced to two pounds. I maintained we could get them even lower, and so they were marked down even further. I said "Lets wait, till the boat is sailing, and then we can get them for next to nothing". The boatman kept coming back, I had lost interest.

We were just leaving, when the Johnny came to the side and said "one pound", the last price I had quoted, and I said fifteen shillings, he said "No" and we lost those lovely shoes, needless to say it was the dog house for me. Through the Nile, which brought back memories of the "Mauretania" in 1945, and on to India. The Officers were very keen for us to do a cabaret on the next phase of the voyage, and in my diplomatic and gracious way, I said "as we could not have our cricket match, it would be impossible for us to do a cabaret."

It was funny how the very next day, I was told that they had found all the netting, and the equipment for the cricket, and that the insurance was alright, and they would be glad if England played against Australia. It would be so good for friendly relations of all the passengers on the voyage. I was "chuffed" to savour the victory, and then organize the teams to facilitate, not only a good and happy afternoon, but another victory, this time for England. We beat the Aussies, very comprehensively.

We stopped at Bombay, and as we arrived that old smell brought nostalgia to my nostrils. It had not changed. Walking about the city, Gwen had a scarf around her mouth and nose, it was over-bearing. The beetle nut was everywhere, Gwen was very upset to see all the crippled Indian children, having not seen this before, she only knew from my comments, and was very disenchanted with the east. Off we sailed again, and it was now the time to do the cabaret requested. Gwen and I with Lionel, presented hits from musical shows with great success, we very spontaneously, concocted a finale for the three of us. It was so successful, that we suddenly found we had a lot of new friends on the journey. Unbeknown to us *Robert Menzies* the Prime Minister, and his daughter had embarked at Bombay. *Bob Menzies* was a lovely man, a warm and friendly Australian, very easy to talk to, a very long serving Prime Minister. He headed a coalition government for 25 years, keeping strong political links with Britain.

He was knighted in 1963. We talked quite a lot, and his daughter Heather was charming. As the "Mengies" tartan was to be worn in "Brigadoon", he promised he would come and see us in Melbourne. Two other delightful people, Dr and Rewa Cohen became very close to us, and we made plans to see them in Sydney where they lived. Cedric Cohen was one of the most eminent doctors in New South Wales. It shows how spoilt we show business people are, from one short cabaret show, we found so many wonderful people, who made our voyage so memorable.

.

The Indian ocean, although very calm, had some swell that made the majority of people feel queasy. We had been invited to a special cocktail party. The food was displayed beautifully, and stewards were all poised with glasses of wine and champagne ready to descend on us. One by one, the room seemed to clear, there was a slow exit, and everyone went to their cabins. Brian Harrod who had been a great help in the cricket match, stayed with me, and by the time the mass exit had been completed, just the two of us were left on our own, with our food and our drinks by ourselves, everyone had gone. As the great line in "Dick Whittington" states "We were the only ones saved from the wreck" Most of the passengers had been very sick, and had gone to their beds. Next morning, miraculously, everyone seemed to be back to normal. What an unfortunate state of affairs, after so much had been prepared for a party, on a very calm Indian Ocean,

We arrived at the Heads of Melbourne in a gale and thunderstorm. It was impossible for the pilot to navigate us into port. We swung on the anchor for a day and a half, and the weather was no better, so the Captain decided to go it alone. without a pilot., we slowly crawled into port. The relief was for all to see. We said "Goodbye" to all our new made friends, and went down the gangway to be met by *Charles Dearden* the publicity manager for J.C. Williamsons.

A podgy faced man with smiling countenance. He told us where we were going to stay, and a small dark haired man who had a very broad accent had a truck to take our luggage to the flat, designated for us in Collins Street. We were to report the day after we had settled in. The flat seemed very bare, the bed was hard, and when we challenged the rent, we were told that the cocktail cabinet was first class. We thought we would get settled in, get on with rehearsals and then find something more to our liking.

We met the company at Her Majesty's Theatre in Exhibition Street. All the formal introductions were effected, and we then met the "Top of the Bill" *James MacGregor Jamieson,* the Director. "Jamie was an American Scot, who had won a preponderance of medals for Highland dancing. He was well known on Broadway for many musicals, but "Brigdoon" was a religion with him. He believed every syllable and quaver that had been written about the show. The whole fey plot was perpetual, and made you believe, to quote the script, "That if you believe in anything strongly enough, miracles can happen".
Jamie believed. and he made sure that we did too. He was a disciplinarian, and in the first few days, he was heard to say to one of his fellow Americans, "If little Miss Overton can learn all her lines, for the first rehearsal, why couldn't he ?", anyway rehearsals went well, and without any contretemps. The first free Sunday I was there, I was invited by the permanent staff of the firm to play cricket for them against some team or other. When Gwen and I got to the ground, we could not believe it, the grass was high, and a coconut batting strip was laid. We had matting strips in Singapore, so that was not foreign to me. The whole atmosphere was wrong for me. There seemed to be endless breaks for scooners of beer, although it was a game of cricket, the play was subsidary to ale. I was asked to bowl, and I took six wickets for five runs, and ended the game rather sharpishly. I said "thank you" for the game, to which they said "Good on yer".

"Another opening, another show."   ***Kiss Me Kate.***
Cole Porter.

I made it clear that I would not be playing again until I had formed my own team from the show, with proper fixtures with good grounds. Gwen and I were able to go to the Melbourne Cricket Ground, to see England win the last Test Match, we had taking quite a hiding that series. It was now winter.

Peter Cuming-Parry and his mother had been very friendly with us on the ship, and he had promised me, that we would have a game of tennis. Peter invited me to his club, I didn't know he was a member of Koo Yong, that was the Wimbledon of Victoria, a very exclusive club. So with my Sharkskin shorts and matching top and splendid tennis racquet, I met Peter at the club and we went on to the court. We knocked up, and I could see that he was not going to give me much of a game, as he was carrying too much weight. Anyway, we were just about to start a set, when an official requested that I should leave the club. Peter being a member was embarrassed, I was very pointedly told, that white was the colour to be worn, and my sharkskin shorts were blue, matching my shirt. Oh dear ! crestfallen, I left these very prestigious courts.

"Brigadoon" opened at Her Majestys Theatre, Melbourne on the 17th March, 1951. The colour and spectacle were received with great acclaim, and the cast did justice to Loewe and Lerner.

Ken Cantril, who had been in "Paint Your Wagon" in London, was playing "Tommy Albright", he was a wooden performer with a bit of a plum in his voice, and Gwen did not find him easy or comfortable to work with. Gwen was first class. Before leaving London she had lessons with our dear friend ***Bill Thorburn,*** to master the highland Scottish accent, so her performance was once again superb. The press wrote " ***With a fine voice, a sound dramatic sense and good looks in her favour, GWEN OVERTON makes an outstanding romantic lead as Fiona MacKeith"*** her accent was very authentic, and the lilt was just right.

The "Taits" were renowned for being frugal. Macquarrie Street was full of medical practitioners. It was alleged that, if you put a penny into the slot for the toilet, three farthings went to the Taits. I was soon to experience the careful outlook of the Taits.

All the press cuttings and past engagements were held in the Publicity Office of the company. I was called before the brothers. It had transpired that, *Billy Shakespeare,* a comedian, playing at the Comedy Theatre opposite Her Majestys, had disappeared. He had packed up his make-up, and left. Nobody knew where he was. Billy had come to Australia to put the comedy in the *The Piddingtons,* a show based on telepathy. *Sydney Piddington with Russell Braddon,* had developed a highly skilled act, while they were prisoners in Changi, during the war. The show was appearing at the theatre across the road. Frank Tait was the spokesman, and he told me of the situation.

"I see, from your publicity, you have been involved in comedy, in a variety mode" I said that I had. "We would like you to go on tonight and do some comedy. As you are in the last act of "Brigadoon", you could easily do two spots of about ten minutes each, and return across the road for your part in "Brigadoon". It was intimated that this could be for the run of the show. There were six weeks to go. I said, that it would be possible. Frank Tait said "We would pay you of course" quickly I questioned "How much" Twenty pounds a week, was the retort. In my stentorian voice, I said "Twenty Pounds ! for two spots a night. My weekly salary in Variety, would be at least seventy five pounds" "Well you see, we needn't renew your wife's contract after the initial six months, or yours. We could send you home". The contracts for J.C. Williamson Theatres were water tight and money grabbing. If there was any problem with artists, it always ended up that the performer paid a certain amount of money. They had worded the contacts very cleverly so that there was always financial kick back.

I was behind the eight ball. Reluctantly I agreed, and put two acts together, which included the inevitable impressions of Jolson, Sinatra, Eddy and Tauber. Two spots going very well, and twenty pounds a week...what more can a fellow want ? And there's more, as *Jimmy Cricket* says. They wanted another five minute spot. I intimated that two was just right for the show, the flannel came with "Your'e doing so well, the public want more" so another ten pounds was offered. Now, what am I going to do for five minutes ? A stroke of luck, *Peter Turgeon,* who played Jeff Douglas and had become such a close friend to Gwen and I, came up with an idea for creating a scene on the Bridge of British battleship. The captain was talking to the crew on the launching of a torpedo at a German ship. Big build up of atmoshere and the positioning of the guns etc., and the tag was "Alright chaps, stop everything...Time for tea.

From this short spot came an eight minute laughter packed opus. I found that while I was taking the micky out of the English, the Aussies loved it, but have a dig at them, and they were not very impressed.

Peter Turgeon and his wife Virginia Richardson, were two lovely Americans. Peter thought British actors were the best in the world, and was very pro British. The stage manager of the show *Edward Hunt,* although an Australian, was the South of England Croquet champion. He set about teaching Gwen and I, Peter and *Ralphine Sprague,* who played "Jane" in the show, how to play croquet. The English rules were very hard, but skilful. In no time we were becoming quite proficient, and Ted arranged that we should play all the clubs in the area. So our beginners team took on all the old ladies, and beat them. It was great fun. They gave us special afternoon teas, and we played for trophies, including engraved boomerangs. So with the croquet, and Gwen and I playing Tennis with Peter and Zelma White, one of the dancers, this honeymoon was a sheer delight. We had also found better accommodation, and Gwen was showing her culinary skills.

There was a funny side, on going into the butchers, Gwen espied meat everywhere in the shop, this was a sight to behold. "May I have some steak ?" she asked, "How much would you like" said the butcher. "How much can I have," said Gwen. "You can have the whole shop" said the butcher with a wide smile. He could not quite understand that we had been rationed when we left Britain, and to be able to order as much as we liked, was quite unbalancing.

Having finished with the "Piddington Show" Two wonderful stars came to the Comedy Theatre. *Evelyn Laye and Frank Lawton.* *"Boo"* as she was very affectionately called by her friends, had a career that was the envy of most actresses. She had played the lead in so many musicals, such as Madame Pompadour, The Merry Widow, Cleopatra, Lilac Time, The New Moon, Betty in Mayfair, and her greatest triumph , Cowards' "Bitter Sweet". Her first husband was comedian, *Sonnie Hale, Mr Hale and Jessie Matthews,* were making sweet music together on and off stage. *Boo* refused to work for *Charles B. Cochran* who presented "Bitter Sweet", as she would work for the same management as her husband. She changed her mind once she saw *Peggy Wood* in the leading role. Later she married the lovely actor of "Young Woodley" and the film "David Copperfield"...*Frank Lawton.* These two charming and delightful people, had come to Australia, to star in "Bell, Book and Candle" and "September Tide" and Gwen and I tuned into them very quickly, and we became good friends.

The licensing laws in Victoria were archaic. The pubs closed at 6 p.m., so the people came out of their offices at five thirty, and whisked down as many schooners as they could in thirty minutes. The results were, the whole of the middle of the road, which was green verge on elongated islands, was strewn with drunken bodies. Boo, Gwen and I would look at a window, while Frank was beset by these drunks. Boo used to say, "Don't look, pretend we are not with him" We did have some wonderful fun with them both.

119

One day we had a mist descend over Melbourne, and the Radio News announcer, intimated that the city was covered in fog, and that it was a "pea souper". It was a slight mist, and the Australian members of our cast, had never seen fog ever, likewise we had a few drops of snow, and the girl and boy dancers went running into the streets, to see what was falling. They had never seen snow in their lifetime so far. Needless to say we had a laugh at the antics of our colleagues.

The Australian Broadcasting Corporation was good to me during my stay in Melbourne. Regularly, I would broadcast in plays, as they would need a cockney character, or a London Bobby, not having these accents on their files.

One of the highlights of my broadcasting career in Australian, was a concert with full orchestra, and a solo performance of the lovely song "Take the Sun" with full choir. This I still have implanted in my memory. I was sorry there were no recordings available of a lovely classical evening. Having an English voice opened doors for me in broadcasting. The Australians, although brash in their behaviour, were very in awe of the accent of people from the "Old Country". The Italians and Greeks worked all the weekend in their shops, but the Aussies shut up shop Friday night to Monday morning, and then moaned about the foreigners making all the money.

The generosity, friendliness, and their hospitality was really spontaneous, and overwhelming. Many families took us out to see places of interest, and generally gave us a good time. Albert & Co published the music of "Brigadoon" and Monsieur Albert, himself entertained aboard his yacht. This was a magnificent vessel with all mod. cons. We sailed around the harbour, with our glasses always full, and food a plenty. The boat couldn't go far, as the back was broken, so they said.

120

We saw Australian rules football between Toorak and Richmond, what an exciting game this is, a combination of soccer and rugby. During all this, I was training the company to play cricket. Ballet dancers were very quick to find expertise, and with their natural fitness, soon became an integral part of our theatre team. The Australians were very clever in providing cricket pitches all the year round. These were malthoid, a combination of earth and rubber and were very true and fast, even *Lionel Baker* who had only played at school, soon developed into a fast bowler. and some of the singers were fairly useful. All in all the team started to progress, and we took on college sides, and started to win. I was very diligent, to see that my dancers did not get hit on the legs, as there would have been hell to pay, if they had missed a performance. Personally I was scoring prolifically, and with many not out innings. In addition I was picking up wickets. Life was sweet.

Big stars who had performed for short seasons before we arrived in Australia, were headed by *Sir Laurence Olivier & Vivien Leigh.*. They were responsible for improving the backstage facilities of the theatres, there were showers and wash basins installed, the Taits were not amused with these demands.

Robert Morley in "Edward My Son" had a very successful time. He was involved in a hilarious contractual episode. Robert Morley was a renowned gambler on the horses. The Tait brigade outlined his shows, calling for a matinee on Wednesdays and Saturdays. Mr. Morley quickly dispelled the assumption that he would be there for a Saturday matinee, as he would be going to the races. He pointed out he would do two matinees, but the contract did not specify which days, so he agreed to play Wednesday and another day, but not, Saturdays. *Arthur Askey* had a comedy hit with "The Love Racket" and we made friends with *Jon Pertwee,* who starred in a David Martin revue at the Tivoli Theatre, *Cliff (Ukelele Ike)* played a season at the Tivoli. He was very popular, as he was the voice of *Jimmy Cricket* in the successful film "Pinnochio"

During the time we were in Melbourne, we got to know the City very well. Living across from the SHRINE, which was a well known landmark, and by the side of the building were the tennis courts, where we played regularly. The city was well formed, with the main road for example, named Collins Street, and a narrower road running parallel named Little Collins Street. The roads were built on squares. Above a very large shop on the corner of Collins Street and Flinders Street, was a solicitors office, named Smith & Emerton. This was the office looking after a Will that had named my uncle and my mother as beneficiaries, (although a small percentage), to the Roycroft Estate. Proceedings for this matter had been started in the U.K. well over two years before, and the solicitors had obviously been tardy, feathering their nests with charges etc. It is quite impossible to describe the expressions of personnel in the office, when they were aware that I was the nephew of Gerald Grestock. There were papers found with prompt alacrity, and the usual "We were just writing to your uncle" rubbish. I was at pains to emphasize how long the delay had been, and my presence hurried up the result. The cheques were received two months later. I am glad that all solicitors are not as leisurely, or are they?

"Brigadoon" had been running very well for five months and there was rumour that the show would go to ADELAIDE, and then the company would rehearse "Oklahoma" while playing the Scottish show, taking both shows to Perth. Our company was very well equipped for both shows. Unfortunately it would be too exepensive to travel both shows, so we missed Western Australia, and Perth once again, missed out on good musicals.

Gwen, unbeknown to me, was plotting a special present for my birthday in November. How do you like it, she only went to see one of the great Australian cricketers of the thirties, who had his own sports store. The name of the man was *Alan Kippax*. He was one of the great players at the time of *Ponsford, Woodfull, McCabe* and the young genius...*Don Bradman.*

Gwen informed him that I was a serious cricketer, and she wanted a good bat for me. He asked if there was anything special about the bat required, she said, "I only know he likes a short handle." Kippax went off to his safe, and brought out many bats. The different weights and grains of willow, were quite apparent to Gwen, but the great man selected a bat, and said "this is the one for your husband.". It was expensive for those days, and Gwen took his choice. Although my birthday was in November, I received this wonderful present before we left Melbourne. When I found out that Gwen had met Kippax and talked to him, I was so jealous, if only I could have met him and had conversed. I scored 112 with the bat on the first outing. It was a beauty. "Brigadoon" was a fortnight away from the end of the seven month season in Melbourne. Ken Cantril who was playing "Tommy Albright" was having some throat and voice trouble, and I was informed, that he would be off and I was to go on. Naturally through the run we had the odd understudy call, and during some of the performances I watched. This was a challenge. I was petrified. Do I know all the dialogue?? have I got all the lyrics firmly in my mind??, and how was my voice going to be? Check all costumes, I was alone in the dressing room. I slowly put on my make-up, I looked regularly at my watch, there was plenty of time. I was trembling and the hands were becoming moist. My dear friend **Peter Turgeon** came into the room, and he started his make-up. He was very thrilled that I was playing the part, the two parts were together a lot during the piece. He could see how nervous I was, and he said, and I will always remember his phrase, *"Whatever happens, remember the curtain will still come down at 10.15."* This calmed me a little. I started to get dressed, did a few scales, started to tremble again, listened to the orchestra tuning up. Peter and I were at the beginning of the show, and I must make sure I waited for the laughs, being nervous you could tread on the funny lines. The orchestra, chorus sang the lament "Brigadoon", the mist descended on the bridge, and the flute played a slow doleful phrase...and...

123

"There's a smile on my face"   *"Brigadoon"*
Alan Jay Lerner.   *Frederick Loewe.*

"Now here's Braemor," the line came out firmly with my pseudo American accent, Peter got his laughs, and all was set fair so far. The music and songs were the same delight as usual, and the reception was the same as any other night. Gwen sang her lovely "Waitin for my dearie" with great response, Lionel had gone home with bonnie Jean, *Olive Lucius* had the real love of her life, I managed the lyrical "Heather on the Hill", and then into the big duet with Gwen. First the verse, and then the chorus, of "Almost Like Being In Love.", all was going well, the moves were spot on, we sang to each other as we meant it. We finished with the top notes and the position with Gwen on the stairs and me at the bottom. What happened next was one of the most wonderful moments in our short singing lives. The big finish, and the audience errupted. The applause went on and on, and cheering began to start, this had never happened before. On and on the applause, Peter was at the gate to get his big laugh, but we could not continue. We stood motionless while the applause went on and on. The one thing you are not taught in a play or a musical, when there is an ovation, is to ad lib, you only know the written word. Finally, the audience were exhausted, and we continued with the show. This was a night to remember. We were just about to go into the last week, when Ken was ready to come back. *Jamie* wanted me to stay on to the end of the final week, and gave Ken a story about saving his voice for the opening in Adelaide. I was so proud to finish the run with my girl. Time now to pack up, and sort out all our possessions, we had acquired extra bits and pieces, and there was extra cricket gear. We took the Overland Express from Melbourne to the charming city of Adelaide. We stayed in a church house of a Bishop, with a lovely housekeeper named Trudi. She was a diamond. The Bishop was away for a while, and Trudi looked after us, she cooked cleaned and everything we required was her pleasure so to do.

Adelaide was an unspoilt city, and we were living above
the delightful area, looking down at the Cathedral and the cricket
ground. The people were as friendly as they had been in
Melbourne, and the show opened to very enthusiastic paper
reviews, and the reception was fabulous. A young couple, John
and Sue came to see the show, and were thrilled with us. They
invited us out to see some of the scenery, and we went on picnics
together. We had a great rapport with this charming young couple.
Their generosity was the hallmark of everything that was good in
Australia.

It was getting close to our second anniversary, and I thought we
ought to have a celebration. Gwen organised all the food, it was a
mammoth task as all the company were attending. I made a very
potent punch, and we had all the usual bottles of wines, and spirits.
With very few exceptions, they all went for the punch. By the end
of the party and the cutting of the cake, people were lying in heaps.
Gabriel Joffe the conductor of the orchestra, was completely
blotto. He would sing in his broken English Hungarian voice, and
eventually passed out, and joined the others, that were inebriated
and ready for bed. It was a tremendously successful gathering, and
the company talked about it for weeks. The show stayed for a
month.

"Brigadoon" was now due to go the Brisbane. It was November,
and the temperature had risen dramatically. With the company
wearing full tartans, it was a very hot and perspiring period on
stage. Salt tablets were issued to save us losing too much body
fluid. We found the show exhausting, and we had to find the shade
as much as we could. Everything was very dry, and we consumed
many gallons of soft drinks and water. It was good for losing
weight, I had gone up to 13 stone with all the rich food. Brisbane
had sensible licensing laws, the pubs closed at 9 p.m. and you
never saw a drunk. I became involved with a tennis club and
played Grade A tennis with the members. Great standard.

Cricket dominance.

You may feel we were a little crazy, but our cricket fixtures were increasing, and we were getting great results, for a team of liquorice allsorts. The big game was against the Brisbane Advertiser, the main newspaper in Queensland. The day was hot, registering 108 in the shade, this figure was significant, as I scored 108 runs in the boiling sun. We notched up a score of 247. The lads were thrilled with their efforts, and when the newspaper team went into bat, they were completely demoralised. We had them all out for 97. So I put them in again. They scored a few more this time, but only managed 138. My innings of 108 in 2 hours in the heat of 108 degrees, took some weight off, in the two innings my bowling figures were 8 for 32 runs. I was very lucky I was in the last act of Brigadoon", for I was shattered.

We had a wooden type bungalow, and there were ants and flying cockroaches, we had monsoon nets over the beds. We would come home from the theatre, put on the light and a black mass would disperse, leaving the floor clear. We had a wild tom cat, who made friends with us. We called him Tiger, he was very timid but after a while he became friendly. One day he arrived at the front door with all his family, a wife and five kittens. Ants were a pest, they tried to get at our milk, so we left trails of ant powder around the milk, so they never crossed the line.

We went to the "Gabba" and saw the first Test Match of the new season between Australia and the West Indies. The dominance of the three "W's" *Frank Worrell, Clyde Walcott and Everton Weekes* the run machines of the West Indies, were a sight to behold. Their batting technique was fast and furious. It was a machine gun way of scoring runs., The Australians were just as quick, and the game was terrific. I celebrated my 25th birthday in the company of the three "W's", and *Viv Richardson and Alec and Eric Bedser.* More than ever before, I loved this game of cricket. It was lucky that the genes were passed down from my grandfather to my father, who played for W.H. Smith and Sons.

Sydney, New South Wales.

The "Brigadoon" eleven was beginning to get a reputation for some good results, and I personally, topped the batting with an average of 104.6. This was because the wickets were hard and true, and with the sun on your back you felt the timing of the ball was automatic. You played forward with confidence and the belief of getting the ball into the middle of the bat. I realised that I had to stay at the crease, as the rest of the team had not a lot of experience and stickability. My confidence was high. With so many not out innings, my average was into three figures. I was now sorting out fixtures for our next stop ....Sydney.

On arriving in Sydney, we looked at an apartment in a new block of flats in Double Bay. We had a surprise of sheer delight. The proprietors turned out to be a couple of 'pros'. One was a trumpet player, and his wife was Valerie Hay who played Kim in "Show Boat" with me all those years before. The flats were very nice and we were soon made to feel at home, with all we required. Val and George were great company, and we felt happy to start the Sydney season. The show opened to very good reviews and all was set fair for a good run.

Peter Turgeon pulled a stroke on the firm, as in his contract he had included a clause, stating that in the event of his wife giving birth, her salary should be added to his. They were Catholics, and they allowed for the possibility. Needless to say the inevitable happened, and Virginia left the show to have a baby daughter, Wendy. The Taits now became the "Furytaits", having to pay two salaries for one person. Trust Peter.

We had caught up again with friends Rewa and Cedric Cohen, who saw us regularly, they helped us to have an enjoyable social life. The radio actors in Sydney had a very fine cricket team. It was a permanent side used to playing together.

127

The actor who ran the side was ***Athol Fleming***, who had been a member of the Stage Cricket Club. ***Garry Marsh*** suggested I got in touch with Athol when I arrived in "Aussie". His radio team included ***Charles Tingwell*** a very good actor who starred with ***Margaret Rutherford*** in the Agatha Christie films. Our side was playing them at Rushcutters Bay and unfortunately Athol couldn't play, he was on radio. All the way through the match he kept phoning to see if they had got me out. Each time he phoned I was still in. I didn't do very well that day, I only scored 35, but we won. My lads were cock a hoop as we were the underdogs.

We are now into December, and it is really hot, picnics, Christmas Day celebrated on Bondi Beach, and the show going extremely well. It was now getting near Gwen's 21st birthday and I wanted to give her a surprise party if I could. I started to plan, after all a twenty first birthday is special. On the day I intimated to Gwen that we might have some people drop in for a drink, she started to clean the flat from top to bottom and I made sure there was plenty of drink on tap. "What is going on?" was her query. I said "Well we are going to Cedric and Rewa Cohen's house for a quick drink, but we must be away promptly as a "few friends" would be in to celebrate. Gwen really tired herself, cleaning and polishing to make everything ship shape and Bristol fashion. We then went across to the Cohen's for 6 p.m. I said as we rang the bell "Please don't be late, please come away when I say so." As we went into the very large house, the whole company had a drink in their hands and sang "Happy Birthday". Apart from the cast of "Brigadoon" there were a few surprises. I had managed to get ***William Hodge*** who starred in the original "Worm's Eye View" in Australia, a good friend, my good cricketing actor friend ***Alexander Archdale***, who played for the Stage Cricket Club in the U.K. Gwen knew him well.

The biggest surprise was **Bob Shakery**. Bob had been a real fan of Gwen when she was in Southend, doing her concerts at a very early age. He was a loyal fan and supported her always. Their reunion was very emotional. Having seen that everything I had arranged was successful, I turned green and was violently sick.

What a lovely day?

Although my batting had caused interest and popularity, I was a little surprised to be asked to play in an all-star *charity cricket match* at the Sydney Cricket Ground. I said I would play and duly turned up with all the gear. This was not like today. We didn't wear helmets and arm protectors. I didn't even wear a thigh pad. I had never needed one. If I had had some advance information regarding this match, I would have acquired a suit of armour. The match for a children's charity was to be the **Lindsay Hassett XI** against **Neil Harvey's XI**. I was to play for Lindsay Hassett. He told me he had heard about my average and for the celebrity side of things I should go in at No.4. I must say I was a little nervous when I saw **Colin McCool** and **Don Tallon** take the field, but the best was yet to come. The commentator announced a special appearance ot **Ray Lindwall and Keith Miller.** The crowd went wild, these players, two of the greatest Aussies, had recently given England, a terrible time. Most of the Australian players that were turning out for this charity were part of the 1948 team that gave England such a beating.

The two teams were a mixture of Test Cricketers, well known politicians and stage celebrities, **Charles Tingwell** and I were the only players that fell into the latter category and we were on opposing sides. The match started, **Lindsay Hassett and Sam Loxton** opened. Straight away Miller and Lindwall were on. The speed of these two put the wind up me, the runs were coming slowly.

129

"What a day this has been, what a rare mood I'm in"
Brigadoon.   Alan Jay Lerner & Frederick Loewe.

The bowling was changed and Ian Johnson an off spinner was
brought on, together with a bowler I had never heard of. Hassett
was out followed quickly by Loxton. I was now walking in,
looking every inch the perfect batsman. I always said "Make sure
your props are smart and you look good". I was announced as
from "Brigadoon" at the Theatre Royal Sydney.

My mind was mentally saying "Not too bad, you can cope with Ian
Johnson", no sooner had I thought that, when the two pacemen
were back again. Lindwall didn't seem to be using his
usual run up, so I surmised he would drop his pace to this young
singing cricketer. The first ball was fast enough for me. I played
forward and the pace beat me all ends up. It took the outside edge
and went down to a very fine leg for four. I managed to get a
couple of balls in the middle and one of the last ball of the over.
Miller was now at me. He came in with his hair like a horse's
mane flowing as he gained speed. He seemed to bowl the fastest
off breaks ever seen, you played forward to what you thought was
the pitch of the ball only to be hit on the thigh. It hurt - no thigh
pad. This was happening with monotonous regularity. Once again
runs were coming off the edge and I was now getting my eye in
and I grew in confidence. Lindwall now went back to his proper
run and the pace was very fast. I remembered all the rules
Compton had taught me and I brought them into play. Many
strokes that brought me runs were my delayed cut through to
where a third ought to be. It was great. I had scratched around
with fluky shots of the edge and suspect timing. I had 23 runs and
was now middling the ball. The crowd was very good, they
applauded as I started to get into form and Miller and Lindwall
were getting a little tired and miffed to see an amateur standing up
and playing straight.

I got to 50 with general pleasure from the crowd and the players, and then on 60 I flashed at a lifting ball from Ray Lindwall and touched it straight into the gloves of *Don Tallon* The scorebook read: *Clive Stock caught D. Tallon bowled R. Lindwall...60.* "What a day this has been, what a rare mood I'm in". Although I have scored 15 centuries in my career, this innings was the most satisfying. I believe the charity did well.

The show was coming to the end of the run in Sydney and there was preparation for a tour of New Zealand. *Robert Moore,* who was not only a good artist, but had a following in New Zealand came in to play Tommy Albright. *Virginia and Peter Turgeon* left for America and home. It was sad saying goodbye to these lovely people. I took over the comedy lead of Jeff Douglas.

The tour opened in Auckland. For the show we had to tour two bridges, a large one for Auckland, Wellington, Christchurch and Dunedin, and a small bridge for Hastings, Wanganui, Napier, Omeru and Timeru and Palmerston North where we had a comical experience. As we travelled a lot of luggage, we packed a taxi full at Palmerston North, and then told the taxi the name of the hotel where we were staying. We got aboard and the taxi went straight across the street to the hotel, a matter of yards. New Zealand was a wonderful country and we were very happy. Desi and Bob Moore showed us all the ropes in this friendly land. In Dunedin, where the accent was predominantly Scots, the young children who had never left Dunedin, had broad Glaswegian accents. The climate was warmer than Christchurch, although further south. Gwen made contact with a relation, an Overton on her Grandfather's side. This was a very enjoyable meeting. The tour finished in Windy Wellington. Bob knew a lovely family by the name of Taylor. They were the premier dry cleaners in the North Island and had numerous shops in the South Island. We stayed with them in a beautiful caravan at the bottom of their delightful garden.

We were so happy and comfortable. Harry Taylor the boss man took to Gwen and I and offered me a position to consider. He had three daughters and no son. He suggested I could start at the bottom and learn everything about dry cleaning. I was hesitant, and we both thought of our families back home. Anyway he gave me until I was 30 to make up my mind, but we turned this generous offer down. The G.O.C. of New Zealand was General Freyberg V.C. and he came back on the "Rangitane" with us. The voyage home was to go through Panama, so in 1951/2 we had gone round the world. The New Zealand tour was the happiest of our life so far. The people were so different from the Australians. So now we were on the way back home and our families. It seemed a long voyage home, very few stops. The Panama canal was very noisy and alive. A night club with strip tease and numerous nationalities, the strippers seemed dirty and over 35. The music was very loud and we were delighted to get back aboard and sail off to the U.K. It was now September 1952. No contracts on the horizon. We slowly renewed old contacts and hoped we would pick up a contract soon, but it was very difficult. All the good shows had been cast. When you are away and out of circulation for 19 months, you are forgotten. There are too many more people looking for work. We couldn't take anything just having played leads in an original production.

It was wonderful to be with the family again. There was lots to talk about and the exploits in Australia and New Zealand were well received by our friends and family. We met dear Fred Wilby again, and he had a pantomime for us, so we were working again until the middle of January. 1953 was to the year of the Coronation of Queen Elizabeth II. It turned out to be a very eventful year. The "King and I" was to be produced with *Yul Brynner and Valerie Hobson* at the 'Lane' and Jerry Whyte the Rodgers and Hammerstein re-producer, wanted Gwen to be in it. but there was nothing for me.

132

Later Jerry wanted me for the forthcoming tour of *"South Pacific"* playing the part of "Cable". This was a tenor role and I thought it impossible, but did not say so. I went off to my teacher RAY, and he gave me a good going over. We went through the finish time after time of the ending of "Younger than Springtime" which was very high for me, but we accomplished a very good vocal ending. It became imprinted in my voice. Years after I could still sing that finish, and not other high endings.

Jerry Whyte called me to the 'Lane' to sing some of the role of "Cable". I was offered the part but I asked for time to give a decision. I had to discuss this with Gwen as in reality, Gwen would be in London and I would be all over the country.

We had to make a real decision that could affect the rest of our lives. We were lucky to have a choice. Was it to have individual careers or a marriage? . What a "Catastroke" as *Jimmy Durante* would have said. How do you know if you are doing the right thing or not? But our hearts told us. We knew that our marriage was more important.

We declined both offers and renewed our contract with Len Barry and the Archie Parnell office. The personnel comprised of *Phyllis Parnell, Len Barry, Jack Adams and George Knapman.* They were good people, and they would try and steer you on the right course. Len fixed us with *Walter Fellows* who presented "Star Wagon" with *Sandy Powell* at the Pier Theatre, Eastbourne.

Walter Fellows suggested we do a week's variety at the Royal Hippodrome, Eastbourne for the Easter week. The top of the bill was *Afrique.* He was born Alexander Witkin in 1907 in South Africa. He trained as an opera singer, he then developed into an impressionist. His famous impression being that of the Duke of Windsor. He was a very successful "Abanazer" in pantomime.

133

The bottom of the bill *Suzette Tarri* was a popular favourite.
The second star on a variety programme, was called "bottom" of
the bill, and the next important usually had the "middle" of the bill.
We were given middle of the bill, obviously to put our names in
front of the Eastbourne public, with the forthcoming summer to
follow.

The running order was established at the band call on the Monday
morning. We were to close the first half. Can you imagine, never
having an act, it was nerve racking to close the interval spot.
Anyway we put some tuneful songs together with a good break up
of tempos and the public liked us very much.

The experience of closing the first half was quite daunting. The
small orchestra was very thin, as I had not learned the art of
orchestration yet. We used printed published parts, and this was
not very satisfactory, as all the instruments were strong on the
melody. Part of my future for orchestration, would centre on the
instruments playing an accompaniment to the voices.

With two strong voices we were over the top of the orchestra, and
we found that the performance could only get better, we invented
movement and started a smooth presentation that flowed with the
music. The experience of musicals then came to be the tools of our
trade. Pace and change of tempo became our trademark, we soon
found the way to rouse the audience to ovations.

During the week we had afternoon tea with *Mary and Leo
Franklyn*. they were the parents of a good cricketing pal *William
Franklyn*, a consumate actor. Bill was a wonderful character, a
very good cricketer, and a good friend.

A double act is born.

"Wherever we go, whatever we do, we'll always go through it together". Gypsy Stephen Sondheim Jule Styne.

Leo was a Musical Comedy star and dominant in the **Brian Rix** farces. A lugubrious face that had you laughing before uttering a word. He had seen us at the Hippodrome. He was appearing at the Devonshire Park Theatre. His strong view was that we should stay a double act, he said "You don't need any microphones, sets, lighting. All you need is a piano and you can get up anywhere and entertain people". He was most emphatic that this was the career we should follow. In hindsight, "Darling Mary and Leo, THANK YOU".

We had now to think of summer. Three programmes and some contrasts to create in our presentation. Costumes to be arranged and purchased. Our combined thoughts were to look good and attractive and smart. We combined so well and we had ideas that were sympatico. Our act had more movement than the usual double singing duo. Gwen was a lovely mover, her dancing was first class and as a singer...........outstanding. I found it very tough keeping up with her. Talking of movement, I remember when playing Edinburgh later in our career,, **Michael Howard,** a popular broadcasting comedian, had a sideline. He wrote for "The Scotsman" under the name of Ian Mackenzie, his main job was to write "crits" on the shows. When writing about Gwen and I in Edinburgh, he said "These two are very nice with good voices, but they move about so much. Anne Ziegler and Webster Booth were never like this". We never wanted to be static.

Rehearsals started at the Pier Theatre, Eastbourne. We met the star of the show..*Sandy Powell.* He was a real star. Gwen was thrilled to meet him as she had been a member of Sandy's gang when she was five. Albert Arthur Powell was born in Rotherham in 1900. He was nick named Sandy because of his red hair. He was the most loveable and kindly man you could have as the top of the bill.

The company became a family. Sandy could show you how to get a laugh without doing very much. A raise of his eyebrows, the moving of the glasses to the forehead to read something and the look while his feed *Norman Meadows* was knocking his brains out with rapid dialogue. Norman in my book, was the finest feed in the country. His boxing trainer showing Sandy how to box was a classic. He physically got himself into a lather while Sandy just looked and reacted, getting the maximum amount of laughs. Sandy was known as "Mr. Eastbourne". Gwen and I were woven into the productions and the sketches. The act was a complete surprise. The reception was fantastic and without any false modesty, the public took us to their hearts both on stage and off stage. We mixed a great deal with the Eastbourne people and became entwined with the family life of the town. This was cemented even more by my membership of the Eastbourne Cricket Club. this team was of minor county standard and we played on the County Ground at the Saffrons. On the Bank Holiday Monday in August against Uppingham Rovers, they were ex-public school, who did a tour each summer, I opened the innings with *Harry Pickering,* who played for Surrey. Harry had a great reputation and all the members built him up as a tremendous fast scorer. They included him in all their teams while he was on holiday. He spent two weeks in Eastbourne every year. As we walked out to bat together I said to him "I am not like lightening, I score at an average pace and sometimes I am a little slow". I suppose with all the hype of his reputation I was a little apprehensive. Anyway we got off to a reasonable start. The Saffrons was a batting wicket, completely flat and true. I was on 30 when Harry had mustered 12. During our stand he said "Whats all this about being slow"? It was one of those days. Harry was out for 53 and I went sailing on. When I got to 92, I seemed to slow right down. The skipper wanted to declare but he wanted me to get my ton. He waited and as soon as I hit a two through the covers to reach my maiden hundred for the club, he declared.

I was quite tired and therefore I was not asked to bowl for a while.
Uppingham were getting on top of us. Mr. Harding the skipper,
was an ex headmaster of Tonbridge. He had a very shrewd
cricketing brain. He threw me the ball and I commenced to bowl.
I felt the legs were going to seize up, but I kept bowling. I finished
with 3 wickets for 11 runs and we won the game. What a day for
me! 3 wickets on a good batting track was very stimulating.

That night in Sandy's closing speech with the "Church Notices"
that's we called the information about the change of programme
and details of Sunday concerts, Sandy said "I would just like to let
you know that our baritone, today at the County Ground scored
100 not out". There was a great reception for this. Sandy got
excited and tried to stop the applause. Once subsided he said "Not
only did he get a century, but he took 3 wickets for 11 runs", More
applause. It was a wonderful day. It was so good to have a
Yorkshireman as a friend. He used to come regularly to the games
to see me play.

In the show we had a lad **Ron Rowlands**. He was described in
those days as a light comedian. One afternoon we were on the
beach, when he arrived with two of his friends. They joined us and
we got to know Mr. & Mrs. Sargeant. To you *Max Miller and his
wife.* This was a tremendous joy to talk to the legend of the Music
Hall....The Cheeky Chappie, but like most good comics he was not
funny off stage. We had a serious talk about the business, and he
was very philosophical about the trends in entertainment. There
were stories about some of the treatment he had during his rise to
fame. If he had been put on by any individual, he sorted them out.
That night in the bar there were many hangers on who wanted to
show off and let people now that they wre friends of Max, of
course they weren't. They would ask Max to have a drink and he
would say, "Thank you, and get one for my friends". In the end
the round would include an extra seven drinks.

The season was great. It was 1953 and the Queen's coronation. Every summer show that year put in a scene to celebrate our Queen and we were no exception. The scene was a room in an Officer's club. We were all in dress uniforms of officers coming to drink a health to Her Majesty. I sang Ivor Novello's "Rose of England".

The opening night I finished the song to wonderful applause and this kept going. Sandy and Norman came on upstage and still the applause carried on. They were doing the "present". Sandy said to Norman "the boy must have sung well tonight" and still the clapping was stopping Sandy from getting out his next line. I was bowing. I even went to the side of the stage and still I was bowing. The whole thing then came to a stop. What had happened was the famous Dorothy Wilding photo of Her Majesty had been dropped in too soon and the applause was for this brilliant picture, and we were all taking plaudits for this lovely personage.

There were some magical moments in the season. A famous sketch entitled "The Leave Train", I think it was written by Johnnie McGregor, but don't quote me, it was a very strong piece of material and it gave Sandy the chance to become a straight actor and squeeze great pathos from his performance. Gwen had the part of his wife. There was a lot of dialogue. Her acting experience was brought to bare. Sandy played the part of Bill, the private on leave. It concluded with 'Sandy going back to his unit and Gwen singing "Bill" from "Show Boat". It was a show stopper.

The press, were kind to us and wrote:-
Gwen Overton and Clive Stock are outstandingly fine singers, their interpretation of the two elderly aunts is an absolute winner and serves the dual purpose of providing plenty of laughs as well as contrasting with the beauty of their "straight" singing. Eric Redfern... Eastbourne Herald.

By far one of the best liked acts in the whole show, is that of
GWEN OVERTON AND CLIVE STOCK. These duettists who
have an air of brightness and charm about them, indulge in a
little marital tiff but patch things up to go to a selection from the
" The Student Prince". Their singing is full of freshness,
brilliance and attack. Eastbourne Gazette.

These "crits" in the papers were very elating as we had only just
started a real double act. During the run of five months, we were
approached by a firm in Scotland. Len Barry had gone up to the
Gaiety Theatre, Ayr. This theatre was owned by Ben Popplewell
and Sons. Ben was no longer with us, but the two sons *Eric and
Leslie Popplewell*, were handling the productions in exemplary
fashion. They were renowned for their quality. They had their
own wardrobe staff, a first class carpenter and *Harry Broad* an
outstanding Musical Director, his library was second to none.

Len was in the office of the brothers and Eric asked of all the
artists he had sent on the current list, who did he recommend? .
Len went down the list and said "Well you don't want that one or
that one, the only act you want, are Gwen Overton and Clive
Stock. They would suit you very well for pantomime". So we
were booked for "Cinderella". Gwen was principal boy, Prince
Charming, and I as Baron Hardup. There was talk of the 1954
season of the "Gaiety Whirl" and this was signed more or less
straight away. There were rumours in Eastbourne that we were not
coming back the following year, as Gwen was having a baby. It
took seven years to the birth. Local people always make up all the
news, when they do not know the facts.

The pantomime at the Gaiety Theatre, Ayr was beautifully dressed.
Gwen's costumes as Prince Charming were out of this world.
Charlie Stewart as "Buttons" was as Scottish as they come and
was loved by the children.

139

Ann Matthew who was his wife at the time, was a very tall and elegant "Dandini". The company was a very happy family, and we all celebrated Christmas. Hogmany was slightly different. As I had jet black hair, I was in demand for "First Fittin". You had to bring the New Year in with either a dark haired man or a piece of coal. Leslie Popplewell and his wife Edna had invited us to their house to bring in the New Year. Eric Popplewell and his wife Rene invited us after we had accepted the invitation from Leslie. It became quite an embarrassing night but it all ended with peace and harmony. The great eating place was the Airport at Kilmarnock. We made many drives to enjoy good food and watch the planes come in to land.

The hospitality of the Scots people was overwhelming, the reputation, that they had been labelled with of being mean, was unjustified.

The charm of Alloway, the birth place of Robert Burns, was completely unspoiled. The rambling small roads were as they were in his day, as were the crofter's cottages. Visitors from all over the world came to see the cottage, where the genius was born, and were captivated by the atmosphere, and the memorabilia of the Bard of Scotland.

ROBERT BURNS.

"Then came, sweet music, inspire my lay" O, Were I on Parnassus Hill". Robert Burns.

The "Gaiety Whirl" was a very famous summer show. *Ben Popplewell* a stock broker from Bradford, came to Ayr just before the First World War. He devised these repertory revues named "The Whirl". Comedy was usually the responsibility of a Scottish comic. The comedy was to be clean and never offensive. Any comic breaking these two golden rules was fired. Our comic was *Jack Milroy.* This 1954 season was to be his debut at the Gaiety and a very strong cast was assembled around him. *Glen Michael* was his feed. The *Edorics*, a very talented song and dance act, were responsible for the choreography as well as their own act, *The Maple Leaf Four,* were the speciality vocal act and Gwen and I had a featured spot in the second half. It was Eastbourne all over again, except that it was twice nightly.The audiences were fabulous, the reception was thunderous. Being a small theatre, the whole atmosphere was so intimate and easy to work.
Every Scots show has a Scots week when the whole company wore kilts and tartans. We had lovely ramps for the whole show to walk down to the sound of pipes, very majestic and soul stirring. As the whole company walked down, the Maple Leaf Four, who were off first, opened the door of the telephone box opposite the exit and as the company came off stage they all piled in to the telephone box. Nobody could move.........Chaos. It was now a challenge to find enough material for the 21 weeks. We had to find 13 different acts, and a repeat for the last week. We had an eight minute act and it had to be orchestrated for an 8 piece orchestra. *Harry Broad,* this fabulous musician took me into his room and library and suggested I adapt orchestrations from his musical selections he had in abundance. He taught me the ranges of the instruments and the comfortable compass they could manage. Harry gave me the key signature for each instrument and the compass and range, that would be comfortable for each musician.

I didn't know I was going to use this chart as much as I did. I was soon taking violin or clarinet parts and transposing them to suit the instruments we had in the pit. My sight reading was ordinary. I learnt it in the choir, but I was now, having to arrange music, to get the best out of a small orchestra. It was very satisfying to listen to the results of my first efforts. You can imagine that we were very quick studies, as we had to find 14 different acts, and it was change every week.

Gwen was now making a dress a week. Like me, she was having to act quickly. We only had the afternoons to do these important parts of our act. A new dress each week had to look new. What a wonderful job Gwen did. We were both working very hard. It was twice nightly. Band call Monday morning, Tuesday morning off, then rehearsal, Wednesday, Thursday, Friday and Saturday mornings for the following weeks show. This would include comedy with Jack and Glen. We had lyrics and words coming out of our ears. It was not unusual at 5.30 p.m. on the Monday night just before the "fust hoose", for Jack to say that the sketch we had rehearsed we were not doing now. Instead you will say something about the man next door and Glen will say, and I will say, you make it up as you go along and the tag will be such and such.........Black out. This at the start was terrifying. It made you spontaneous and it was the greatest experience for coping with all situations. We would not have missed this education for anything. So we did thirteen different acts without repeating.

Gwen and I decided to even change the act again for the last week, another dress to make and more orchestrations. It was worth it as we discovered the best act of the season, and we opened with it at Aberdeen. The show was extended to go to Aberdeen and Glasgow. Jack Milroy was a great hit and surrounded by a first class production and strong cast, he went to the top of the Scottish artistes, popular list.. A very funny comic, but because of his lightning delivery, he couldn't travel south.

The "Gaiety Whirl" was a high class and superb show.

On returning home to London we felt we had really worked our socks off. We had been rebooked for the "the Gaiety Whirl" for 1955 but we needed to find some other engagements to keep the wolf from the door.

Poppet, known as Josie Bradly kept on at us to join the Concert Artistes Association. This was an association of Artists in all branches of entertainment. It was founded in 1897, its principal object was to raise a Benevolent Fund to safeguard the interests of its members. It owned 20 Bedford Street, Covent Garden, its own West End club, where you could perform for agents to see your work. We were not keen on joining at the outset, but we eventually filled in the form. *Josie Bradly* proposed us and a lovely lady and clever comedienne, *Rowena Vincent* was our seconder. We had to do an introductory performance on a Monday night in front of all the members, This was to pass hopefully, for membership. Rowena had never seen us and was scared stiff in case she had seconded a turkey. " Ro" was as petrified as we were.

During our act she stood alongside and I could see her face light up. She was a very good looking lady and highly respected in the Association and a prominent Committee member. This performance was to change our whole professional life in the theatre. Within the C.A.A. there were about 42 Concert Agents who had all sorts of dates ranging from small concerts, Masonics, Rotary Clubs, Smoking Concerts, Livery Companies, Council functions, Conferences and Mayoral celebrations.
Smoking concerts, were very popular after the first world war, when many singers who had been in the war returned to sing once more. Many of them had lost legs or arms and luckily had voices that were above average. They could earn a living.

143

Unemployment was rife, so the lads from the service at that time found it difficult to get work. Among the members and the agents were many characters, I would make this book like the Encyclopedia Britannica, if I included all the stories. An agent Edith Price was known as "Cut Price". Her usual saying was "It's alright dear, it's on your doorstep, so you will do it for two and a half guineas won't you". When you got there it was 2 spots and a finale. Talking of finales, Evelyn Norris (Lemon Hart Rum) always finished with "We'll Meet Again" at every show. Some agents were pianists as well, so you had to have them for the job, even if you were not happy with their playing.

Lily Denville, a very short sighted agent, with thick lens glasses, was a crazy woman driver who would take her hands off the wheel while turning round to her terrified passengers. A little like Mrs. Malaprop, she would tell of her latest driving accident. There were several. Her description would be thus "It was a foggy night and before I knew where I was, I had gone slap bang into one of those bollocks in the middle of the road" (ooh- painful). *Tudor Evans* of the Welsh Guards was a very popular baritone. He played the lead in "Kismet" at the Stoll Theatre during a very prestigious career. Tudor liked his tipple and after a successful show for the forces, he attended a party,. determined to drink them all under the table. When it was time to leave he could not be found anywhere. After a search he was discovered blissfully snoring on the floor outside the "Gents". When he was woken up, he sat up, rubbed his eyes and said "Was I going in there or coming out?"

Among the C.A.A. list of agents was a Mrs. Bess Richards, her late husband Murray had started the agency, and she carried on the business. Bess became a good friend and booked us a lot. Her niece was *Gillian Lynne*, a very fine choreographer who had a brilliant career in West End Musicals and Films to her credit. Bess said she wanted us to hear a pianist who she thought would be good for us. His name was *Trevor Smith.*

Accompaniment by Molly Snooks.

He read a bit, played a bit and was willing. Trevor came to our home and played for us. I was a little naughty. I gave him some new manuscript to read. It was an accompaniment with full orchestral figures. I wanted the sound to be the orchestra and the third part of the trio. Our voices contained the melody and the harmony while the piano played the third part.

It was slightly embarrassing. Trevor was obviously nervous and played quite a bunch of "wrong uns". Despite this we could see that the lad had talent and provided he had time to look at the music, he coped very well. Gwen and I used to laugh when he had a new introduction to play, he would go at such a pace, you were not sure what he was playing. However, Trevor Smith became our permanent accompanist and nobly he did. It was wonderful to have a complete unit whenever we appeared. Having a double act and material to span 15 - 30 minutes, within our profession we became an established duo to be incorporated in any special concert or show. We appeared with *Dickie Henderson, Russ Conway, Ken Dodd, Leslie Crowther, Ken Goodwin, John Hanson, Al Read, Howard Keel, Norman Wisdom, Sandy Powell, Jack Radcliffe, Donald Peers, Roy Hudd, Bob Monkhouse, Tommy Trinder, Ted Ray, Arthur Askey, Rawicz and Landauer and many more superstars.* If you gave a reliable and successful performance, the "Stars" were pleased to have you on the bill. Our professional life seemed to take on a pattern, summer shows, after dinner entertainment, and pantomime. We were engaged through the year.

In 1955 we returned for the summer in the "Gaiety Whirl" at Ayr. It was a very hot summer. Once again Jack Milroy was with us, we had the Four in a Chord as the speciality vocal act. We were so well established with the Scots audience, that as we walked on stage, we received an ovation. The sun shone all the time. We were hoping we would survive. The Ice show down the road eventually closed. The business increased and we seemed to be set for a long and happy season.

145

The cricket season was going well with the Ayr Cricket Club, although I could only play on Sundays, the show being twice nightly. Cricket with the Ayr Cricket Club was the most peaceful and serene I had ever played. The setting at Cambusdoon was beautifully landscaped. It was a bowlers wicket, and I found it very hard to get scores over 60. It was the only club I didn't score a century for, and I played for eight different clubs. The general opinion amongst the cricketing fraternity in England is that Scotland do not play the noble game. Nothing is further from the truth. I went to Dumfries to play against them at that time. The club had just celebrated 103 years of existence. The Queen had visited in the centenary, to open a new pavilion. The standard at Ayr was very high, and when I was fielding with a twelve year old boy, by the name of *Mike Deness,* you can see I was in good company. We had a professional at the club, *Charlie Oakes* of Sussex. He was coaching and training Mike Deness for greater things and we know the story. Young Mike captained England and Kent scoring 25,000 first class runs and 4 test centuries.

Charlie Oakes, for one Sunday asked me if I would play for his professional team against the club. It was for his Benefit. He said "You won't get a bat with my County men batting, but you will get a bowl." How right he was. I bowled all the afternoon ending up with 16 overs, 4 maidens, 38 runs and 6 wickets. It was a little soft and this suited me. I was now ready for a rest as I knew I would not bat. Jack Oakes, Charlie's brother, John Langridge, Colin Smith of the West Indies and the wonderful Rohan Kanhai, who was the professional for Aberdeen. The so called "pros" found it was not an easy wicket, and were all out except for Kanhai. I joined him and what an experience. We ran many fives, he was so fast. They would put a man directly behind the bowler on the rope. Kanhai would make it a half volley and drive to that boundary. He would walk to the pavilion knowing it would probably be caught, making sure he walked behind the batting crease. The ball would sail way over the fielders head for six. He did this several times ending up with 78 not out.....great.

A fire catastrophe.

"I'm on fire, I'm a flame"   ***Tough at the Top***
Sir Alan Herbert.   Vivian Ellis

On Tuesday the 2nd August, 1955 at 5.40 p.m. just before the first house, I went into the box office to book some tickets, having done this, I opened the side door to see the stage on fire. It was not red flame, it was white. The flames were shooting up through the top of the flies. In panic, I ran into Carrick Street and shouted "help". There was not a soul anywhere near. I ran round to the stage door thinking of Gwen as she was in the theatre doing her practice. Gwen had managed to get to that infamous phone box and call the fire brigade. She had to leave quickly as the flames were crackling round her. Luckily the Fire Brigade responded, even though the phone was off the hook. She took one of our trunks out of the dressing room, into the street only to find there was nothing at all in it. Jack Milroy came up the street, looking at the flames with tears in his eyes. The press the next day had the picture of Jack looking so distraught that he looked absolutely devastated and ill with trauma. After all it was his season up in flames. It was ironical that the Chief Fire Officer had given lectures on how to put the fire out at the Gaiety, as he knew it would happen one day. His idea was to make sure the fire curtain was down so that the draft would shoot the flames through the top of the glass roof and out into the air. This is exactly what he did but in doing so he nearly lost his life. Two girls were in the dressing roon at the time and nobody knew they were there. Luckily they were rescued.

The fire at the Gaiety Theatre, Ayr was one of the greatest tragedies that befell our profession in the middle fifties. It was a summer show that was held in the highest esteem throughout theatrical history. The whole company was left in sadness and dismay at the finish of a season that had beaten the heatwave, and enjoyed the greatest success for what would have been an outstanding production.

"If music be the food of love...play on" **Twelfth Night**
William Shakespeare.

Being out of work in the middle of a summer season was going to be traumatic and financially problematical. The after dinner season didn't start again until the end of September. A stroke of luck manifested itself. The Edinburgh Festival was about to start, and it was suggested we go to the Gaiety Theatre, Leith for three weeks. The show to be called the "Festival Show" starring *Jack Milroy, Glen Michael, Gwen Overton and Clive Stock* and the support would be different for each week. We signed for the three weeks and went to this filthy theatre. It had been closed for a long time and needed a good spring clean. The show was an immediate hit. Jack was an instant success and *we* had a ready made public because the audiences loved musical comedy. We started to incorporate comedy with a topical flavour. This was to stand us in good stead when we returned to London's cabaret scene. Well dear reader, don't take my word for the success of the show....it ran until the middle of December. Out of tragedy, luckily came a triumphant 20 week season.

In the August I took my driving test. I had a two hour lesson the day before the ordeal. I was horrendous. I stopped traffic on hills, and gave the tram drivers a scare in Princes Street. My tutor said I had no chance at all of passing. I said to him "Bad dress rehearsal, good performance". The next day I passed.

We lived in a caravan just outside Edinburgh, sharing the same site with Glen Michael, his wife Beryl and his small daughter Yonnie. It was great fun and the outdoor life was good for us. We played special games of football which gave us regular exercise. It was a very happy time. Glen took us around in his Austin Atlantic with white wall tyres. It was a little hairy as he was always running out of petrol. When it was time to go back to London for Christmas, we hired a dark green Ford Zephyr.

My first long drive.

It took just about all our costumes, music (which had grown considerably) and our clothes. What a journey home..?
It was quite a large number of cases. The journey just before Christmas was going to be a great ordeal for me as I had only just passed my driving test in the August. Since then, I had not driven at all and the thought of hundreds of miles to London was daunting. We started off at the crack of dawn, the plan to follow Glen. Off we started and Glen was like a flash. He cornered like a racing driver. Trying to keep up with him was scary. I was driving like a maniac to just keep within sight. Very gradually I gained more confidence and managed to hold the road. It was obviously time for coffee around eleven o'clock, we stopped at a hotel in Morpeth.

Whilst enjoying our coffee, an A.A. man came into the hotel and said "Is there anyone with an Austin Atlantic with white wall tyres here ?". Glen said he had and the A.A. man said "Well there was a car following at high speed with flames coming out of the exhaust". I said "That was me," so we went outside to the car and as the A.A. man lifted my bonnet, there was an explosion and rusty water went everywhere. It was a hose that had split. "Well that's the cause." he said. "I have to fix a new pipe." This he did and while doing this operation he cut his hand. So now we had blood, rust and water all over the inside casing of the engine. We thanked him and gave him something for his trouble, and he took his leave. We then drove off and must have covered at least 275 miles when we stopped. Glen said he would have to find an hotel as his daughter Yonnie was exhausted. They found a place nearby, they asked us if we were going to stop and in true pioneering fashion, we said we would go on. At least we knew we had our home if we arrived back, and I found our way to Hampstead. We said goodbye and on we went. No sooner had we gone a couple of miles when we hit the worst "pea souper", I had ever experienced. The fog restricted us to a snails pace and following the cat's eyes we were becoming very sleepy. There was one moment when I felt a bump and I had gone up on a roundabout.

If a motorbike hadn't come round the corner with his orange lights, I would have been stranded for some time. Nearing home, there were orange street lights to help us. We came to a fork in the road and through the fog, I thought I recognized some shops. The right hand road was the one to lead us up to Finchley Road. Luckily my sense of direction had not failed me, and we were on our way to Mill Lane where we lived.

Tiptoeing into the house, as not to wake my parents, for they had to wake up early in the morning for newspaper deliveries, we finally, around midnight, got into bed, utterly shattered. In bed I felt we were still in the car and the bed was moving with the rhythm of the engine, and the lights were still coming at me. Eventually we were both spark out. The welcome home from my parents was tremendous and we had to tell the story of the first long drive ever from the north. We were home in time for the Christmas festivities and it was a family "get together" enjoyed by all. 1956 was brought in with a few 'sherberts'. We did a few after dinner shows and then it was time to get into the well packed car for the drive to Edinburgh and then stop with a friend before going on to Dundee. We were joining Jack again for a short season at the Palace Theatre, Dundee and then the summer at Aberdeen. We started off to the North and all was well, until we met some black ice, we managed through that, the car was behaving. Up through Northumberland and on to the outskirts of Edinburgh, we took the ring road and just as we were approaching the big complex of Marconi, the engine started to miss and we were slowing to snail pace. The car came to a standstill and would not budge. I alighted and managed to lift the bonnet to look inside not having a clue what I was looking for. I couldn't see any water anywhere. There was a car on the other side of the road, it turned to see my distress. He drove in front of me and stopped and asked where are you going and I said "to Barnton about 4 miles to go" Taking off his webbing belt, he tied it around his back bumper and our front bumper..

Too close for comfort.

We gradually started to move off, although it was a strain for his car pulling a heavy load. We were on the last stretch when his water started to boil and he had to stop. The weight had started to take a toll on his radiator. A policeman on a bicycle passed us and must have realised after going some distance that we had not only broken down, but that we had not any numbers to show that we were being towed. We waited a few moments while his water cooled. Sitting quietly and being patient in anticipation of the last part of the journey, we spied through the side mirrors as we were packed up and could not see out of the rear. Our steadfast bobby, pedalling like the clappers, getting nearer and nearer. This we both thought would be the final straw of being taken to the police station with it now being around midnight. As the copper was about to dismount and say the usual "hello, hello, hello", our fine saviour started up and we gradually pulled away. The policeman was now disorientated as he was half way off the bike and rolling to the ground. We were going slowly to start, and by the time the Scottish policeman was pedalling, we picked up a little speed. The bobby was accelerating and had us well within his sights, he was exhausting himself trying to keep up with us. Our cars were creating a few lengths clear, like the Boat Race and we could see him far away in the distance, he kept going. I suppose he thought we might break down again. Safe and sound and thanks to our very kind chap, who we learned was in the Army, and his webbing belt, we landed with Phoebe and Jack for a good nights sleep.

The next day we called the hire firm to take back the car, and we assembled all our luggage and props for the journey on the train to Dundee. This would be an adventure, as we had never played Dundee, we had heard mixed reports about the place and it would be interesting to see for ourselves. One good thing we would not have a great deal of rehearsing, as we would be doing familiar sketches with Jack.

A new production on the horizon.

While we were rehearsing, we found that there were quite a few cats in the theatre. Being cat lovers, we made friends very quickly, so much so that we would be singing during rehearsals, with the cats on our shoulders. There was a wonderful warm atmosphere at the Palace Theatre, Dundee. The audience was probably the best of the Scottish tour. During the run, Boo Laye and Frank Lawton came to the town. Evelyn Laye was starring in "A Wedding In Paris". This wonderful lady was also looking after Frank as he wasn't very well. Frank, bless his heart, came to see us one night. It was a great night as we had the longest reception for our "Kiss me Kate" finish ever. Frank came to see us after the show. He thought the evening most educational as he had never seen a Scottish revue before. A lot of it he didn't understand. He was very animated by our act, which of course, he had never seen before, only seeing "Brigadoon". Frank was most complimentary. What a lovely man. that was the last time we saw him as he passed away very soon after. Luckily we did see Boo again. On we went to Aberdeen.

It was now definite that Gwen was pregnant. This was joyous, although we were in Aberdeen. How long could she last before leaving the show? This we had to play by ear. Very skilfully she was able to let her dresses out at the back and could carry on for quite a while. During the run *Mary Lee*, who was Jack's wife became very ill and couldn't perform her task as comedy woman. This was a trauma. Jack called the company together, and asked all the girls if any one would step in and keep the curtain up. No Scottish pro would volunteer. In the end Jack looked at Gwen and she being the trooper she always had been, and always would be, said she would do it. The comedy parts included red noses, horrible make-ups, red bloomers and dreadful clothes. I must say, and with complete impartiality, Gwen was brilliant. The company, especially Jack, were thrilled to pieces and very grateful. This triumph was despite the fact that at the time, Gwen was having bouts of sickness, rush off stage, one big heave, and then rush back.

Little Mary Lee came back, and was not particularly grateful..
You would remember Mary as the lead singer with the Roy Fox
Band. Dear reader. If you can, then you are my age, or maybe
more?

Gwen, despite her resolve, couldn't cope any longer and it was
time for us to leave the show. The relations with Scotland and all
the Scottish audiences was special. One of the main reasons they
took to us was that we were not doing the Scottish music. We
were an attacking act with movement, comedy and above all
American musicals. It was very sad to say farewell, especially to
Jack and Glen. These two were a super double. They were the
first to be *"Francie and Josie"*. The feeling from the management
demonstrated the goodwill we had built up, and they wished us
well. There were many presents, especially for the forthcoming
production of the infant Stock.

We returned early May and it was time for the last run up to the
birth. While we experiencing the excitement of our first child,
there was apprehension. Having worked together for over three
years and established ourselves as a successful duo, we were in a
difficult position, myself now a single performer with no real track
record. What to do now to earn a living was the question? As a
double we were successful and marketable, but as a solo
performer, it was very precarious.

By the strangest piece of luck, dear old *Fred Wilby* was producing
an afternoon television programme called *"Treasure Chest"*. This
was to be a women's programme including knitting, household
gadgets, entertainment and tips for cooking etc. The host of the
programme was *James Norbury*, a famous figure with the woollen
giant Paton and Baldwin. He was an outstanding knitter, and each
week he introduced a new pattern for the ladies.

I was to include two songs each week, requested by the viewers. The mandate for the choice had to be a fairly popular song and an impression of a famous Music Hall performer. I would be dressed for the latter. It was a thirteen week series for A.T.V., recorded in the Old Hackney Empire. The straight songs were fairly standard but the impressions of *Sir Harry Lauder, Will Fyffe, Talbot O'Farrell, Al Jolson, Nelson Eddy, Richard Tauber, G.H. Elliot, Frank Sinatra, Donald Peers, Paul Robeson, Arthur Tracy, Cavan O'Connor and Clarkson Rose* were more difficult. I remember writing to "Clarkie Rose" to get his permission to do "The Girls of the Old Brigade". He was not keen on this, but after some smaltz and flattery, he reluctantly gave his consent. The dressing of the famous stars was an interesting operation. Many old photographs were perused, and the applicable suits were given to me to wear. It was difficult because I had never seen Talbot O'Farrell perform. There were some ancient recordings, so I had to do the best I could, the grey top hat and long grey coat were very smart, and I felt very aristocratic. How near I was with the voice was open to guess work, but Fred who had seen Talbot O'Farrell on numerous occasions, declared that it was very near.

This series with a restricted audience, was a life saver. It meant that we could keep the wolf from the door, and I could be at home for the birth. It also meant that I could play cricket for the Stage and Brondesbury Cricket Clubs.

Through the Concert Artistes' Association and the various agents, I picked up a few dates but not many, as the winter season was over and it was now summer. There were a few Sunday concerts and these I could fit in with the television shows. I found a soprano who would sing with me. The agents always wanted a soprano and baritone so that the management could have two solos and one double. They thought it was more for their money. I was not finding the lady singer very easy to work with. Gwen and I had such a rapport, and this was completely instinctive.

Playing cricket for Brondesbury was easy, as the ground was only half a mile from home, It also gave me a chance to get to know the local people, and Middlesex County used Brondesbury as a nursery for young players, and the fostering of very young talent.

The Stage Cricket Club has given me some of the most rewarding and happy moments in my long cricketing career. It was founded in 1930 by W. Earle Grey. Bill was a darling of a man steeped in Shakespeare and mad about the game. There had been another club prior to the "Stage", namely the "Thespians". They had *Sir C. Aubrey Smith, the Livesey Brothers, Jack, Roger and Barrie, Jack McNaughton and many other actors of note. C. Aubrey Smith* was a giant as a cricketer and he went off to Hollywood to start his own side with *Ronald Colman, Reginald Denny, Basil Rathbone, Boris Karloff, David Niven, Errol Flynn Robert Douglas, Nigel Bruce* and other film idols. A strange episode was that *Garry Marsh* who at one time was called the "The Stage Cricket Club" was to go to Hollywood on a contract. Harold his "man what does" told me that just as Garry was about to leave for America, he had a bout of nerves on two counts. 1, that he was nervous about his ability as an actor, and don't forget he had become the wonderful "baddy" especially in the *George Formby* films, and 2, he was to lose his cricket season. He decided not to go, and *Herbert Marshall* went in his place.

It was a known fact that the majority of the Surrey fixtures were held through the cheery personality and generosity of Garry Marsh. His buying drinks for the opposition and his consumption of Booth's Gin was legendary. He was Captain many years and after his lunch and the imbibing of numerous gins, he would bowl over after over to sweat out the liquid. Of course the opposition piled up many runs, and sometimes put the game out of our grasp. Garry would say "Give them a few Cockie". This all helped to keep the fixture warm for next year. The serious cricketers of the regular team, began to get very disgruntled with too many runs to chase.

155

Garry was very generous to actors that were down on their luck and he would pay all their expenses if they played for us. One such actor was *Geoffrey Barrie*. He was a first class cricketer, a Yorkshireman and the cousin of the famous *Len Hutton*. He was a fine right hand medium fast bowler and left hand bat, very difficult to dislodge. He was never in work. Garry thought it worth it to have him in the team. There were characters in the team when I played from 1947. *Leonard Brett*, a T.V producer, a suspect wicket keeper, *Abraham Sofaer*, a classical actor who had the dirtiest whites and looked slovenly at all times. "Sofi" as he was affectionately called, was secretary of the club for quite a while. He bowled round arm, and his best ball was his "dipper". *Kenneth Milne Buckley*, T.V. producer and husband of *Sylvia Peters*, a well known announcer. *Anthony Huntley Gordon*, stage director of the "Mousetrap" for many years. *Henry Hepworth* an actor who was probably the finest all-rounder we ever had. His brother John used to play as well, before they went off to New Zealand. While I was away in Australia new blood made themselves felt, there was *John Slater, Edward Cast, Tony Rowe, Sam Kydd, Gavin Doyle and William Franklyn* who gained publicity as the "Sch..weppes, you know who!" He was a fine athlete. I used to play him at tennis with personal success, but he out did me in the longevity stakes. I gave up playing cricket at 70, this was an ambition of mine. *Oliver Gordon* a play director used to take 100 wickets every season up to the age of 70, so that was my goal. I know for a fact that Bill was still playing at 76. *John Slater* a hard working film actor, always working. You would see him regularly in British films, usually a cockney spiv or villain. Johnny was one of the nicest cricketing friends I knew. He had his own net in the garden where he would play with his sons. One memorable innings for Johnny was against the Metropolitan Police. I opened, we lost quick wickets and at number 7 the bold Slater ambled to the wicket. He usually got on with it straight away. We put on 100 runs in exactly 40 minutes. I had scored 34 of this partnership and Johnny had scored 66 when he was cleaned bowled.

I went on to a ton not out. The innings together was great. We ran many twos that would normally be singles. *Sam Kydd* another busy actor played when he had the time. *Edward Cast* opened the bowling with Bill Franklyn for the 1st eleven. These two in tandem with the new ball were a force to be reckoned with. *Geoffrey Chater* a regular television actor was a class bat and good cover point, and in the early days *Trevor Howard* turned out for us. He was an exceedingly good cricketer and went to play for Barnet. The Stage played at Lords every year, while other clubs had to wait for one in four. We played the first Tuesday in the Cross Arrows fortnight every year. The first game I remember in the middle was a win by 5 wickets and the top scorer for the Cross Arrows was an actor *Jack Livesey* of 52. Another time against *Freddie Titmus* and **Don Bennett**, Garry and I had a big partnership, because the wicket had been pitched near to the Tavern. My late cut come dab through third man gave us an easy chance to run five. Off Don Bennett particularly I kept running fives. Garry was a big heavy man and it was getting to the crunch where he could run no further. It is a wonder that he did not pass out. *Brian Rix, John Alderton, Tony Britton and Philip Stone* all played *for* us. Philip actually joined the Stage in 1947 before me, but unfortunately he went to a sanatorium so I did not meet him until around 1956. I was skipper that year, and I brought Philip on first change with his off spinners and as they say, he would 'do the Business' for me. *Eric Delzenne* an electrical engineer for *Harold Fielding* became secretary and he played regularly. Frank Taylor, who was with me in 'Oklahoma' was a spinner. He had been a prisoner of war with the Japanese and had lost his teenage years. He was a Scot who could really hit the ball hard, he left us and went to live in Australia.

Abraham Sofaer, he with the beautiful voice, was reading a book by Ranjitsinhji. He gave chapter and verse of how to play the rising ball, especially bouncers. Sofi would say in stentorian tones "Ranji would whip the ball off your nose like so". We were playing Merrow, near Guildford.

We were losing wickets to this fast bowler, each time, we lost a wicket, Sofi would say,"Now Ranji would have done this, and Ranji would have done that, in his book he says you must always pull off the nose". The wickets were tumbling and the drooping shoulders, dirty whites, and bat trailing on the grass with tie tied around the grubby flannels, walked to the wicket with head bowed low. He took his guard. The first ball flew over his head, the second missed his ear by a whisker, and the third took his castle, with the bails flying yards. He turned slowly and crawled back to the pavilion. As he was within yards of all the members and in true thespian style, he put out his arms so that everyone could see him and in great declamtory voice said "*I must have misread the book*".

Dear reader, I am talking about players during my time with the club. I save the best to last. *Hugh Goldie*, an outstanding batsman and wicket keeper. Like me he was ex RAF but not like me, he had a DFC and Bar. Also like me he was a member of the Middlesex County Cricket Club. When he played his first game for us, it was on the County Cricket Ground at Horsham. What a paradox, here was Hugh, a brilliant wicket keeper rushing up and down the square leg boundary, picking up and throwing in, all in one movement, while Leonard Brett was allegedly keeping wicket. It was not long before Hugh became the opening bat and the wicket keeper. It was then it became a regular practice when we were both available at the same time, that Hugh and I would open the innings. One Sunday against Stoke D'Abernon we opened. Hugh had scored 32 before I opened my account. He played his square cover drive to the boundary and although there were fielders there to stop the boundaries, the ball would hit a bump or the legs of the fielder or go through the hands and Hugh had 8 fours in no time. When I was out we had an opening stand of 208, which is still the Club record. Those who were watching thought the bowling must be easy.

Hugh and I, had mastered the lifting ball, when the rest of the lads went in, they sort of made a quick exit. The team crumbled and we were all out for around 278. Hugh was a complete man of the theatre, from actor to stage director to assistant producer, to director producer. He was Director of Productions at the Theatre Royal, Windsor for over 12 years. He became a qualified Umpire for Middlesex County League and played for many clubs in Devon and Somerset, North Yorks, and Durham Leagues. You can feel I had a lot of time for Hugh because he was not only a good craftsman within the theatre, but he was a thinking cricketer and I identified with that. *Eric Goldie,* Hugh's brother was a singer with the BBC singers for many years. He was a spin bowler, and although he was small, he could play an off drive with the best of them. He wore glasses, and it always fascinated me the way the peak of his cap rested on top of his glasses. His wife Joan was a darling. We still have the whisky decanter they gave us for our wedding gift. Eric and I were the only singers in the club until *Roger De Courcey* joined us. Roger was a very good baritone before *Nookie* discovered him. A good bowler, and a long handled batsman.

Lauri Lupino Lane ran a side called "The Gaieties" started with members of the shows at the Victoria Palace. He played for us in some of our mid week sides when we were short. For a big man he was very light on his feet. He had great elevation.

Russell Napier known for playing inspectors and detectives, was a main stay of the club with organization, and the getting of teams together. Leg spin, quite useful and a very nice guy.

The regular players were very keen. We met once a week at the *Gover-Sandham School* for sessions with the two great cricketers. They really made a difference to our playing skills.

So we are in the season of 1956. I am playing for Brondesbury C.C. and skipper of the Stage Cricket Club. On the ninth of June, Gwen is taken into Elizabeth Garrett Anderson's hospital at Belsize Park. I was pleased to take her in as I felt that once the baby is on its way she is in safe safe hands. Her Gynaecologist was a clever lady called Miss Barnes. This lady had a great reputation and was highly skilled. I went off to play cricket at Brondesbury and received one of the few ducks of my career. It was probably retribution for leaving my wife in hospital and going off to play that ball game.

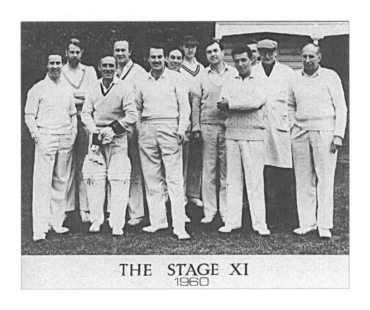

THE STAGE XI
1960

Yours truly. Alistair Boyd, Sam Kydd, William Franklyn.
Bruce Beeby, John Slater, Roger Kimber, Edward Cast,
Brian Jackson, Umpire Jack and Russell Napier.

The heir to the Stock dynasty.
"Like a tree he'll grow, with his head held high" Soliloquy.
Carousel... Oscar Hammerstein and Richard Rodgers.
On the 10th of June, a son was born to us. **Richard Beresford**
Clive Stock had arrived safe and sound to swell the family.
Naturally all parents think their child is the best thing that has
happened since **W.G. Grace,** but he really was a bonnie lad. Gwen
had given me yet another present, a healthy boy to carry on the
name, and thank the lord, she was fit and well, after a rough time.

All the usual family problems followed, with nappies and lost
sleep, and bottles etc., Gwen was just a fantastic mother, and
Richard grew and blossomed in the usual sequence of weight and
size, and was perfectly normal in every detail. It was now, with
Gwen out of action, how to earn a crust on my own. A part from
singing in a few concerts, I got to know **Conrad Leonard.** He was
a pianist, composer, and accompanist. He played for me now and
then. Con was an arranger with Lawrence Wright, the music
publishers. Musical scores were piling up, and he needed another
pair of hands, so he brought me in to assist, by getting me to copy
scores. This meant there was a large manuscript from which all the
parts for the musicians had to be copied. I set to work on this job,
and I would write to 3 and 4 in the morning. In 1956 you received
3 shillings a bar for piano parts,, 1 shilling and sixpence for a
violin part, and if double stopping 2 shillings a bar, all the other
parts were 1 shilling and sixpence. I did a whole score for
Mantovani for a broadcast, and this gave me quite a good income.
It helped me out considerably during this single period.

It was quite an experience, at first I was cramming too many bars
on a stave, and it was bunched up. I soon learned to space my bars
to the customary four to five bars, and this of course, increased
your fee for the number of pages. Having learned from Harry
Broad, it became a "good little earner".

161

You'll never walk alone.

It is amazing how the odd concert here and there increases the income, there were little old folks shows, and concerts put on by members of the C.A.A. I fitted in with my odd impressions, and rendering of character songs, like "Devonshire Cream & Cider"

Singing with a different soprano now and again, was not very enjoyable, I missed my partner. We were a proper double.

All was going pretty well, until a concert on the first week in August, when the soprano I was to sing with, contracted laryngitis. The agent asked if Gwen was fit enough to step into the breach, and being the trouper she was, back she came, and we once again were re-united in song. In hindsight, Gwen always said she came back too early after the birth. Engagements started to flood in once more. The advantage of being an established double act, is that you can be booked anywhere, either on your own, or with other acts in a variety of presentations. One day we had a call from *Gerald Sanderson.*

This man was an impresario, who had presented Gwen in concerts, when she was a 12 year old soprano. He had arranged for her to sing with *Harry Davidson and his Orchestra,* on numerous occasions. There were other bands she sang with, i.e. *Harry Roy, and Blanche Coleman and her all girls Orchestra .* I had never met Gerry, but he had heard of our act, and he renewed his friendship with Gwen. He asked us to sing at the opening of a new club in Jermyn Street. It was to be opened by my hero. *Sid Field.* He enjoyed our show, and Gerry told us that Sid was in the bar, but would not be staying long, probably ten minutes, he was tired and was playing in "Harvey" at the time. Ten minutes !, we chatted for nearly an hour, what a lovely time, he was super.

One of our first theatre concerts, was with our good friend *Arthur Askey.* He told of how he would do six shows a night, these were usually masonics or private functions, in his day he got the princely sum of one and a half guineas. one pound, eleven shillings and sixpence. Out of this fortune he paid his commission and pianist. His accompanist was *Sydney Jerome.*

There was a tariff in those days, One and a half Guineas in town, Three Guineas outside i.e. Croydon, Clapham etc., Arthur told us that he was doing a show at the Holborn Rooms, when after the show he was asked by the secretary, if he could do 12th November at Arding & Hobbs at Clapham, Arthur looked in his diary, you always had to have your diary with you, he said "Yes but it would be three," and he put up the three fingers to rubber stamp the amount of three guineas. Evidently the day arrived, Arthur was as usual triumphant, and when he picked up the envelope with his fee therein, he found THREE half crowns. I made sure that after that, I always counted the money in the envelope, with guineas, the odd ten bob note could be missing. Working with Arthur was always a joy, we saw him many times throughout his life. I mentioned *Sydney Jerome,* he was married to a beautiful pianist, *Kathleen O'Hagan.* They ran a very good agency, and we had numerous engagements from them. They were both first class pianists, and having either one accompany you was a real pleasure. Syd was a mad golfer, and I remember being at his funeral with all my pals from the VGS (Vaudeville Golfing Society) when *Walter Midgeley,* one of our very best tenors, sang in the church, It was so beautiful, that we were all in tears. Hard baked comics and magicians were all moist of eye.

The passing of Syd was a very big loss to all of us who knew him, together with his sense of fun. He used to say to me when he was playing for us, and espied my busy parts. "Why do you write piano parts like this,? There are only two of us that can play them". He meant, Kathie and himself. A lovely pair of people.

163

The diary of *Gwen Overton & Clive Stock* started to fill up with
dates, so that we were doing 3 shows a night, consisting of a
permutation of "Master's Songs" at the Installation of a new
Master in masonry, and Masonic Ladies Festivals. Gwen was a
natural for the rapport in these private functions. It all depended
on friendly contact with the audience, and above all the Festival
secretary. The whole success was like a snowball, one function
recommended you to another, and so on. In the late fifties, a ladies
festival could have three acts for cabaret, a seven or eight piece
band, a toastmaster and a five course meal. By the end of the 70's
it was a trio, no toastmaster, maybe one cabaret act, or as the
talented *Gordon Turner, the man with the white piano,*
always said "Its either me or the fish course"

Gwen and I were booked at the Savoy for the Acton Lodge Ladies
Festival. When we arrived we found that there were five acts. To
open were the *Stargazers.* followed by *Helene Cordet,*
The Beverley Sisters, Carole Carr and Gwen and I to close the
cabaret around 12 midnight. Now this is for an ordinary Lodge
Ladies Festival. 400 people. They were all big stars of the day, and
we had to follow the Lord Mayors' show. The audience were
exceptional, and all the acts before us were successful. The
toastmaster announced us, and on we went. Well.! It was just
sensational. We had an ovation that went on and on. There was a
large bouquet of flowers at the end for Gwen. The Master of the
lodge a big man, said, when the applause had subsided.", Would
you like to hear them again ?" there was a big "Yes" from all
assembled, and we came back at 1 a.m. in the morning. We tried
out for the first time our "Kiss Me Kate" medley, and this was a
magic moment. So magical that we had our fee doubled. (Fancy
two guineas all in one go). I am kidding.
The Masonic world was a large enterprise, in London and the
Home counties there were thousands of lodges. I had many dates
at the Connaught Rooms in Great Queen Street, London.

The main pattern was for an Installation meeting to sing the "Master's Song and then do an act afterwards. Entering the main entrance, the uniformed steward at the front, checking everyone, to see if they were bona fide, would ask me "Where are you tonight ?" came my reply "I'm in the Derby room" "Oh what time are you on" "8.30 says I" and off I would go to the Derby Room. The function was always late, and often the fellow at the desk would phone up, "Are you going on now ?", I would tell him, they are running 45 minutes late. He would say "Will you go the York room they need some one now." I would take Trevor and off we go to the York, and do one that we were not scheduled for. I have known this to happen regularly, and another one would come up, and I would do three a night. The functions were always late, as a Grand Officer would be on his feet, with verbal diarrhea, delaying my entrance to sing my spot, I would commence with.. "Tonight I was going to sing for you the top of the hit parade" but its gone down to Number 9. Doing two "Master's Songs" and one Ladies Festival, or one "Master's Song" and two Ladies Festivals, was dependent entirely on the skill and goodwill of the toastmaster, and his rapport with the client. There is no doubt in my mind, that the doyenne of all toastmasters, was and is, **Bryn Williams.** He was quite easily the most versatile controller of a function on the London scene. When I say "versatile", I mean he was at home with all types of function. In the early days **John Mills** (not the actor) was renowned for the handling of the Manson House and City dinners, but he was not very comfortable with the ordinary Lodge ladies night. Bryn was always at ease with everyone. He would make sure that he put us on at the time we were booked for. If it was late, I would say, we will have to go for the next show. Bryn always made sure we were on and away to the next one with time to spare, thus enabling three shows in the one night. In those days you had the Piccadilly Hotel, the Criterion, The Monico, The Conaught Rooms, Hyde Park and Park Lane hotels, Savoy, Grosvenor House all in close proximity, and you could park. Now, there are very few functions, and the parking is horrendous.

Performing the "Master's Song" for me, a non mason, meant that I had to wait outside before I was allowed in, to sing. This did not seem right, as I liked to have a show flowing without any stops where nothing happened. My dear friend and pianist, *Trevor Smith* suggested that I join his lodge in Croydon, Ernie Turnbull was to be my seconder, he was the friend that introduced me to the insurance company. a very nice man. I intimated that I didn't want to join a theatrical lodge, in hindsight, I was right. So on the 4th February, I was initiated in to the Composite Lodge No 7162 to start my career in Freemasonry. More of that later.

Because of the tremendous numbers of functions, we kept an up to date diary, this would have the material we performed and what we wore. Gwen of course had many dresses for all types of engagement, and I had apart from the normal Dinner jacket and full Midnight blue tails. Wine tails and shoes to match, white tuxedo, Scottish tartan D.J. with velvet collar and shot facings. A mohair brown full dinner jacket and slacks with brown suede shoes, and a lighter blue full dinner jack and slacks. Black suede boots. A well known agent once said to me ," You are a flashy bugger", so I said "Yes. and when other performers are trying to catch me up, I will go a stage further." Our dress and presentation, were a highlight of our career with the after dinner world.

1957 we were booked again with *Sandy Powell and Norman Meadows* at Eastbourne, another lovely season, Great cricket at the Saffrons, and with the kind friends of Eastbourne. In the height of the season we appeared on Sundays as well, this gave us an opportunity to include some new material. The highlight of the season was to commemorate Sandy's 1,000th performance at the Pier Theatre, Eastbourne. For this show we had the guest appearance of *Norman Wisdom.* Sandy had evidently given Norman good advice when he was starting out. Keep it clean and never be offensive. Norman had always been grateful for this rule of comedy, and had kept to it. It was a lovely night.

There was a new musical coming to the Palace Theatre, London called "Where's Charley" a musical version of "Charley's Aunt" Gwen and I were called to the Palace to audition for the show, we did not get the job, as they said we were too operatic. We found out we had been recommended for the show by NORMAN WISDOM. What a very nice gesture on his part.

Richard had come away with us for the season, thanks to help of Gwen's mother. Mrs. Overton was a tower of strength, and looked after our son, and a most unselfish act, was that Gwen's Dad, travelled up and down to Eastbourne from London, so that Mum could come away and help us out. What would we do without the help of our parents, When we returned home after the season, then my Mother and Pop looked after Richard when we went out at night to do our after dinner shows.

We had appeared at many Concerts for different charities, one of our favourite appearances was for the Caxton Convalescent Home. There were always big stars on these Sundays. On the 13th October, we appeared at our beloved Drury Lane. Our friends *Dickie Henderson, Arthur Haynes, Toni Dalli,* were among the artistes included. The highlight for us was our finish with a "Oklahoma" medley with Harold Collins and his orchestra. All the stage hands and the managers of the theatre were at the side, all those that had been with us with the original show. Luckily the audience were completely with us, but all the staff and ourselves, were tearful with emotion for the memories we all held together. These special moments only come once now and again.
The Convalescent shows and the Stars Organisation for Spastics brought us together with special friends like *Russ Conway, Leslie Crowther and Dickie Henderson.* They worked tirelessly for the charity, and we were pleased to give them support. They were very cooperative when I presented shows for charity in the future.

Ernest Thompson was an insurance man, from top to toe, and when he tried to get a trombone insured, and nobody would cover the risk, he thought there was something wrong. He found that it was almost impossible to insure actors, artistes and musicians. *Ernie Turnbull,* my friend, being in the same office building, mentioned that I had been in Lloyds and that I was a professional performer, and maybe I could help. Ernest and I met, and we floated a company called *Theatrical Profession Insurance Service Ltd.* I became a director, *Jack Train* then joined the Board, *Sir Tom O'Brien,* who was then the secretary of the Trades Union Congress, joined the Board of directors. Our first Director's meeting was chaired by *Stuart Robertson,* a well known Bass Baritone, who was the brother of *Anna Neagle.* The firm was now open for business. It started well, Ernest, with a good typist secretary, looked after the actual cover of policies. The Nation Life insurance company was the main underwriter. Their rates were competitive, and artists were covered, all was going well. Then Stuart resigned as he was very involved in *Anna and Herbert Wilcox's* film company. Then came the new Chairman, my film director of "The Small Back Room" *Michael Powell.* He was a very experienced operator. We greeted each other warmly, although I always felt I was not important, but we became better friends, when he realized that Gwen and I, were a very busy pair, and well known in the world of the Savoy and the leading London hotels. He was a bit of a snob.

In the film world, there is always a problem with film finance. Every film that is produced, has to have what is called, "End Money". 60% has to be deposited before the cameras roll. So Michael Powell, knowing the film world completely, wanted to set up a film finance company, independently of the insurance side of the business. The rewards could be great, and so we voted to let Michael acquire as much finance as he could, for the Film industry's end money.

Bob Monkhouse was approached with regard to a puppet type television show, really the forerunner of the "Muppets". Bob had the scripts and the ideas, and was willing to discuss the possibilities. **Jack Hawkins** was coming in, because there was a need for a Film Distribution company. We were on the brink of an empire. It seemed to me that there was too much "running before we could walk" syndrome. The idea about artistes' insurance was being obliterated by these names joining us, even **Anthony Quayle** came to a few meetings.

Gwen and I returned to Eastbourne for the 1958 summer season. once again it was one of the happiest shows, as we were with two very close friends **George Clarkson and Gail Leslie.** The show was up to its usual high standard and there was plenty of golf and cricket. The four of us were inseparable, and we made financial budgets every week, as we could never keep to our restricted spending limits. Richard was two, and he loved his "Jige and Klee" as he called them. Richard loved the sea, and he was growing. His hair was blonde and curly, he put up with people saying "Isn't she lovely", he would say in a large voice "I'm a boy", he was once asked if he would like a brother or a sister, ?, he replied, "My father and mother are too busy", he enjoyed being with the show personnel.

Back home for the preponderance of bookings that had come in for the London hotels. Meetings for the insurance firm, Captain of the Concert Golfing Society, life was hectic, and then we were off to the Theatre Royal, Bath for pantomime for **Frank Maddox**. This was "Puss in Boots". Frank had rules that had been a tradition from his father, **Reg Maddox.** There was an unwritten law, that all the principals were to meet for drinks on a Sunday morning. This was not on as far as we were concerned, as we wanted to see our lad. We drove like the clappers after the show on Saturday night, so that we could see our son's lovely smiling face on Sunday morning. This was like a tonic to us.

169

"Something for everyone, a comedy to night" A Funny Thing Happened on the way to the Forum.   Stephen Sondheim.

The other rule was that if the company had a party, the men went in one room, and the ladies in another, this had been going on for years. We soon changed that. We enjoyed the pantomime, and we were booked for the following year at the Kings Theatre, Southsea. *Frankie Howerd* was to star in the same production. Frank was going through one of his very depressive phases. Nothing seemed to be going right, and into the bargain, he had just lost his mother. At the end of the pantomime there was a spot for Frank, like the song sheet, but not quite. Frank was at the harmonium, and at the last moment, because there was no one else, Gwen joined him. Now usually Frank had everything scripted. It was completely ad lib. The harmonium rolled down to the footlights, there were verbal digs from Frank to Gwen, it was all "make it up as you go along time" the laughs were enormous, it was different every night. Gwen said "Thank goodness for Scottish weekly revue"

Frank would often phone up to come for a meal, when he was in the lonely mood. He would arrive, and one night, he said that he must see the television programme "H.G. Wells' Things to come" We had a good meal, Frank sat in the chair, and went fast asleep. and missed "Things To Come". At three in the morning, he woke up, and wanted to play cards. We had taught him to play solo in the pantomime, we were not in the mood for cards at that time.

It was well known that Frank went for an audition at RADA, but his nerves got the better of him, and he began to stammer and stutter. This was not the ideal situation to play Shakespeare, but he did play "Bottom" in " A Midsummer Night's Dream" at the Old Vic. His successes were numerous, and he will always be remembered for "That Was The Week That Was" "Up Pompeii" and "A Funny Thing Happened on the Way to The Forum", He was a very talented comedy character, and Gwen and I liked him.

"A land unknown to prose or rhyme"   **Epistle to Hugh Parker.**
Robert Burns.

1959 summer season was at the Gaiety Theatre once again with
Jack Milroy. It was a little incongruous finishing the season with
an orchestra, and returning to do an Installation Meeting in
London, with a piano. I remember arriving back from Scotland to
do a "Master's Song" at the Abercorn Rooms in Liverpool Street.
I had always prided myself that I had always remembered my
lyrics, although it was a fear that one day I should black out
altogether, I had always rhymed "moon and june", anyway at this
particular Masonic gathering, they were rather white haired and
immobile. I said to Trevor, it looks like a touch of the "South
Pacific" and off. But I said, if they should have a rush of blood,
and they show enthusiasm, I shall go back and tell them all about
Robert Burns, who rode on horse back to his lodge in Tarbolton,
all the way from Alloway. I gave Trevor some manuscript that I
had written with a voice line on top. I shall talk about the great
man, and build an atmosphere on the horse and Burns riding
through the lanes and byways, by the Crofter's cottages, and then I
shall say "I will leave you with the immortal words of Robert
Burns...so we did the "Master's Song" alright, and then we went
into the "South Pacific" medley. There was nothing for "This
nearly was mine" they started to move and get quite interested in
"Younger than Springtime" and by the time I finished "Some
Enchanted Evening" they were cheering and shouting........."Get
Off" and "Encore" and other jocular phrases.

The applause was unbelievable from these elderly gentlemen.
Of course I am now drunk with power. I'm now going to tell them
about Robert Burns, if it's the last thing I do. I go back to the
rostrum, and tell them, I have just returned from Ayr, the
birthplace of the Bard of Scotland, Brother Robert Burns. I have
got them entranced about the horse ride from Alloway to his lodge
in Tarbolton, they are hanging on every word, I say "And so I will
leave you with immortal words of Robert Burns"....and nothing

The words had gone, Trevor gave me the arpeggio more that once, he didn't know the words or the tune, I did the usual "Talk among yourselves" and finally dear reader..............I leave you with the immortal words of **Robert Burns. :-**
Then let us pray, as come it may, as come it will for a' that.
That sense and worth oe'r the earth, shall bear the gree and a'
For a' that and a' that its coming yet for a' that.   *That.*
that man to man the world shall oe'r
Shall brothers be.. for a' that.

It was a nightmare, I was so embarrassed and hoping it would never happen again.

When Gwen and I were in pantomime, we would always try and get home on the Christmas Eve, so we could see Richard on the Christmas morning. When we did "Mother Goose" in Torquay the whole town was covered in snow, nobody could get into the town, and nobody could get out. Undaunted we set off after the show, taking with us a dancer, who had an audition. Barely two miles out of Torquay, the road was packed ice, the further we went, the road became narrower, the snow was so thick, you could see signposts just sticking out above the snow. For a hundred miles it was a nightmare, if a car came the other way, there would have been a big accident. Nearer London the road cleared, so the last few miles were bearable. We dropped off the dancer at St. John's Wood and arrived at home in Hampstead around three in the morning. Tired out and full of tension, we got to sleep around 4.30 a.m. The greatest reward was the little face of Richard when he saw us in the morning of Christmas day, there are no words to describe how we felt, it was worth all the hardship of the dangerous drive, needless to say we were off on Boxing Day for the matinee.

During the pantomime, at the Kings Theatre, Southsea with **Frankie Howerd,** New Year's Eve fell on a Sunday, and we were booked to do the New Year cabaret in Chelmsford.

172

There were 5 acts booked including the clever *Betty Smith*. jazz musician supreme, who had been with Gwen, when she was with an all girls orchestra. The temperature fell, and all roads were iced over. We set off in good time, and slid all the way to Chelmsford, we turned a complete circle at one time, and found our car was facing the way we had come. When were arrived for the cabaret, only two acts turned up, what happened to the other three "Turns", we never found out. We saw the New Year in, and now we had to get to Southsea. Overnight it had snowed to at least four inches deep. We decided to go by train, so we walked to the station, and found that trains were not running. We went home for the car, and very slowly drove to Southsea for the matinee. The time was flying by, and we didn't seem to make any progress, finally we reached Southsea. The company were waiting for us, the Overture began, and we dressed with alacrity in time to make our first entrance.

Having a double act, you never knew where you would appear. An unusual engagement was to appear at Bingley Hall in Birmingham. This was on the lines of the Ideal Home Exhibition. There were three shows a day, performed in a little theatre in the far corner of this huge venue. 1 hour for the first show, 45 minutes for the second, and 30 minutes for the last one. *George Bolton* a lovely man with a huge voice, was the comedian. He had spoken to *Ted Ray,* and by mutual agreement had *Robin Ray (Ted's son)* to feed him. This was Robin's first stage show, and very efficiently he performed. H. Robinson Cleaver accompanied the show. The show was so good, that the punters were not looking at the exhibition, they came to see the show. We did another the following year, but with *Jimmy Clitheroe* as the comic.

A very enjoyable engagement and a good relationship with *Robinson Cleaver,* this was later, to become an outstanding partnership.

The Pavilion Theatre, Glasgow.

1959 and 1960 summer seasons were again at the Gaiety Theatre, Ayr, one with Jack Milroy and the other with Johnny Beattie, a rising new Scots comedian of clever and wordy comedy. His parodies were exceptional. Eric Popplewell, as the season was coming to an end in 1960, called Gwen and I to his office to have a drink, he had been " over the moon" with the season. He said "I am thinking about asking you back again for 1961". We said please do not, as we will not be coming back. That was the last time we played the fabulous Gaiety..Ayr. We really had enjoyed this wonderful theatre and the town, we felt the time had come for a change.

During that season we had an overture from Eurie Scott, who owned the Pavilion Theatre, Glasgow. We had played the Pavilion before with Jack Milroy. This show was to be titled "The Four Star Show. The comic had not been cast, but the three were **Donald Peers, Gwen Overton & Clive Stock.** We put off signing the contract until we knew who the comic was going to be. We told Eurie Scott that we would not work with Lex Maclean or Johnny Victory. We were getting to the end of the season, and still no name for the comic. Managements have a ploy, to keep you waiting until the last minute, so that you will sign, being frightened that you will be without a season. The Scots comic was eventually contracted. It was **Johnny Victory.**
Well dear reader, you can imagine, how Gwen and I felt...a little betrayed to say the least. The difficult situation was that Johnny and Donald did not get on at all, and Gwen and I were the mediators. We were good pals with Donald, and we became surprisingly enough, close colleagues with Johnny. The first half finale was a "Dial M for Music" scena. The audience would call out songs, and one of us or both would sing the request, the big advantage was that I knew the key of each song. Johnny was very impressed with this, at the end of the scene he would do a religious monologue to a great reception. He always gave us the plaudits with a personal call at the end.

174

Johnny was a gruff man, bordering on the uncouth, but a good performer, what a tragedy he committed suicide in his caravan in Dundee. Scottish theatre missed him greatly.

Pantomime seemed to call us once more, and we were delighted when, that wonderful gentleman **Derek Salberg** invited us to play in "Mother Goose" at Torquay. **Bryan Burdon** son of the great comedian **Albert Burdon,** played Mother Goose. This was the first time he had ever gone into frocks and dragged up. He hated it. He would come off the stage and throw the wigs and exclaim :- "I'm not going to play bloody dame again". Contrary to that bold statement, he is one of the best dames in the U.K. Big **Fred Emney** was the star of the piece. He hardly had any lines to deliver, except under his breath, he would say "Look at the little perishers, I hate bloody kids". He would strut around with his Pomeranian "Enoch" under his arm, completely incongruous, a giant of a man and a minute dog. Some of our Concert Agents used to say, "Why do you go away for pantomime ?. you'll miss a lot of work, agents won't book you". We used to say, provided we let everyone know when we go away and when we are coming back they will book us, and they did.

"Babes in the Wood" at the Alexandra Theatre, Birmingham had very happy memories, and some hilarious moments. **Ronnie Carroll** was the star of the piece, but he was one of the biggest "Corpser's" in the business. It was not unusual to hear the introduction to "Moon River" played five or six times. Gwen many times whispered to him "Take a grip on yourself". The scene in the woods was horrendous. **Arthur Worsley,** was playing one of Robin Hood's merry men, together with his famous dummy ..... "Charlie Brown". Charlie was dressed in Lincoln green, complete with the famous Robin Hood style cap. Anyway, back to the woods. Ronnie had the storyline about the wicked uncle and the babes, who were in danger. Ronnie looked at Arthur, and the face of Charlie Brown leered at him,   Ronnie was speechless.

175

Arthur was renowned for never speaking, so the dummy took over
the whole plot. He would say to Ronnie "Look at me son, when
your supposed to be talking". Ronnie never said another word.
The whole company was standing in the wings. Charlie Brown
carried all the dialogue, it was made up, as he went along, the
whole story about the wicked Sherriff of Nottingham, and the
babes was told by this mischievious life like dummy, and bore no
resemblance to the plot, everyone was in hysterics, and the robbers
Gordon & Bunny Jay couldn't enter for laughing, needless to say
our "guvnor", Derek Salberg was not amused. *Arthur Worsley* was
a brilliant ventriloquist. *Ed Sullivan,* the American top television
presenter, stated on his coast to coast networked show, "That
Arthur was the greatest ventriloquist of all". He had the title of the
"The World's Youngest Ventriloquist in 1935".

Summer season in 1961, back to Scotland and Aberdeen with Alex
Finlay. *Donald Peers and Alex Finlay* proposed me for the
Vaudeville Golfing Society the popular golfing fraternity of
our profession. Two lovely gentlemen, never to be forgotten.

We were now getting busier than ever, Pantomime for Derek once
again this time at the Alexandra Theatre, Birmingham, a full book
of after dinner engagements, many meetings for the Directors in
the Insurance Company, there had been some problems while I
was away in Scotland. It seemed, we were short of money, and it
was serious. While in Glasgow I wrote a report with my thoughts
regarding the way the business was heading. It was five pages
long. It was read thoroughly by the Directors.

At the beginning of 1962 it was obvious, that there was a
discrepancy, and the Nation Life who financed our insurance side
of the business, were wanting some money. There was a series of
meetings, pointing out, that unless bills were settled, there would
be serious consequences. There were delaying tactics. Being away
I was very much out of the run of things.

An opportunity arose for me, and I had to make a calculated decision. *Rex Leslie* was a baritone, who started a Concert Agency. *Bob Monkhouse* worked for him regularly. Rex had some nice connections, and as he was thinking of retiring, he offered me the chance to buy his book. I had advice from other agents, who pointed out that I would lose a lot of work, as they would think I would filch their bookings. It was also suggested that artists, particularly singers of the "Master's Song" would not pass on engagements, fearing that I would take them into my agency. Deep and logical thought was given to this possible project. I decided to go ahead. So I purchased REX LESLIE CONCERT DIRECTION for the sum of £200. Rex, booked Gwen and I for one of his best clients, and informed him, that I was taking over. The client said to me, with reference to our act that evening for his firm's dinner. Very bluntly, "If you are not going very well, get off. but if you think they are enjoying it, stay on a little longer", these first words were rather hard to take, we were not looking forward to the show, and this man was a prospective client. Anyway we went on and paralysed them, the chairman of the company, got up from his seat and took our hands, bringing the applause up even more, after plaudits from him, he asked the crowd if they wanted more, and they unanimously shouted "MORE". Luckily I had found out that the Chairman, had just seen "The Sound of Music" and Gwen and I had just completed a new vocal arrangement of "Climb Every Mountain". This encore could not have been better timed, so we finished in triumph. That was the night I became a friend of Roy Culver, and we cemented my new position of agent. My company was named DERWENT ENTERTAINMENTS LTD. and was registered.

The year of 1962 was to be a momentous turning point in our professional career, and our private life. We had now signed with a new agent, the well known broadcaster *George Elrick.* The Agents Association had launched a new contract for sole agency agreements.

The five year contract had a six month trial period, it was written into the contract, that a certain sum of money would be secured by the agent on behalf of the artist. If that amount was reached and secured for the artist, then the contract would go on for another four and a half years, if the agent had not achieved the nominated sum, then the option was with the artist to terminate the agreement. At the end of the half year trial, George had not reached the estimated amount, he was very busy looking after *Mantovani.* So *Max Jaffa,* who was also under contract to George, agreed that Mrs Elrick's wee son George, had really tried to obtain engagements, but without any luck. Gwen and I decided to let the contract go the rest of the term.

Into the office came our dearest friend *George Clarkson,* who naturally spent time on our future. Unbeknown to us or George, a certain *Charles Aitken,* who was then General Manager with Catlin's in Llandudno had been trying to get us with the firm for quite a while. He found that every time he suggested us, or any one, the Catlin family would be totally contrary, and vote for an opposite suggestion. So Charlie Aitken, tried a new tactic, and intimated to the firm not to have us, we were too expensive.

Mrs Elrick's Wee son, George.

Our Agent for many years.

GEORGE ELRICK.

"This land of song, will still be singing" We'll keep a welcome
Lyn Joshua, James Harper, Mai Jones.

The ploy worked, Catlin's were interested, and George went to see
the firm. They acquired references from the Popplewells' and
Sandy Powell and we were contracted by the famous Catlin family,
to appear in the "Catlin's Showtime of 1962." at the Arcadia
Theatre, Llandudno in North Wales.

We had never been to North Wales before, but everyone told us
that we would have the best summer season of all time. We were a
little suspicious, as when you are given such glowing reports of
anything, it doesn't always come up to expectations.

In 1960, the Catlin family had decided that they would no longer
present shows themselves, and would lease to another impresario,
to present the summer show in Llandudno. In their calculations
they determined their last show would be in 1960, which was a
record breaking revue starring *Wyn Calvin.* They sold all their
costumes and props, and kept some scenery in the scene dock at
the back of the theatre. *Bryan Blackburn & Cyril Stapleton,*
presented "PIERROT 61" starring *TED ROGERS.* Paul Catlin,
Grandson of Will Catlin was responsible for the new management
taking over. It was mounted with modern structures, including
scaffolding for the base of the scenery. The whole show was right
up to date and modern.

The usual public who would come regularly to Llandudno did not
care for it, and it was a failure. Catlins decided to present the show
of 1962, themselves, which necessitated purchase of costumes and
props. It was really like starting again. They hoped they had not
lost too many of their regular patrons, and strove to give the public
their usual high standard production.

So we are now off to Llandudno. The Arcadia Theatre had a charm of its own. I don't know that I remember appearing in any theatre the shape of this unusual venue. An eight foot apron with the orchestra in the pit, side stalls facing into the front stalls in tiers, and the back stalls raked to the back of the theatre. BUT this place had atmosphere. It was built in 1894. It was to have been the extension to a second pier. It was built by a company led by *Jules Riviere.* He had been a woodwind player in the Pier Orchestra, the Pier Company had engaged him as resident conductor. The eccentric 75 year old, was sacked by the Pier Company and not to be outdone, he formed a consortium, and built, what was to be called the Victoria Palace. It became Riviere's Concert Hall. When he departed it was renamed The Llandudno Opera House and Hippodrome. In 1915 it was renamed the Arcadia and became the home for Will Catlin's Pierrots.

Will Catlin was a tremendous pioneer of entertainment. He was shrewd and with acute business acumen.. This was amply illustrated when *Arthur Haynes* came complaining to Catlin that his billing was the same size as all the other artists. The posters were promptly changed to read *"Will Catlin presents Catlin's Follies with an all star cast".* Will Catlin was born in 1872, and in 1952 he passed quietly away sitting in his car on the lovely Llandudno Promenade, whilst holding his wife's hand. So one of the great pioneers of seaside entertainment took his final curtain.

In 1962, The Arcadia ,had a the seating capacity of 1,345 seats. Llandudno was lucky to have the Grand Theatre, the Pier Pavilion, the Palladium Theatre, and the Odeon, that became the Astra Theatre, plus the open air Happy Valley. These live theatres were all successful and healthy, and doing well. The producer of the show was Harry Mitchell Craig. He had been a tenor with the Catlin's shows in the past. He married one of the Catlin daughters, known as Topsy. Harry would sit in the stalls, with his flat cap poised in the centre of his head, and would go to sleep.

Responsible for the scenas and the opening and the finale, were *Averil & Aurel.* They were the dancing act in the show. Averil was a soprano, and an attractive dancer. The comedians were ...*Felix Bowness.* together with *Tom Mennard. Tommy Rose, Harold Taylor and a very strong cast. Averil Jean* wanted to be in all the production scenes, and really she produced herself out of the show. This was good for Gwen and I, as we were used in the comedy, and our act was fresh when we had the third spot in the second half. It was a great spot, and we registered with our new resort immediately. The visitors to Llandudno were discerning and liked good music. We were thoroughly spoilt, and we found mixing with the town, brought many joys with the local families. They were a very caring people, and I found my way on to committees for local charities, as well as National fund raisers. There was a hard core of ladies who were completely committed to doing charity work. In the year 2002, Councillor Brian Bertola, who was Mayor at the time, told me through visiting so many organisations during his time as Mayor, he never realised how caring the people of Llandudno were. I said "They were the same in 1962, forty years before.

During rehearsals I was asked to go to the cricket club. I always wrote to the club of the town for the summer season. I would always give my references including centuries scored and clubs I had played for. I arrived at the Llandudno Cricket Club, where the President, Chairman and full committee were waiting. I kitted up, and then the Captain led me to the nets, where the first team, were practising. I remember clearly, the officials lined up in front of the wooden pavilion, with its white picket fence and the Llandudno flag flying in the breeze. I was expected to bat and ball, to show them if I was good enough for a place, in this very strong side, at the time. I went into bat to face the bowling of all types. My stomach was in knots, this was far worse than appearing in front of 3000 people. I was so nervous, I kept saying to myself you have faced Lindwall and Miller, this is easy.

I batted well and dealt with all the bowling hurled at me. I was asked to bowl, and I hit the stumps at regular intervals. I passed the audition, and the President said that I would fit in well with the current side. I then told him I could only play Sundays, and if they wanted me on a Saturday, I would have to leave at 7.30 p.m. at the latest. This was unacceptable, so I resigned myself to Sundays only. I was put in the second team for my first match, against the Rydal public school. As I scored 100 not out and took a wicket, they had a re think about my playing until 7.30 p.m. I then became a regular member of the first eleven, and the antics that went on when I was still batting at 7.15 and trying to get myself out to get to the theatre, were hilarious. I would dance down the wicket to have a swipe, it would come off the edge and go for four, I would go forward and play an air shot, so that I should be stumped, but the wicket keeper would miss it altogether. Many times I would go on to 50 trying to get myself out. Needless to say my Gwen would be champing at the bit, when the curtain was about to go up and I rushed in. What happy times.

The show had three different programmes. On the first programme dress rehearsal, Gwen and I started our opening number, which was our own duet version of the quartet from "Kismet" by name "And This Is My Beloved". We had just started when Averil Jean went to Mitchell Craig in indignation, he then stopped our rehearsal. He said "You can't do that number, Averil is doing it in the eastern scena", I said "O.K. We'll do it in another programme", this seemed to be acceptable. The procedure was that after a performance, we would do a dress rehearsal for the next programme, which would go into the early hours of the morning. We would have something to eat and drink. The stage staff would bring in the new cloths for hanging, while the current programme was taken out to the scene dock,.we would then do a dress rehearsal, with orchestra for the new show, together with new costumes. For the third programme, we had decided to open with "And this is my beloved". We started with the introduction.

"Stop the rehearsal" the high tenor voice of Mitchell Craig had got higher, "You know that song is already being used" I stiffened and said "If you remember we came to an arrangement that we could do it in another programme, this was agreed. Averil with scowling face, said "You cannot sing it". Charlie Aitken was up at the back of the stalls, waiting for me to blow my top. What happened to me I will never know. I said "Right ! you can jolly well wait, while I write a violin part to another opening number..."Only a Rose" The orchestra were not amused at the delay. I also was not amused, and nobody interjected, for they knew I would probably land out at anything in my way. On the surface it seemed that I had infinite patience. This action obviously went in our favour, as Gwen and I were invited back for 1963 and 1964. Felix came with us also. The shows were very strong, in each season we had solid acts, that were tried and true. In 1964 we had our friends *Tommy Wallis & Beryl.* This highly versatile act had been at the Gaiety Theatre, Ayr, with all those changes of programme, it gave them a wonderful and varied repertoire.

Well dear reader, you may have wondered what had happened to my best friend, *Don Weston.* He had continued singing for a while, and then went into the box office at Wyndham's Theatre in London. A short stay there, and then he became the Manager of the Savoy Theatre. This was a prestigious appointment, and we were all very proud of him. A firm by the name of Webb from Wolverhampton, were building a holiday village at Burnham-on-Sea and they advertised for a manager. From over 200 applicants, Don was on the short list of four, what a feller ?

Don Weston was engaged as the number one man. The village was built from scratch. There were villas, caravans, bars and a very large ballroom. He landscaped and furbished the ballroom theatre in naval decor. Don had been in the Royal Navy. Gwen and I went down to see him at work, out of nothing he had built a wonderful leisure complex, we were so impressed by his expertise.

183

From being a singer to this creator, it just didn't seem possible. We were so pleased for him. We congratulated him warmly. Don gave me the job of putting in an entertainment for the summer. I assembled a unit headed by **Danny O'Dea,** of "Last of the Summer Wine" fame. This was very successful. We stayed the weekend with Don and June. Don had married **June Bishop,** a super performer. June had been with me in "Tough at the Top" she had a wonderful sense of humour. Her triumph was as Principal Boy in pantomime. Just before leaving Holimarine, during the night, I had terrible pressure on my temples, and the room was coming in on top of me, as soon as I returned to Llandudno. I saw Dr Ian Wynne Hughes, who diagnosed high blood pressure and Hypertension. I went on to 100g Salupres, one every day. I had to be reconciled to a pill every day for the rest of my life. I was so grateful to Ian Wynne Hughes, who had set me right, he was a very good young doctor, who sadly died at a very early age. What a great loss to the people of Llandudno.

In the 1963 version of the summer show, on the dress rehearsal **Lettie Laughton,** who was a niece of **Charles Laughton,** was ill and could not open the show, she was in all the comedy. GWEN learnt all the dialogue and on the opening night, she was ready. What happens ?, Felix and **Tommy Rose** make a complete hash of the script, and Gwen is prompting them, and they were supposed to know it, once again, as Sid would have said "What a peformance" All the time we are enjoying the summer in Llandudno, we are taken to family homes for afternoon tea. The Curate of Holy Trinity Church arranged all these meetings. We are really getting interwoven with all these wonderful people. The Curate Owen Jones had only recently taken Holy Orders, He had been a Director of Chanel No 5. in Croydon. Once he had guided his two sons through college, he resigned and studied, so that he was ordained in the Church of England. "O.T." as he was affectionately called, became the Actor's Church Union priest.

"O.T.", was responsible for the tremendous liaison, that we enjoyed with the people of Llandudno. These regular enjoyable get togethers, were a great help to the full houses we had during the seasons. Some of the families we met, were very involved with the town, either as shopkeepers, hoteliers or both, and were Councillors. The refreshing resolve of the councillors was the way, no matter what Party they represented, they would vote together for the good of the town. Two friends I had, namely Harold Neville, a Tory, and Algwyn Hopkins a Socialist, would regularly vote together if a resolution would be an advantage to Llandudno. The same cannot be said forty years later. The Party Whip, took over. The summers in Llandudno were golden, the sun seemed to shine a lot, the cricket was fantastic, we had a very good flat, halfway up the Great Orme, so that we looked across from the West Shore to Conwy. The view, gave us a panoramic sweep of the bay, making it the Naples of the North. One of the happiest times was the association with a very lovable labrador. He had been neglected, and as Gwen and I were animal lovers this smashing dog took to us. He belonged to the owners of the accommodation where we stayed. For two seasons you would have thought "Duke", belonged to us. He had when a pup, been lying out, near the road, when a van ran over his front paw. I don't think his owners really knew at the time, consequently, he always suffered from rheumatism. He adored us and we adored him. It was quite comical when my nephew came to see us. He had been walking on the beach, and he espied Duke, trotting on the sands. Grahame, thought he is a way from home, I'll take him back, so he struggled to move Duke, and found it so hard to pull him up the Great Orme to our flat. He was totally dismayed to find that when he reached us, it was not Duke at all. He had brought a strange labrador to us, and Duke was with us at the time.

I have mentioned the Neville family, they were chemists, and added to them were the Roberts...David and Joan, sons Michael and Andrew, and daughter, Judy.

The families were the backbone of the town.

The Roberts family were responsible for very high quality shoes.
Harold and Beryl Travers, sons Tony and Simon. Beryl's brother
was Russell Gradwell. He was the Chairman of the Welsh
Badminton Union for five years, he had played for Wales and had
captained North Wales for many years. He joined the RAF in 1941
and by 1944 was flying Lancasters with No 9 Squadron. In July
as they were bombing the target, the plane caught fire and the crew
bailed out. Russell came down near Beauvais. He and the crew
evaded capture, and were accepted by the Resistance, 8 weeks in
hiding before being liberated on the 1st September 1944. We in the
Arcadia used to meet Russell on a Thursday night, when we did
the draw for the Llandudno Swimming Pool. He became a
Councillor and then Mayor in 1979. His own hotel was the
Elsinore, and in 1990 on the retirement of Jim Williams, Russell
became chairman of the Llandudno Hotels and Restaurants
Association. Jim Williams and his family were corner stones of
the town. The quality of the Councillors of the Llandudno Urban
District Council was first class, they worked hard for the good of
the ratepayers of Llandudno. It was a weekly meeting in the
Elsinore, with Val and Russell, who brought a party to the theatre
every Monday night, after the show, the highlight was seeing
various members of the cast, with their top lip paralysed with the
Merrydown Cider consumption.

Catlins had the right formula regarding the Arcadia. It should run
the summer show for five months, and then close the other seven
months. There was no business in the winter months, so the
summer was the income.
One of the most pleasant duties, was to arrange the church service
in the middle of the summer. I included each theatre, so that we
had soloists from each venue. You had the comics reading the
lessons, the singers enjoying the other side of their
musical experience with the hymns.

Sport being my strong point, I arranged a tennis tournament between the Grand, Arcadia, Palladium and the Pier Pavilion. Two pairs from each theatre, on a knock out basis. *Bill Maynard, Greengrass* as he is better known today, was a very good player. He and *Terry Scott* did battle on many occasions, Bill had a blonde dancer as his partner, and he used to give her hell, if she missed a short, consequently his company at the Pier, were not very enamoured with Bill, and did not support him. Gwen and I got to the semi final against *John Gorrie* and an Australian actress, they were both good players, after a gruelling, best of three sets we managed to get through to the final. We were now to play Bill and his blonde in the final. You would have thought it was Wimbledon, we were all nervous, and the crowds had gathered, obviously each theatre came to support their own cast members, except for the Pier Pavilion, who openly supported Gwen and I. We started on tender hooks, and Bill was the only one to win his service. It looked as though Gwen and I were going to lose this one. The blonde dancer began to be over anxious and was losing easy points. Maynard was really furious with her, and his game started to suffer. He could see the trophy disappearing from his mantelpiece. Gwen had a very deceiving forehand, and this upset the comedian. We won two sets to one, and the win disturbed our Bill. He had been itching to take me on at singles, and I was very ready to oblige. He was a good player, the rallies were long and fast, but my consistency got the better of him, and I beat him in two sets. It was a very satisfying day, and my darling must take full marks for rising to the occasion. The pressure was tremendous.

After the 1963 season we returned to London and immediately started our after dinner functions. We did many shows with *Ted Ray, Tommy Trinder, and Bob Monkhouse.* Ted had a tremendous spontaneous wit, he had a filing system of gags in his head, so that he quoted immediately. Gwen and I had dinner with him in the Randolph Hotel, Oxford. We cemented our friendship.

We all knew the same people and therefore had so much in common, together with golf. It reminds me that my good friends, **Donald Peers and Ted Ray** took on **Bob Hope and Bing Crosby** in a golf tournament, and beat them, they were no mean golfers.

Into 1964 and there was bad news ahead. The Theatrical Profession Insurance Service was in real trouble, it was inevitable that the firm would go up the spout. Just before we were off for the 64 season at the Arcadia, all the Directors had notice that the company would go into Receivership. So I started rehearsals for the season full of tension, apprehension and nerves, not knowing what the form was to liquidation. We had no date for making an attendance at the Board of Trade. So the season started, Felix was once again, principal comedian, apart from Gwen and I, we had one of the most polished magic acts of all time *Alan Shaxon & Anne.* There were lovely people and we have been friends for 40 years. *Bill Cameron* a real double for Fred Astaire, *Tommy Rose* one of our real female impersonators and feed for Felix, and *Tommy Wallis & Beryl,* they play instruments, dance and sing, this was a fantastic act for all the public. The 64 show was only second to the 1960 show for attendances.

Although I was scared of the outcome of the crash of the insurance firm, I had a wonderful lift for the cricket season. I was selected to play for the County, this was a tonic, for at 38 I was a County Cricketer, saving the side in my first game.
The County of Caernarvonshire played Flintshire, and I had been asked to play. They batted first, and I was lucky to get Stan Baker, a Worcestershire opener, trapped LBW. This really made not the slightest bit of difference to a side that was packed with batting, they eventually amassed 286. We started badly, and lost four wickets for "flumpence", I went in at number six, we were finding runs hard to come by, and then we lost two quick wickets, leaving me with numbers 9, 10, and 11 to come. The scoreboard showed 143 for 8. Now they started to tempt me with the spin bowlers.

County Cricket for Caernarvonshire.

Tossing it up in the air, so I would go "Whacka the ball" and get myself out. I was so tempted to have a real slog, but I restrained myself. On the board 174 for 9, and the last man in with me. I managed to shield him, and kept the bowling. It was now starting to get dark. The ball was against the background of trees, I was using all my experience to stay, runs were not important. Stumps were drawn at 10 minutes past 8, I had survived with 31 not out to draw the game. Eric Johnson, a solicitor and President of the club, was over the moon, as it was through his support I was selected. He sort of said "I told you so".The North Walians were a little clannish, and being an Englishman, they liked to keep the side Welsh. I was accepted, and became very much apart of North Wales in general, and Llandudno in particular.

Before the end of the season, which went to the first week in October, I went to the Lodge of St Cystenin, as this was the only lodge that started their meetings early. They accepted me straight away. I went to the meeting, and then around 7 p.m. I went off to the theatre. They were a great example of good Freemasons, the bond of friendship was extended most cordially, and there was no differentiation between the Welsh and the English. I felt very comfortable and happy with this lodge.

Our accommodation for the 64 season was in Carroll Place, with two very sweet ladies. They had a lovely flat for the season, and they made us very welcome, and Richard was the apple of their eye. Rosamund Kempson was a physiotherapist, and one of the leading specialists in her field, she was related to *Rachel Kempson,* the wife of Sir *Michael Redgrave.* Llandudno was lucky to have such an able lady. Her friend Jane Paul was a strong type of woman. I think together they really adopted Richard. While we were at the theatre, they used to take him to the cinema to see the Beatles, which would not be their cup to tea. They were really lovely, and it was so good of them to look after a 8 year old boy.

A new member of the family.

While at Carroll Place, our adopted labrador found us, and didn't
want to leave, this situation was beginning to tear us apart, and
when we went to see his owners to say "Goodbye" at the end of the
season, "Duke" with both front paws on my lap and looking into
my eyes, made it almost impossible to leave.

The lady of the house was expecting a baby very soon, and she
kept saying "If he gets any hairs on the baby, he'll have to go",
Gwen said "With Tom out all day, how are you going to manage,
with a baby, a four year old daughter and Duke". There
was a long pause, and Gwen said "I think it would be better if we
took him with us" This was agreed, so leads, official pedigree
certificates were found and without coming up for breath, we took
this adorable dog with us. The show was to end the next day, and
Duke went into dressing room and under our dressing table, and
never stirred right through the whole performance. It was as
though he had been with us all his life.

You can imagine packing the car. We had not had any idea that a
large dog would return to London with us. Gwen made about a
foot square space for him to sit bolt upright, we made many stops
on the way south, and we arranged for my mother to meet us on
Fortune Green with our spaniel, so they could get together before
going in the house. Mother was the epitome of a caring animal
lover, in fact cats and dogs came before most human beings.
Duke, now home with us was a very happy canine. We had an
awkward moment, when we had a call, saying, the daughter was
missing Duke, and wanted him back. They used to feed him on
corn flakes when they thought to feed him at all. No way would we
let him go.

Through my agency ***Derwent Entertainments,*** I was picking up
all types of bookings, from Masonics, Variety, Concerts and of
course big firm's conference entertainment. One of my favourite
friends, and one of the most versatile performers of our time was
Roy Castle, his talent was abundant.

Roy Castle the most versatile of all.

Roy did many shows for me, and every one was a triumph. His success brought about many more dates, which was good for my company, and good for him. When you have such a performer working for you, who becomes an Ambassador, as well as displaying his own talent, he creates trust and confidence for the client to use your company for further engagements. When Roy passed away, we lost one of the nicest men to walk a stage or cabaret floor. Another such person was **David Nixon,** he always did a super show, but had me biting my nails. He would be due to go on at 10.30 p.m. and at 10.20 he would not have arrived. I would stand outside the Savoy or Grosvenor House, and with his usual cheery smile, he would arrive at around 10.25, and all would be well. How I never had ulcers, I do not know,

Another artist, who should have given me ulcers was *Al Read.* I had booked him at the Majestic Hotel, Harrogate. There were five acts together with accompanying musicians. The form for this function was always, artists to sit down to a seven course meal, then a break for the speeches, and then the entertainment.
Just before the meal I receive a telephone call...."Mr Read is going to be late, he has broken down at Doncaster" It was his manager. "Can you tell me how long is he going to be ?, " No time could be given. I said "Well there is a little time, as apart from the other acts on the bill, we have not started the meal yet. "I will call you, when we are on the way" I thought well that is that, we should make out alright. On with the meal, *Ted Durante & Hilda,* being an acrobatic comedy act, could not eat too much but they were tempted and partook of the scrumptious meal, together with the delectable wines. We are now on the sweet, and another call to say that Al Read is on his way, he has just started. I inform my client with the situation, and we hope Al will make it.

The speeches go on, and there is no sign of our top of the bill, the first act has just started, and *Al Read* bursts in, and wants to go on first, he has another show in York.

191

"Al, there is no way you are going on first, you are top of the bill"
"I must go on next" he said. I am hot under the collar, I see
Freddie, my client, and he agrees with me, he goes on last. "Look
Al, I have booked you through **Bernard Delfont** , and you must
close. What I will do is see that you don't go on for any finale, and
you can get away". He had to settle for this. Successfully he
closed the show, and stayed for the finale and drinks afterwards.
So York lost out. He had tried to do three shows in the one night.

Al Read, had a meteoric rise in show business. From Meat Pies he
had became a household name in entertainment, within four years.
his catch phrases "Right Monkey" and "You'll be lucky, I say
you'll be lucky", became every day sayings. He was a tremendous
comedy character on radio. He was a specialist in sound.
Television was not as comfortable for him. He excelled with the
man in street.

Gwen and I were booked with him at a Rotary function in
Blackpool, at the Norbreck Hotel. We were met by Gwen's cousins
Lester Sharpe and Iris. Lester said to us, "You're going to like
this man". Al was with his manager and the pianist, and he was
giving instructions in Pseudo French. This took a long time, and
we were the only act that needed music. At the end of it all, we
hardly had time to have a rehearsal. We were not impressed.

Dickie Henderson, was a delight to have working for you, his easy
style was infectious, the public felt at home with him, he gave
them a very comfortable feeling, a real casual entertainer, as was a
lovely man and friend, *George Martin.* His topical comedy was
masterful. How he kept so up to date, I don't know. He told me
"You know the old gags are the best, but the secret is to place them
in the right spot" and George was brilliant at the gag for the right
situation. Gwen and I thought this man was one of the greats, both
on stage and off.

Bob Monkhouse was a tonic to watch. One show with Bob was at the Grosvenor House for 1100 butchers. I was asked to compere that night, and during that superb act *Robert Harben*, Bob was writing names of the secretary and other characters of the firms, with this big, thick black pencil, he incorporated these people into his act. He pulled the house down, to coin a hackneyed phrase. A brilliant comedy wit.

Having been a member of the CAA for ten years, I was inveigled on to the Committee. They met every Thursday. The CAA being founded in1897 had a very large membership, and we administered a healthy Benevolent Fund, also responsibility for Sickness Grants, Legal and Medical Consultation. We owned the building 20 Bedford Street, London WC2. These committee meetings were very busy directing policy. Committe members like *Pamela Cundell, Rowena Vincent, Jack Crosbie, George Rissen, Avril Fane and Gordon Holdom* at that time were at the forefront of the success of the enterprise. I joined to learn about all the facets of this very popular association. Except for the summer, I was a regular attender. The secretary was a full time employee. Her name was Carmel Maguire, who later married *Hubert Gregg,* who was President for a short while. Other Presidents were *Arthur Askey, Leslie Crowther, David Nixon, Webster Booth & Anne Ziegler, Roy Hudd, Cardew Robinson, Jimmy Perry, Jack Warner* the list is endless. I eventually became Chairman in 1975. The position started off with a trauma, we had three burglaries in two weeks, so I had to arrange steel bars on all the windows. The bar stock was worth a pretty penny, this start to my reign was not inspiring. It settled down and I enjoyed the responsibility. The CAA boasted many very talented acts of all ages. Their experience was formidable in Summer Season and Pantomime. Many acts were exclusive to the after dinner, and concert party scene. Artists like :-*Bradley Harris, Jack Crosbie, Norman Caley, Brenda Armstrong, The Garland Sisters, Barry Johns, Bob Heath & Paula Scott , Syd Marx, Sandy Sandford, Linda Mason.*

Gordon Turner Harold Taylor, Calvin Kaye, Arthur Gerard, Michael Bailey, Ming Chow, Vince & Rita Starr and many others, they were all artists who could hold an audience. Gwen and I were so pleased we knew all these lovely people. Alas they grew older, many went to the green above. The green was the green sward, the turf that Shakespeare performed his plays on. It was awkward at times in the club, as artists who were friends, wanted me to book them through the agency, it wasn't always possible, as at certain functions they were not suitable.

If you were really conscientious about your bookings, and the desire to get the best that was available for your client, and to advocate the old adage "Horses for Courses" you would draw on your own experience of performing in all the regular venues. You knew that an intimate act like *Freddie Sadler,* would not register in the Grosvenor House ballroom, whereas he would be very successful in a small room, where the audience would be close by as in a drawing room. There were very few acts, that were at home in small rooms as well as large ballrooms. I remember driving to the Trentham Gardens near Stoke, which was huge. The bill consisted of *The Bedlams, Musical Clowns.Harry Smith-Hampshire & Doreen Casey, World Ballroom Dancing Champions, Syd Marx, musical comedian, and Gwen and I.* The floor space was the size of a skating rink, and the audience was miles away. Gwen and I were to close, *Stanelli and his Orchestra* provided the music. Each act died, now they were all tried and true and normally winners, we thought it a real paradox, that they should fail.

We started our usual spot, with little or no interest, so we reverted to a string of choruses, which they all sang. We got off with a fair reception. All the artists were very despondent, and to add insult to injury, we went all those miles for fifteen guineas, less commission, and in our case, pay for our pianist.

Our good friend Trevor Smith, was due in Covent Garden market at 4.30 a.m. so he slept on our couch, before getting involved with all the vegatable produce. He often used to stay overnight when we did a long journey for a show.

There was no doubt in our mind, that performing on the after dinner set up, gave us a full education to entertaining different types of public, in different venues. It made you versatile, spontaneous and very quick in assessing the type of material you needed for the range of different functions.

"Our good friend, and accompanist : **TREVOR SMITH.**

What did we see, we saw the sea. ?
"And the Atlantic isn't what its cracked up to be"
Follow the Fleet. *Irving Berlin.*

Now into 1965 and no word of the liquidation of the Insurance firm, we carried on with the three private functions a night and any extra concerts, and there were many. Early in the New Year, we had a call from the Bernard Delfont office to see if we would consider going with the Cunard Line. We successfully negotiated a contract for the whole of the summer. It was for two ships, the *Franconia* and the *96,000 ton Queen Elizabeth.*
The first three crossings of the Atlantic, were to Canada. Liverpool to Montreal. The second trips were from Southampton to New York.

This way of life was quite different from usual entertaining. The band accompanying us on the "Franconia" was very sub standard, to be kind. We had to have extra rehearsals to give any sort of polished show. It was a little precarious, we even changed key to the drums on occasions. We settled down and found the passengers were delightful, of course the passengers were very much 1st class and tourist in those days. Cunard were fair, we had a good salary, and they gave us a tipping allowance for the gratuity for the stewards etc., we were not overworked. We saw Montreal, Quebec and we took a trip to Ottawa. We had lived in London and had never seen the changing of the guard, this we saw in Ottawa. On the way back to Montreal to catch the ship, we experienced the severest electric storm ever. The coach was travelling at speed, and the thunderbolts and lighting seemed to be getting closer, as we went around corners there were fires at the roadside. We clung to each other independently thinking, we may never see Richard again. It was scary. What a relief to board the ship again and return to England.
It was now time to board the finest ship in the world at that time. The fast, majestic, cream of the Cunard Line, was a different kettle of fish. The whole trip was organized. The eight piece orchestra travelled with us to each class.

There was real 1st class, Cabin Class and Tourist class. the musicians were tried and true readers with experience of musicals and variety. To sing was a pure pleasure. There were many celebrities on these crossings to New York.

We were thrilled to sing for *Mary and John Mills.* They were a real "pros" audience. I am not sure what *Leopold Stokowski* thought about our style of singing from musicals. with comedy parodies thrown in. Not many people realized this brilliant and outstanding conductor was born in London, I know I didn't. What a fabulous export. A world beater.

The people generally, had not conceived the possibility of flying, the ship was still the favoured way of going to America. When we reached New York we were finger printed, and numbered, photographed, and made to feel like criminals. All this was for a Seaman's union card. You were not let on the ship without it. We had 48 hours in New York on each turn round. A highlight was to see *Virginia and Peter Turgeon.* They took us to Sardi's, the famous eating house where all the actors went. We met *Melville Cooper and Charles Korvin,* but the magical moment of all was to meet *Frederic Loewe. Fritz* had been away from New York for over 18 months. He had serious heart problems and was ordered to not only take it easy, but to keep away from the City. and the hectic environment. As we had been in "Brigadoon" it was fantastic to meet the composer of the show. He was very interested in us, and Peter filled him in on our background. To meet such a composer, and have sung his music, is the greatest experience. Peter took me to his club. The Players Club at Grammercy park, was the equivalent of the Green Room Club in London. I was shown right through this venue with its history and atmosphere. I was very disappointed that I missed *James Cagney* by a few minutes. The room of *Wilkes Booth* was kept in the original state of his day, it reeked of the smell of bygone times.

Gwen and I saw "The Roar of the Greasepaint-The Smell of the Crowd" starring *Anthony Newley* and our dear friend *Cyril Ritchard.* The show was absolutely marvellous. Quite one of the best Newley-Bricusse ever wrote. It was great to see Cyril again and recall all the lovely memories. The leading lady was *Sally Smith.* a lovely artist. She was staying with one of my cricketing pals *Brian Jackson,* we chewed the cud till early in the morning then we returned to the ship.

Two other shows we saw on Broadway, were Richard Rodger's "Do I Hear A Waltz ?" not a very successful show compared with his blockbusters, like the "King & I" "South Pacific" Oklahoma" " Carousel" etc., but "The Man of La Mancha" starring *Jose Ferrer.* was a tremendous musical, based on Don Quixote. after seeing this, and returning to London, we contacted *Bernard Spear,* to tell him that there was a great part in "La Mancha" We had met Bernie with our very dear friend *Joe Church* in 1963 at Llandudno, they were together at the Pier Pavilion. When "The Man of La Mancha" was produced in London, with *Keith Michell and Bernard Spear,* we sent a telegram to Bernie on the first night, saying *"There is justice in Showbusiness after all".* Bernie was a real star as Sancho Panza.

After the second trip on the "Queen Elizabeth" we arrived home to find my mother was in hospital. She had an operation for cancer of the bowel. One of the top surgeons in London had given her forty eight hours to make up her mind as to whether to have the operation or not, intimating to her that it was life or death. My mother hated anything to do with illness or hospitals.
Thankfully she decided to have the operation. Gwen and I went to see her. The look on her face when she saw us, was full of the feeling of security and peace. Pop had lived with this terrible situation. He could not contact us on the ship. Mother grew stronger each day, and learned to deal with the awkwardness of the colostomy, this was 1965 and she lived with it until she passed away on May 23rd 1989.

She was a very strong minded lady and had physical strength to match. Pop somehow, financed the operation, and this had quite a knock on effect. The business was not doing all that well, and finances were very stretched. Anyway we were so happy that mother had come through, and was back to her old form.

Off we went for our final crossing to New York. Two days out of Southampton, the weather seemed to be stormy, and worse........... this very large ship was about to be tossed about like a paper boat, on the edge of a hurricane. The "Queen Mary" had been in the middle of it. Hurricane "Betsy" was horrendous. I managed to get out on deck, with permission, to film this enormous ship being thrown about. Waves came over the Bridge and smashed all the windows, there was glass everywhere. The Bosun, who was the original at the launching, kept saying "Stay down girl" evidently if the Screw came out of the water anymore, he said we would turn over. The ship was dipping, so that you watched the whole back end of the ship rising up out of the water, it was frightening.

That night, the Captain asked us if we would go on in the Cabin class to give the passengers a bit of a lift. They brought the 1st and tourist class into the Cabin ballroom. Most passengers were sick and in their cabins. The show was a triumph, because through the elements, we increased the amount of spontaneous comedy. Through the movement, we lost all the musicians, with the exception of the piano, the instrument was screwed to the floor. We would start by the piano, and end up running towards the end of the floor. Gwen ended up more than once, in the lap of a passenger. The second time she landed, she asked the passenger to have a port and brandy, ready for her, on her next visit. The more we were thrown about, the louder we sang. It was a worry, but the outcome was enjoyed by everyone, and the Skipper was very grateful.

We were now well established with Cunard, and did cruises at the festival times, Easter and Christmas. The happiest time was with Richard, one Easter. *Joe Church and Pat Stark* were as they say, in the jargon of today, were an item. Gwen and I loved these two, and Pat who was not besotted with children, had an admirer in Richard. She was very struck with him, and he has been very fond of her to this day. Joe and I cemented our friendship, we talked about the Grand Order of Water Rats. Joe being a good sportsman, partnered me in a tough match of deck tennis against the Officers. We showed them we were no "Willy Woofters", and beat them, comprehensively.

Richard had a great time on board, he made friends with other lads of his own age. He would leave us notes to tell where he was, and when he would meet us. Cruising was a confined business. You were with the passengers nearly all the time, but you would meet some very kindly and interesting people from all walks of life. Of course apart from the exciting New York, the short cruises in the Mediterranean, gave us the sun, and the attractive places in the Balearic Islands. One cruise, we were in Casablanca, and all Richard wanted to know, was when were we going to the bar. It was the Casbah he was thinking of. Pat gave him a coke, and he was quite happy. The lovely performers with us, gave us great joy. *Rawicz & Landauer* wonderful, Marion and Walter became very good friends, and it was hilarious to hear Marion say, in a very broad continental broken English accent, :- I come to England, I foreigner, I be here years, and I still "Bloody foreigner". Their playing was superb.

1966 arrived, and most people thought of the World Cup, and how we won this prestigious tournament. The summer season at Eastbourne with Norman and Sandy was as enjoyable as ever. Cricket at the Saffrons was a little more energetic and taxing, I was now forty, although very fit. In the month of August, there was a match every day, I only missed the one matinee days. The highlight was another century for the Club.

FRANKIE HOWERD with his manager Dennis 1958

ROBINSON CLEAVER & CLIVE STOCK'S "SHOWTIME" LLANDUDNO, 1971

The record breaking show with Wyn Calvin, 1971

Richard with John Hanson. Palace, Morecambe, 1980

*Vicki & KEN GOODWIN
on our 50th Anniversary, 1999*

*Vanessa & Freddie
(Parrot Face) Davies, 1983*

The "Big House"
Dilkusha,
Rhos-on-Sea.
1979

The Cricketing Generations,
Craig, Richard & I, 1996

The Mediaeval Court Sherriff,
Ruthin Castle, 1988

The American Heavy Weight, Ernie Shavers. 1989

BOB HOPE becomes a Water Rat. London, 1991.
Photograph by Water Rat Doug McKenzie

With King Rat FRANKIE VAUGHAN & Stella 1998.
Photograph by Water Rat Doug McKenzie

A fifty year friendship with HOWARD KEEL. 1947-2003.
Photograph by Water Rat Doug McKenzie

Above: *With ROY HUDD &
BOBBY ROBERTS, 2000.*
Photograph by Water Rat Doug
McKenzie

Left:
Richard with RUSS CONWAY

Five Generations of the family.
Gwen and I with Auntie Sis, Jadzea, Jordan, Calista and Richard,
Kay, Kerry, Laura and Craig.

Stock

Coat of Arms

We had the arrival in England, of **Tony Grieg** from South Africa.
He was to play for Sussex. **Jim Parks** brought a team to play
Eastbourne, mainly to give Tony Grieg practice on the English
wickets. Eastbourne was a good example, and he took full
advantage of the true wicket. We played during the week, so our
side was not as strong as it was normally. Grieg went though us
like a knife through butter. I was quite frightened I should get
maimed for the show at night. He hit me on the thigh, (Where
Keith Miller had hit me before), it was painful. The ball was
flying off the edge of the bat, I only hit one in the middle, and that
was trying to get out, a big hit to extra cover, caught well, and I
was so grateful to be walking back to the pavilion. I was top score
with 15, they slaughtered us.

The Pier Theatre, Eastbourne gave Gwen and I wonderful times,
the happiness was perpetuated by Norman and Sandy, 1966 was
the last season we did for this lovely pair, and for enjoyment was
just second to Llandudno. May they both be smiling down on us.
1967 and we were in the Ocean Revue at Clacton with our old
friend **Billy Burden.** Both 1967 an 68 seasons were produced by
our talented **Frank Adey.** Two very happy seasons **Bob Marlowe
and Jenny** were the dancers, and **Don Mclean** was at the Westcliff
Theatre. This gave Don and I plenty of chance to play tennis. Don
was one of the best squash players in our business, along with
Tommy Steele and Leonard Rossiter. Don was a good tennis
player, but the two games were different in technique, and I could
always beat him at tennis, but I never played squash. He made me
laugh while we were playing, he would run for a ball and say
"Most comics want to play the London Palladium, but I want to
beat Stock at tennis". He and his family were lovely people.

At the end of the 1967 season, the Official Receiver sent for the
directors of the T.P.I.S. Ltd to appear at the Board of Trade. **Sir
Tom O'Brien, Michael Powell, Ernest Thompson, Jack Train,
Phil Burn and myself** sat in the front row of a line of seats.

It was like being at school.with a tall desk in front, we sat, waiting like naughty schoolboys, for the Headmaster. If there could be proved any fraudulent transactions in our business, serious consequences could follow, and although a limited company, we could be liable for the debt of around 28 thousand pounds. This was a large sum in those days. Because of the report I had written while in Scotland, and because Sir Tom had read it, as though he were a trade union official, fraud was ruled out, we only had to pay the individual Bank Guarantees commensurate with our shareholding. That was quite enough, to pay in full. It left us without a penny. I learned from that experience, never depend on other people, go it alone and do it yourself. This practice I put in to policy for the future, with viable results.

After this tragedy, there was more to come, Dan Jenkins, our dairyman next door but one, came running into the shop, to inform my father that he had seen that our property was to be sold. He promptly received a letter with details that our property, was to be auctioned with 138 other properties, in the forthcoming January 1968. The auction to take place at the Piccadilly Hotel. It would take two days. Our property would be under the hammer on the first day. We were sent a beautiful brochure, with all the properties for auction. I telephoned to the Auctioneers to see if they would accept an offer prior to the 12th January, 1968. No deal, they would not be interested. I don't know where I thought I could raise the money, after the demise of the Insurance firm.

The whole situation was urgent, as this Leasehold property was our home and living for my parents. Gwen and I set about raising some money. To put the kybosh on credit, the Government had placed a moratorium on all loans and borrowing to the limit of four thousand pounds. At least we could start from scratch, we had nothing. "With a little bit of luck" Gwen and I were appearing at Hendon Hall, in cabaret for a finance company.

We were booked there regularly. Victor Bianchi the General manager, used us and the agency, probably because we were so close to the venue. It was cabaret time for the North Central Finance Company, we made contact with the Managing Director of the firm, and he was very sympathetic to our plight, venturing to suggest he could help us to the limit of four thousand pounds, if all the paper work could be effected satisfactorily. So we were off on our quest, so with family borrowing on the Overton side, and odd bits and pieces, plus the regular earnings of ourselves, being very busy. A sum was finalized in our mind as to our limit.

Christmas was busy, and the impending auction was gradually looming. Our solicitor *Ian Nairnsey,* son of Doctor Nairnsey, who lived close by, talked about the usual procedure of these auction transactions, and I intimated the maximum price we could go to. Sitting in Piccadilly Hotel, a venue Gwen and I only knew from appearing in cabaret, I felt nervous and twitchy.
I telephoned Gwen, and told her of the atmosphere, I said I would do my best, and if we were meant to have the property, then we would secure the shop and the property, this was a fate feeling.
The auction commenced, we followed each property by the shiny attractive photographs, and excellent presentation. The properties ranged from Oxford Street to Paddington and Hampstead. We were the twelfth item on the programme, No 8, was a similar property and that finally went for a staggering amount, if ours went for anything like this figure, we might as well leave. In no time it was upon us. The auctioneer talked about our property, and said that it was in excellent repair, and that we would be vacating in seven years, being the expiry of the lease. Rents could then be increased. I wished he had not been doing his job so well. The bidding started and stopped, so the fellow said he would take bids of five hundred pounds, and then two hundred and fifty pounds. I felt we had lost it. The bidding stopped, we looked as though we had lost, sadly dejected was I. Ian timed it beautifully, he bid another five hundred pounds, and that did it.

I had made my parents safe.

The property was ours. I phoned Gwen, there were tears of joy, and I thanked Ian for his gamble. Now I have to amass the finance. The Finance company provided their maximum, provided I was to be included as a partner with Pop. Being the younger man I would provide the future. This was all regularized, and I set about getting involved in the shop. The first job was to refit the shop, so as to increase the turnover. We found special shop fitters, and this would cost. My dear father was not in favour of spending money we hadn't in our hand. I managed to have the shop gutted and the new fitments went in. The turnover increased immediately. It was obvious Gwen and I could only have a spasmodic input, owing to our engagements.

The business did pick up. Pop was getting extra tired. For thirty years he had been getting up at 5 a,m, every morning, with the exception of Christmas Day and Good Friday. This was driving him to exhaustion. There was no respite. Mother helped with the papers first thing in the morning, but otherwise she would not serve customers. Mrs. Carter had been our assistant for many years. Great loyalty, and genuine fondness for my dad, she did all she could to give him relief, we all could see that he was not as well as he had been.

With all our engagements being in London in the winter, it meant that we could help out with shop from time to time, and not going out to work until around 8 p.m or sometimes later, we saw Richard a little more, even though he was at school. The Hampstead School was well equipped, but the teaching staff was always changing. His education was sadly lacking and he was not happy at this school. He had good friends, especially one Christopher Tucker, who lived opposite us. They were inseparable. The summer was close, and we were booked at the Ocean Theatre, Clacton for a second season. The Catlin family had a record breaking season in Llandudno, in 1968. They decided to sell the Arcadia Theatre, to the Llandudno Urban District Council.

Gwen and I came to the Pier Pavilion for a Sunday concert at the end of Catlin's 1968 season, at the Arcadia. We saw the last night, and I was very upset to see the finale line up, with Harry Mitchell Craig squashed into a corner by the proscenium, without any kind of prominent position. Even if it had been in name only, he had been the producer for Catlins for at least fifteen years. it was a very insignificant farewell to a good servant. Tears came,
It made me realize how you can be left behind so easily, so I made up my mind that I would direct the last night like a production in the future. If, I was in the position of producer.

1969 arrived and the Council in Llandudno leased the theatre to **Robinson Cleaver.** Robbie contacted me and asked me if I would put a show together to include Gwen and I, and would I produce the whole enterprise. He had evidently been in the Arcadia in 1963 when I was taking hold of the proceedings while Mitchell-Craig was asleep. Robbie told me that he had made his mind up, that should he be in the position to present summer revue, I would be the one to take charge. So now it was challenge time. Could I do it ? To be principal comedian, I hired **Bryan Burdon.** Having been with him in pantomime, I knew his track record, and I knew that his warmth would readily permeate through to the visitors who came regularly to Llandudno, The Queen of the Welsh Resorts. Bryan was an immediate success. **Leslie Adams** was the comedy support. A very experienced raconteur, very good with words. He was originally to be a dentist, he certainly could get his teeth round long words with great clarity. with additional comedy from **Cyril Jackson** multi-instrumentalist, known for his clown antics with the successful duo **The Bedlams. Ken and Anna Alexis** were the dancing act and the choreographers, with eight **Cherry Willoughby Dancers, Tony Bradwell and an 8 piece orchestra,** and the popular **Chas McDevitt & Shirley Douglas.** This lovely and talented couple, were versatile, and their music was easy on the ear. A class act. add to the cast **Gwen and I,** who had a ready made audience from other seasons.

I was devising and producing talent and above all, my friends. One of my popular offerings, was a tribute to one of the great composers. This meant I could use all the company. Another great asset was that Bryan could sing, I mean really sing. I made sure he did.

Being my first production, you can imagine I had prominent memories of personal enjoyment, and this show would stay in my mind forever. Robbie had a lease with the Council for 3 years, so we became business partners and we created the firm..
R.C. Productions. R for Robbie and C for Clive. This new enterprise meant that I was now responsible for the Pier Pavilion as well. It was my intention to bring the Sunday concerts at the Pier Pavilion up to date. Our stalwarts like ***Semprini, The Beverley Sisters and Russ Conway*** would be fine in June and September, but I wanted to bring in a few comedians and flavour of the month entertainers, and a few Television favourites. This was a task I would relish. Luckily Robbie went along with all my bookings.

Bryan Burdon starred in the 1970 season with Gwen and I, and the three of us built on the the previous season. I brought in a lovely musical act ***Cathy Downey & Glyn Evans. Cathy*** was a superb dancer, so she was featured strongly in production. For a speciality, we had ***Yuri and Tonya*** from the Russian State Circus, I still kept 8 girls, add to this the foremost Xylophone act in the Country...***Jackie Allen & Barbara***, together with ***Bill Cameron*** our Fred Astaire dancer, who also was responsible for the choreography, the Arcadia "Showtime" show was probably one of the most successful entertainments on any coast. I was not completely happy with the M.D. for 1969, so ***Charlie Stewart*** recommended me to ***Gil Roberts.*** Although I had not seen Gil, having Charlie's suggestion, I was confident of musical excellence, and so it turned out to be. There are certain "Pros" who you know you can trust with experience, for recommendation. Gil was wonderful, and we worked together very amicably.

Llandudno lies on the Creuddyn Penisula between the Great and Little Ormes, two headlands formed from carboniferous limestone. Over several millennia the geology of the two Ormes has produced a distinct amount of rare plants, one plant Wild Cotoneaster, has its sole British location on the Great Orme. However, Creuddyn is strongly connected with early Welsh history through the ruined site of the castle at Deganwy.

The first hotel to be built was the St. George's in 1854. Children evacuated from the bomb-stricken English cities spent their war years in Llandudno, and the Grand Theatre was used by the evacuated BBC Variety department for the show "Happidrome" with **Harry Korris.**

With Bryan for two seasons, I didn't want him to out stay his welcome, and I hoped to bring him back for another two seasons. So I said to him we would leave the next season. For the 1971 season Charlie Aitken and Robbie wanted to bring back **Wyn Calvin.** I was not too keen on this, as Wyn had 1958, 1960 and his record breaking season in 1968. I was afraid that we should have a lot of the material he had performed previously, especially as there were only two seasons in between. Wyn had a famous story about two lions walking down Mostyn Street, that every one used to quote. I had to bare in mind, that a large majority of our audience came to see us every year. The visitors would arrive in the town, put their cases in the hotel, and come straight to the box office, and book for the three programmes. They knew the quality of the show. This meant we had to ring the changes. It is always harder for comics to find new material. Singers have a much wider choice.

During the season, we had the tragic news that **George Clarkson** had died. We were devastated . Richard was very upset, he adored "Jige" as he called him. After George stopped dancing he became secretary to **Des O'Connor.**

George had had a heart warning , this had been diagnosed "all clear" and Jige was not to go back to the doctor for a year. Whistling along the corridor in the television studios one day, he dropped, and that was the end of one of the loveliest human beings we had ever known. Gail was shattered, and coped with the bereavement magnificently. We are so pleased to see her at regular intervals. A wonderful lady.

During the 1970 Bryan and I did more doubles, that it became hilarious. Bryan had gags that basically were very short with a good tag. We ad- libbed through these short interludes with a great rapport from the audience. He was superb to work with, and he never minded me getting a laugh for myself, because he'd top it immediately. Great experience and a happy time.

At the end of the 1970 season, Wyn came to have a meeting with Charlie, Robbie and I. Wyn said frankly to me, that he understood I was not in favour of his return. I told him my concern was that I thought he would use the same material, and I didn't want that, for he was so familiar to our audience. It was quite an embarrassing situation. I had directed two successful seasons, and I had my own style of production, and I would continue with the format that would include the characteristics of the performers I engaged for the season. Wyn, very graciously, intimated he would be willing to fit in with my direction. I conceded that the odd old gag would return, but I wanted a new approach. The contract was signed for the 1971 season. It was now a question of the ideas, I had for this very talented man.

A very enjoyable pantomime ensued, and with the London scene as busy as ever, time was flying by, and although I had some ideas for the Wyn season, work was getting in the way of writing the script.

208

During the London season, we found that we were doing many more engagements in the Livery Company Halls. We had an engagement in the Inn Holders Hall. When we arrived we found that the room was inhabited by very elderly gentlemen. *Billy Cater Smith* was playing for us, this was unusual, as we always had our own Trevor. Eventually we went on, a very small rostrum that really only took the piano, and we felt very cramped. While singing I counted approximately 22 men in dinner jacket and tails sitting leisurely after a good meal. The Rt Hon, *Clement Atlee* was asleep, and round the bottom of the table at silly mid off, was a very young *Donald Sinden.* he was just making his name in the theatre. Against the rest of the men in the audience, he looked like a Peter Pan. We took a polite bow, and went off to another room. We were just lifting a glass of "sherbert", to our lips, when *Donald Sinden* came rushing out to see us. He could not believe that we could actually get up on a box, and sing to these old codgers. He said he wouldn't have been there except for his father in law being a member, and he brought him. "How do you do it?", he spluttered, "I couldn't do that for a million quid" He was full of admiration for anyone who could have courage to entertain in those surroundings with such an inanimate bunch of blokes.

The Guildhall, Mansion House and the Livery Company Halls were among our regular venues during the winter months. We appeared before the Lord Mayor of London regularly. Two events at the Mansion House readily spring to mind. I had just finished a very involved piano part for "My Fair Lady" and we were going to perform this for the Lord Mayor. Trevor had rehearsed this complicated arrangement, and so we commenced the performance. The sustaining pedal fell off the grand, and the piano became a real honky-tonk sound. Trevor was horrified, especially at the sound of this very effective accompaniment, on such an instrument. Because "Fair Lady" was so popular and current, the audience gave us a tremendous reception. *Emile Littler* was a guest at the function, and he came to congratulate us on a wonderful performance.

A very busy time and preparation for the 1971 season at the Arcadia.
We said "Didn't you hear the sustaining had fallen off, and it sounded like *Winifred Atwell's,* other piano". He had not noticed the dilemma we were all in.

Another Lord Mayor of London had engaged GWEN to sing at the Mansion House one night. The Beadle came to her, and informed her of the procedure for the evening after dinner. You go on at approximately 8.30 p.m. After this there will be a speech from the Managing Director of the Company thanking the Lord Mayor for attending. Then at 9.30 p.m. I go to the Lord Mayor, this is the regular form, and I say "Lord Mayor, what is your pleasure, and he always says, "My carriage", and then he leaves." Gwen sang her 20 minutes to a very warm reception, and then left for the dressing room. The beadle on the stroke of 9.30 p.m. went to the Lord Mayor and said "My Lord Mayor what is your pleasure ?", The Lord Mayor in a very clear voice, for all to hear, said "I would like to hear that young lady sing again" There was panic, the Beadle ran up to the dressing room, only to find Gwen in a state of undress, getting ready to go home. "Quick,!" he says," " the Mayor wants you back for another spot", like lightning, Gwen put on a second dress, she always carried more than one, and raced along the corridor, telling *Kathleen O'Hagan* the programme she would sing, as they hurtled on. This was a very happy night....eventually.
The whole after dinner picture, was a case of more you were seen and heard, the more bookings came in. It was a giant snowball. Christmas had come and gone, and although I had mapped out some of the three programmes, I was no further on with the first half finale of the opening programme. This had to be a true blockbuster of a scene. I telephoned Wyn with the other productions, the programmes were all set, except this one piece. I knew the whole theme I wanted to convey, with the music of *Franz Lehar's "Merry Widow"* but I couldn't place it on paper. Many a time I had my fingers on the keyboard to type, but it would not come. Time was running out.

Then one afternoon just after Easter, it all came to me, and in two hours I finished it. On the phone to Wyn to tell him the final dialogue complete with the musical score. I finished talking to him, feeling a bit devoid of all energy. There was a long pause, and I thought he doesn't like it, I knew it was good, and then in those stentorion tones, he said " Brilliant ! I am absolutely sympatico. It is a replica of a period in my early life, and it is weird to think you have recaptured this memory ". I was now even more assured that this scene would be magical. It was now time to think of how I was going to dress this extravagant musical, for it was a complete play with music.

Having friends in the whole business was always an advantage, I contacted my friend in the wardrobe department of **Richard Stone.** I wanted four immaculate uniforms, eight fabulous satin crinolines. and a large "crin" for Gwen as the lead character. I also wanted them at a cheap rate of hire, as it would be for 20 weeks. Richard was very generous, and these lovely costumes were mine for the season. Good friends.

It was a superb cast I had assembled. I cut to six girls, as the minimum salaries had shot up. British Actors' Equity had made a big mistake. Instead of making small increases each year, like the Musicians' Union had done, they loaded a £14 increase per girl. They had also brought about for managements a higher and lower minimum. If you could satisfy the lower minimum, that is:-
1. Seating capacity under 1,000. *2,* Less that 12 in the cast.
3. Outlying population of less than a million. Then you could pay the lower minimum salary. We could not satisfy any of these criteria, so we paid the higher minimum, we had to cut our cloth accordingly. We hired *Aubrey Budd,* who had just finished at the London Palladium, as our Principal dancer and choreographer. *Roger Carne,* a super ventriloquist, *Margaret Schonbeck*, simply a very talented all-rounder. *Syd Marx,* six foot six of mirth and melody.

He was very short in height, and played many instruments. He was hilarious. I brought back *Jackie Allen & Barbara* who had been such a success in 1970. Gwen and I to play our last season for a while, and the Welsh Prince of Laughter *Wyn Calvin.*

Rehearsals commenced two weeks before the opening saturday night. The comedy bits all fell into place, the acts knew their own material. The big production took a little extra time. the Lehar music scene had been titled *"The Not so Merry Widow"* *Gil Roberts* and the orchestra had a very full book musically.

It started with Wyn and Roger as two old men, coming to listen to the band concert. Wyn had a wonderful make-up, and Roger just managed to get a wig on in time, as he had just come off from his act. The usual gags about the tuning up, the music they were going to play, Wyn threw in a good one that always tickled me. "I don't know this one "Refrain from spitting" and then they were to play a selection from the "Merry Widow". Wyn, then told Charlie, how, many years ago he was in the show, and fell in love with Maria, the leading lady. I played Wyn as a young man. From songs from the "Widow", I had picked out the lyrics that fitted the situation. With black outs, cutouts and secretive lighting a wonderful atmosphere was produced. The famous "Women" number was performed by *Syd Marx,* who had a lovely tenor voice. I had to bully him not to be funny, as he was dressed in a tremendously smart uniform, tailored to fit him. His wife Dolly, would watch every performance, and think that's my immaculate Syd. She had never seen him so smart. The sad dialogue where I leave Maria musically, while Wyn recalls his pain and anguish at their parting. Just as the mood is sombre with sorrow, I opened up on full stage in a ballroom with practical candlearbra, rostrums and chandeliers right across the proscenium arch, and the whole company in the uniforms and crinolines swirling round to the "Merry Widow waltz. Gwen singing at the finish with the old man joining her vocally, and with an extended vocal finish, the tabs closed.

There was a one second pause, and then the audience erupted. It was the biggest reception for a first half finale I ever heard in the Arcadia or any other theatre. The scene was timed for twenty minutes, but we had to accept that the show would come down a little later than the other two programmes every night. Our usherettes, kiosk and bar ladies, watched this scene every performance. The hard work and diligence had all been worth this triumph. *Trevor Cresswell,* from Bury, had built and painted a beautiful scene. To think the top priced seat was only fifty pence.

With the exception of the Sunday concerts we promoted ourselves, there were no other live shows on. The Pier Pavilion was turned into a cinema by *Alan Hutchinson* , he had around 30 cinemas in the Northern area, so there was no real opposition.
The Arcadia held 1,345 seats and we averaged at just over 1100 seats a night. It was the record of all time, and still remains so until 1995, when the "old girl " closed forever. The last night was a production in itself. So popular was the show, we had to have two last nights. The success of the season led to a further lease of the theatre, although of course, the Council raised the rent for the next three years.

Gwen and I were truly part of the town, and we started to negotiate to buy a house, we had had some very nice places to rent for each season, we now thought it would be better to have bricks and mortar, if we were to continue to have our summers in Llandudno, and it looked as though it was a likely possibility.

Naturally I was still playing cricket for Llandudno, and I had a good season. At the end of the final fixture, there was a special trophy meeting. David Roberts, who had been a President, sadly passed on. He was a lovely man, and the cricket club was a poorer place for his passing. His son Andrew however, presented a batting, bowling and promising newcomer award.

An all round super season.

This trophy would be in father's name, for the 1971 season. Andy as he was affectionately called, presented me with the Batting prize. As he gave the shiny trophy to me, he said "This is not for the hundred you scored against the Cheshire Officers , it is for the fifty eight you hit against Styal", I had forgotten all about that. The side had fallen apart, and only two players reached double figures, and I just stayed there to achieve some sort of respectable team score. The trophy alas, was burnt in the fire. Andrew, very successfully carried on the family business, he is responsible, to this day, for providing the best shoes in the area.

At the end of September and the record breaking season, Gwen and I, decided that we would buy that house in Llandudno. It transpired that we bought in the Oval . The business and completion of the sale went through within six weeks. We bought from a lovely lady named Miss Dale. She knew us from the theatre, and we tuned in to her immediately. Her garden had a written plan where all the flowers and bulbs were placed, and the names of each were delineated on an immaculate diagram. Gwen, in her usual efficient way, made the house perfect for our habitation. We were excited to feel we had a home of our own for the 1972 season. The name of the house was *"Dilkusha".* which is Urdu for "Place of Happiness"

Our permanent home was of course 83 Mill Lane, West Hampstead, London, where I had lived since 1938. With the auction being successful in our favour in 1968, circumstances changed with retirement of my Pop. There was no way Gwen and I could carry on the running of the shop, so we decided to sell. We made sure that we looked for properties that were close to London, we agreed that the Surrey area would suit us. Eventually we found 304 Malden Road, New Malden. The selling of the shop was not without difficulties and delays, we pressed on and by April,1972 we were domiciled. Richard had his own room, and we gave my parents separate rooms, so that they were self contained.

There was plenty of room also, for two cats and two dogs. Duke and mother's dog, a blue roan spaniel, by the name of Pepys, settled in straight away, and the two cats, Figaro and Joe had a little more difficulty, as Figaro was blind, and he really had to sort out his bearings. The garage was large, and I had it lined with hardboard and papered, a carpet on the floor, two very large desks, one for me and one for **Betty Lunn,** a very excellent secretary. Betty was the daughter of **Wilby Lunn,** she was running a floorshow called "Cavalcade". she was my right hand, and helped to make, **Derwent Entertainments Ltd.,** up and running.

The agency thrived, and my day would be in the office until around 4.30 / five o clock, and then off to do a "Master's Song" or Gwen and I would be off to an after dinner function.

Richard had come from a very over crowded school, named Hampstead School. He did not do well there, the classrooms were far too crowded, and the teachers changed every few weeks. He was pleased to be in New Malden, and entered a very personal school. Beverley by name. When he arrived there, they were prompt in telling him, that he was four years behind, so he got his head down and started to catch up. Like father like son, he was outstanding at sport. He hadn't played rugby before, but this didn't phase him. The headmaster praised him for his sporting achievements. He left the school well equipped to take on the commercial world. Richard was the first to admit, that he was not a performer, not a singer, not an actor, and would not follow in our footsteps at all. You can imagine how delighted we were when he landed a job at the London Palladium. He was to be a showman backstage. His first show was the **Larry Grayson** show. Larry said to him "I know whose son you are". **Tommy Steele in "Hans Christian Anderson"** was the next show on the stocks. All the while, he had to do televisions' "Sunday Night at the London Palladium" this meant working through the night, laying floors and erecting sets.

Tommy Steele was very good to Richard, he let him have his dressing room to get some shut eye. The names Richard worked with read like a who's who in variety...*Frank Sinatra, Count Basie, Mike Reid, Bruce Forsyth, Michael Crawford* and a host of others. He enjoyed this side of the business. Gwen and I were secretly pleased he had some attachment with the profession we loved.

One day Richard telephoned us in Llandudno, to say that he was leaving the London Palladium, he wanted to talk to me, not his mother. He informed me that he had fallen for *Kay Winnett,* one of my usherettes. "I have given in my notice", he said, " I leave on Friday." I was very annoyed and upset. I said "You can't just leave like that, the London Palladium, the No 1 Variety House of the world". " I am leaving", he said, and that was that. This he did, and arrived in Llandudno. Fine, while Gwen and I were there for the summer, but of course, he fell on his feet, Gwen's mum and dad lived up there, and they took him in, and he was looked after, and spoilt.

Derek Barsham, better known as "Master Derek Barsham" a boy soprano, was well known with the usual boy solos, and he made many recordings, and though a world beater as a treble, his voice when broken, joined the hundreds of thousands of baritones on the market. He was rather like *Ernest Lough,* inasmuch that the new voice was not as outstanding as before.

It seemed to be, the pattern that a strong treble had thick vocal chords, and when changed into manhood was usually a baritone. Derek changed his name to Mann, so he was now on the market as *Derek Mann.* He was a go ahead fellow with bags of enterprise, I used to book him for Masonics. One day he suggested I join *The Savage Club.* This was a prestigious and exclusive club for the arts. It was divided into categories for membership under sections like :- DRAMA, MUSIC, POETRY, ARTISTES/PAINTERS.

It always reminded me of the *Vic Oliver* gag "My wife had posed in the nude for a painter, I know that lots of girls pose in the nude for painters, but this one was a house painter" I don't wish to know that...Derek proposed me into this fantastic club, and *Gordon Marsh* was my second.

My first visit to the club in St. James, made my jaw drop. That night in the club I was introduced to :-*Soloman, Max Jaffa, Jack Byfield, Alan Cibell John Wilbraham, Mark Hamburg,* and my old friend *Sir Alan Herbert.* My good friend *John Wade* said to me "What do you think of this lot ?" I said I was most impressed.

The club had a house supper each month, when those that attended were at the mercy of the host for the evening, so you made sure you brought your music. The accompanist was first class, the superb *Leslie Murchie.* I went to my first house supper, only to find the host for the evening was Sir Alan Herbert. I knew he was bound to pick me out sometime in the evening. Feeling timorous, my confidence was low, he saved me for the last spot. Well dear reader, I was overawed by my peers, and they had never heard this new member before. APH introduced me from his show "Tough at the Top" and he hadn't seen me since 1949. I kept my act short, my axiom was always leave them wanting more. I included some of the lyrics of my host, I was quite emotional, thinking of APH, *Vivian Ellis* and "Cockie". I registered well with the members, and as I was coming back to cries of "more", I saw, out of the corner of my eye, *Owen Brannigan* nearby. Owen had been on tour, and this was his first time in the club for a while. I knew Owen, he had been with Robbie and I in Llandudno for concerts. Feeling elated with my reception, I announced I thought it would be a fitting finale, to hear Owen Brannigan after a long absence. This was well received, and Owen finished off the evening to a great reception. He did not tell me off for throwing him in the deep end.

Rubbing shoulders with all these classical artists, made me realize that I was like the old saying "Jack of all trades, and master of "some". These clubs were all very well, but you needed time to cement relationships, and most of the members were drinkers, and I liked a drink, but I didn't make a career out of it. Of course you made many contacts, and you never knew when they would be useful to you. I attended when I could, but with the Concert Artistes' Association, Rotary and Freemasonry, and all the theatres requiring my attention, I had to give priority to earning a living. So my attendance was minimal.

It was now obvious to me, that the after dinner scene was starting to contract, the number of functions were reducing, there was a shortage of money, and entertainment was always the first to be cut. Bands were suffering by being reduced to electric keyboards and drums. Lucky for me, there was a new Master every year, so the lodges still wanted the Master's Song, each Master would have a Ladies Night, though this depended on the wealth and the depth of the Master's pocket. Parking in London was a headache. It was great if you had bookings at the Piccadilly Hotel, The Criterion, and the old Monico. they were close together, so one parking place could do you for the evening. To be at home, and sometimes go off at 9 p.m. and then return home at 11 p.m., was perfect.

During the winter, I was off everywhere finding new costumes and thinking of the 1972 season. I went to Worthing to see a Black and White production of "Salad Days". The scenery was all black and white, and looked very strong. I went backstage to see the scenery, I noticed that all the cut outs and flats were made of four ply wood, the rostrums were strong enough to hold a full company, and the cut out trees were very well done. I then asked, "What to you do with this scenery when the show is finished ?" "We throw it away", came the answer. I said, "I'll have it" So for seventy five pounds, it cost me for the transport, I had procured some wonderful sets for the coming season.

The Arts Council did not utilize, or use their sets for further productions, we private managements had to make the most of what we had . I started to enlarge my operations. The Floral Pavilion at New Brighton came to me for a summer show, I added the Pavilion at Cromer and with Burnham-on-Sea established, my personal company was growing.

Ken Roberts was the comic for 1972, together with ***Brian Stephens,*** an impressionist. To feed Ken was a difficult spot to fill., but an idea came to me. Behind the Arcadia was the Grand Theatre, and they had repertory in the early sixties, the company was run by ***Derek Pollitt.*** Derek was a first class actor with a great sense of humour. I wondered if he would fit the bill, or should I even ask him. Plucking up courage, I suggested he might like to feed Ken. He thought it a great idea, so problem solved. Bringing back ***Jackie Allen & Barbara*** was obvious, and I added ***The Gaytones.*** four ladies who were maestros of the trombone. I had a strange modern singer named ***Simon Jons.*** He was born in Sweden. He was very unreliable, so much so, that he went around Llandudno and ordered suits and other clothing, and did not pay his bills. He ran up hefty debts, and gave the shop keepers a cock and bull story that I had not paid him, and I had left town. Despite the inconvenience, I sacked him on the last week. Robbie and I went round and settled his debts, we could not have our names associated with dishonesty. He was the only "wrong un" I ever booked.

I had seven lady principals, four men and six girl dancers, this meant clothing 13 ladies and 4 men. This was an expensive show, shoes and tights as well as sets of costumes and some intricate scenery. It was a challenge to be more successful than the record breaking 1971 season. It fell short of that season, but as a show. it kept our reputation in tact. With all the worry of production, seeing that lights were right, scenery in place, all the publicity etc, I felt it was too much, so Gwen and I stood down.

Pauline Whitaker was a soprano of very good quality, having made herself a hit in pantomime with *Arthur Askey & Dickie Henderson. Aubrey Budd and Margaret Schonbeck* ,were jointly responsible for the choreography and *Gil Roberts* was with the stalwarts in the pit.

Well dear reader, you may be saying to yourself, this was a one man band as a management, it was to a certain extent, but I must point out that I had a superb Wardrobe Mistress in *Margaret Best.* When you have limited resources, you need loyal help, and Margaret was all things to me and to the artistes. Efficiency was her middle name. Her father, *George Nussey* was our stage manager. *Freda Sands* controlled the box office, so we were a complete family.

It was now imperative that I found efficient and loyal staff for the other theatres. Having the financial input in Llandudno, it was important I was in the "Queen of the Welsh Resorts" most of the time. So calling on my old friend *Claude Worth* who had been with us in Scotland, to manage the New Brighton operation, I was well served, and the extra shows were successful and accident free. For Cromer my old friends and comedian *George Bolton and Barry Johns* were a tower of strength, with a good support, there was little hassle to put the blood pressure out of gear.

After Christmas, we carpeted the house in The Oval. We started to make it a proper home, although we were only there for six months a year. This house was very convenient for me, as I could change, and walk straight out on to the cricket ground. We were in a Cul-de-sac, in a very quiet area.

Duke loved going out on the Oval for a run and a romp.
We were not there long, before the business of booking the 1973 production was upon us, so back to London.

In March one of the most outstanding achievements of my life so far, came to fruition. After a long procedure of a couple of years, I was initiated into *The Grand Order of Water Rats.* This was the most prestigious organization in our profession. At the time there were only 140 members in the world. This exclusive Order was founded in 1889 by a few Music Hall Artistes, that developed into a tremendous charitable and benevolent fund for artistes who were down on their luck, or were ill and not able to carry out their profession. The "Rats" as they were called not only looked after their fellow "Pros", they raised funds for very expensive instruments needed for hospitals. It was also responsible for looking after families of Water Rats who passed on. I had an occasion to support an ex Bluebell, who was going to commit suicide because of her husband beating her, her children not allowed to go to school, and her accommodation in Rhyl was dreadful. The Rats sorted her out, and she had a nice flat, the children went to school, and her desperation was turned into hope and happiness. I was so thrilled to be accepted by the Water Rats. When you sit in Lodge, and a big star name is turned down, your chest expands with pride. I would now do my best for this fantastic Order, with all the comics and first class performers together, we could raise coins (we called money coins) and have fun doing it.

In the winter of the year, Gwen and I were asked by *Jack Howarth,* ", Albert Tatlock, in Coronation Street" to appear for SOS Stars Organization for Spastics at the Opera House, Manchester, with *Leslie Crowther, Russ Conway, Barbara Law, The Fortunes and Dickie Henderson, with Cyril Stapleton* and his Orchestra. On arrival we were ushered into the dressing room of *Eartha Kitt.* This charming lady had left drinks and ice in her fridge and a bottle of Brandy. With a little note "Dear Mr & Mrs Stock, have a lovely concert", what a super thing to do. The concert was memorable.

Reviewing the local paper, my attention was drawn to an article, with photograph of *Ian Garry.* Here was a performer who had appeared in the West End's "Music Man, No Strings and Sail Away" put with this, shows with *Barbra Streisand and Ginger Rogers* And then his wonderful performance in the film "Hello Dolly" directed by *Gene Kelly,* here was a talent and a man after my own heart. We negotiated, and Ian was to appear and do the choreography for the 1973 edition of "Showtime" others in the company were :-*Vera Bennett & Michael Chivers, Norman Caley, Gwenfron Hughes, Vince & Rita Starr and the chance in a laughtime...Bryan Burdon.*

During 1973 another honour came my way. I was made Chairman of the Concert Artistes' Association, it was to be a very busy year, and the Annual Dinner in March 1974 was a big responsibility for me. I had to propose the toast to the Association. *Arthur Askey* replied. I sang at the end of my speech, and Arthur had quite a lot to say about it, he was not going to follow such a performance, and the laughs came thick and fast. Other speakers were *Bill Pertwee, Esther Rantzen, and Dick Emery.* It was a wonderful night for Gwen and I and our family.

We decided for the 1974 season we would have *Bryan Burdon* for the last time. This time, Gwen would be in the show on her own, this would be the first time we were not singing together. Contracts were always signed well in advance, this was my way. I engaged *Jackie Allen & Barbara,* they had a great following. Robbie and I were very much at home in Llandudno. The press had let it out, and I still don't know how they found the information, that Robbie and I had raised over £20,000 for local charities. It was part of our interest to support well known charities. Save the Children, Mencap, R.S.P.C.C. and many others. The Royal National Lifeboat Institution co-opted me on to the Appeals Committee. Russell Gradwell had something to do with this new role, I feel. It was a great stimulus helping all the local volunteers who worked so hard for others.

On the 26th April, 1974, Pop died, he had been diagnosed with cancer of the lung some months before. He was very poorly toward the end. Gwen and I kept analysing his life and the lack of fun in it. He had worked solidly until he was 75 years of age, and just when he retired to enjoy some sort of free and relaxing life, he left us. It all seemed so unfair. He was a great example of the hackneyed expression, "The salt of the earth" he was kind, very patient and tried his hardest to provide for his family. Having been a prisoner in the first World War, he made us all feel, that he did not worry about anything, but he did, his children were everything to him, and when he could see that each of us were solid and successful human beings, he felt that he had been a success as a father. My sister Beryl, adored him, and I am so grateful that he gave me an example of being a good citizen and that old phrase "Of playing the White Man".

Gwen was particularly fond of him, and in his last years did many kind gestures to make him more comfortable. He was a very modest and gentle man. Having just moved to New Malden, we didn't know any people locally, so his funeral was a very quiet and sparse affair. His good neighbours and fellow shop keepers came over from Hampstead to pay their last respects. My task was now to attend to his affairs. Although he and I were a partnership, his personal tax had to be sorted. This was a headache as he owed a large amount to the Revenue, this I paid off at so much a month. How sad it was to think of his passing, with so little to show materially for his life, but so much we owe him for his example as a fine human being.

From this sadness, I had to prepare for the 1974 summer season, this was slightly different in content, inasmuch, I made the second half. a cabaret type scene. With *Ian Garry and Janice Armstrong, Gwen* with her attractive spot on being a girl, and *Jackie Allen & Barbara* overtures and the playing of tiny xylophones by the audience, *Willie Wyse* a Scottish tenor, and *Christopher Connah.*

Chris, was from the **Black & White Minstrels.** They both gave grand support to our comic BRYAN. Gil Roberts had retired, so I brought an old friend to join us as Musical Director, **Les Brown.** Les was a very experienced Musical Director. He had his own band in the after dinner world, and he lived in Greater London. This meant that I could go to see him with routines I wanted to do. Les was a great animal lover, and we had a long friendship, for which I will always be grateful.

During the run at the Arcadia Theatre, Llandudno, I was running across to the Pier Pavilion, Cromer to rehearse "Showtime" with **George Bolton, Steve King, Tommy Elliott, John Murphy** and full supporting artistes plus **Brewyeen Rowland** and the Showtime Dancers. The show opened on the 6th July, 1974 to rave notices, eclipsing the popular 1973 version. I went into the Sunday concert while I was there, to keep my hand in, so to speak. Returning to Llandudno, I popped up on the Sunday show on 18th August, with **Semprini.** Albert was a consummate pianist, who pleased everybody. He was born in Bath, of an Italian father. He was an expert conductor gaining experience in the important opera houses in Italy. The Arcadia show ran on to the end of September, and on the 23rd September, Gwen and I celebrated our Silver Wedding Anniversary luncheon at the Lodge in Tal-y-Bont. Without any rehearsing Les Brown became the toastmaster and presented all the toasts. All the cast were there and Robbie and his wife Molly, and Gladys & Charles Aitken, it was a very happy celebration of what had been so far, a truly wonderful life together. It is quite remarkable to say, that we had never had a cross word at any time. Considering Gwen and I were in each other's pockets all the time, it was a tremendous achievement.

1975 was once more a busy and notable year. My dear friend **Joe Church** was installed as King Rat, This is one of the most prestigious positions in showbusiness, and during his year of office, Prince Charles became a Companion Rat.

Robbie and I presented "Showtime 75" at the Floral Pavilion, New Brighton. Starring *Roy Lance and Johnny Lancaster.* The accompanist for the whole show was *Nigel Ogden* he had never been associated with a summer revue before. He was one of Robbie's organist pals, and Nigel found the whole season an education, and it stood him in good stead, when he continued his career with the B.B.C as the resident organist in *"The Organist Entertains". Nigel* was a very excellent organist and an extremely nice individual.

At the Arcadia, Llandudno at Easter, Gwen and I starred with the fabulous *Syd Marx. Syd and I* opened the show with a funny double. The Minting family came into this show, they consisted of *Norma Hughes* a very attractive soprano, with her children, Janice, Judith and Jill plus dad...*Roy Minting,* an ample magical and comic entertainer. Of all the families I have ever met, the *Mintings* were quite the most family orientated, the bond between them was quite outstanding. They endeared themselves to Llandudno, and I had them marked down for the future.

At the Pier Pavilion, Cromer I presented *Clifford Henry* in his one man show, with *Ann Harriman* an outstanding voice. This was a self managed show, and saved me travelling across, from west to east.
At the Arcadia, the flagship so to speak, we brought back the ever popular *Wyn Calvin.* To bring strong support we had two good friends in *Ted Durante & Hilda.* Ted was quite surprised that I got him singing, he had a fair baritone to help the productions, we also had the surprising vocal power of our dancer and choreographer *Ian Garry* . Ian had developed a high baritone, capable of reaching a top B flat. Add to this, a little lad from Rhyl who played solo piano, a great asset, for the Charlie Chaplin tribute, as the "Kid". *Willie Wyse* with his strong tenor tones to help lift all the vocal productions that became my speciality.

During the rehearsals *Les Brown* stayed with us at the Oval, while he did the orchestrations with me, he unfortunately, was not with us for the season. Gwen and I had the biggest heartache for years. Our dear labrador *Duke,* was very ill, Les and I put him on a deckchair, and used it as a stretcher. We took him to our vet, the very clever Med Humphries, who said he could keep him alive for another 24 hours, but he would only be putting off the inevitable. So this darling dog, who had been such a bright spark and loveable, and a loyal companion, was to leave us. We were heartbroken. He was so theatrical. He used to tag a sketch by coming on stage with his lead in his mouth on a certain cue. The amazing part of his theatrical sense, was he only had to do this in number 1 programme. He took no notice of the Number 2 and 3 programmes, he only got ready for number one. He was the favourite with all the company and the local population. He was buried at the Crows Nest, Meds house, with Rajah, Med's great dane, who he played with. Two pals finding peace together.

The 1975 show was well up to standard of the past seasons, there were some lovely pieces. It included a lovely tribute to *Charlie Chaplin.* He had just been Knighted and we had Wyn as he was in 1975 receiving the telegram, and Ted as the "Tramp" with the kid. Another first half finale was the Welshman in London, which included some Oliver music by *Lionel Bart.* The show once again rose to our expected popularity. There is nothing better in the theatrical world, than to have your show, received with long and loud applause.

In October, on my return to London, I was installed as the Master of my lodge. The great leveller in freemasonry is that all have the chance to become Master of their lodge. Rich or not so rich ascend the ladder of promotion dictated by the date they joined, it is a chronological progression that is only interupted by illness, or moving far away from the Country.

Master of the Lodge.

The general public have preconceived ideas about masonry, and they sometimes, are scared, because of ignorance, thinking that we are clandestine and a religious order, which is farthest from the truth. We believe in God, and the ritual teaches us a way of life. If you think about the goodness of morality and the charitable deeds we observe. You can liken our precepts to the Ten Commandments. You can't go far wrong with those, but the one truth that so many people forget, is that we are an organisation that gives so freely to charity. Life boats, Schools, medical equipment. The Royal College of Surgeons. You name it, you'll find that Freemasonry donates large sums of money to these very well deserving institutions and life saving charities.

Being Master, meant much learning, and when you absorb the dialogue, it is the most stimulating feeling. My personal experience was to come to lodge, when you were under pressure with business meetings, appearances and voice worries, to sit there in lodge, and feel the relief, and the tension subsiding and floating away. I couldn't be without my masonry. There were many first class human beings I encountered in the course of my visits to lodges. None could compare with **Ralph Hearsum,** he had been a friend since the late fifties, and his guidance and help prepared me for the tremendous strides I made in the Province of Surrey. His wife Rene was a wonderful friend to Gwen and I, and we have shared many memorable times. Whenever we went to London for any functions or meetings with the Water Rats, we stayed with them. It was like being at home, and we were very excited when we knew we were going to be with them. There were many times when it was imperative that we had to be in London, and this could only be achieved by Ralph and Rene's good graces.

After the Installation meeting was the usual dinner. Except in this case, we had over 120 sitting down to dine, and some of the brethren were Water Rats.

They included the King Rat *David Nixon. Joe Church, Don Smoothey, Johnny Lancaster and other Rats,* with a high ranking Officer, the founder of the Stage Cricket Club *Bill Earle Grey.* The speeches were fabulous, and the comics were on top form, after David had finished his verbals, and very funny, I called upon Bill to finish off, he had such a tremendous knowledge of *Shakespeare.* He quoted the Bard with appropriate speeches to suit the occasion. He was so successful that my rats and all the meeting stood to him, which is very unusual for this type of meeting.

Robbie and I during our presentations of our Sunday Celebrities, regularly engaged *Russ Conway, The Beverley Sisters, Semprini, The Llandulas Male Voice Choir, The John Morava Pier Orchestra and other favourites.* In 1975 I booked for the first time *Tom O'Connor,* he had made such a hit on television with "Name That Tune". We put a choir with him, to keep our popular singing contact. On the 15th August at around 7.15 p.m. the show started at 8 p.m. One of our regular patrons came to the Box Office to collect her usual tickets. Just about to leave, she turned to Willie, our box office manager, and said "By the way, What time is the conjuror on ?". Willie said "I'm sorry, there isn't any conjuror on the show tonight" she said "Oh yes there is, its on the poster outside" Willie explained, that we were not allowed to have any props on stage. The Sunday concert laws were governed by the Chief Constable of Caernarvonshire. There is no cross patter, dancing, or costume changes or magic allowed on Sunday. I was in the back counting the ticket sales.
The patron was having none of this, she made Willie come out of the box office to look at the 12 sheet on the Pier rail. "Look see," she said, " there it is" the poster read :- *Robinson Cleaver & Clive Stock present Tom O'Connor, star of television, Robinson Cleaver organist in over 1000 broadcasts, The St. Cecilia Singers directed by Ronald Smith. to include the MAGIC OF IVOR NOVELLO.* That was her conjuror..Oh dear. Tom O'Connor dined out on that story for years.

The Pier Pavilion had for the past four years had odd shows for the summer, and two seasons with *Alex Munro*. My old friend Alex had been exceedingly successful at the open air *Happy Valley* but he was not at his best with a production show. The Pier Pavilion being a 2000 seater, needed colour and lots of artists on stage. The five handed show without scenery and girls was lost, and Alex was not happy at the poor business. Robbie and I were still presenting the Celebrity Sunday Concerts, so we decided to bid for the lease of the Pier. We secured this for the season, with an option for another three years.

The Pier Pavilion was a large and prestigious property. Talking of property, Gwen and I had another rush of blood, we sold the Oval and bought Queens Court Holiday Flatlets. This was a dominant building in the Craig-y-Don area of Llandudno.
We took over this existing business of 15 flatlets. with many bookings already secured for the season. We must have been crackers. We were both in the Arcadia 1976 season, and to take on another business.!!! I did say I would help with the flats, but of course producing and running the theatres, no chance, My darling took on the flats single handed, she was marvellous. Never having been involved in anything like this, how she coped, I will never know. The guests loved her. Irene Allen of *Jackie Allen & Barbara* saw Gwen cleaning the step one morning, she exclaimed. "A star from Drury Lane should not be doing this". Of course rehearsals started and Gwen spent her time between the theatre and the flats. Very tiring in a heatwave.

We had booked that super comedian *Bobby Dennis* for the 1976 version of "Showtime" at the Arcadia. Gwen and I came back after a break of four years. *David Andre,* a talented impressionist, son of the very versatile *Victor Seaforth* (known for his Hunchback of Notre Dame characterisation) *Silvari & June, Alan Beale* an instrumental virtuoso.

229

Jimmy Webster a tall debonair dancer and choreographer. *Janice Armstrong* a lyric soprano, who was the wife of our reunited Musical Director, *Les Brown, with the orchestra* assembled to make a very strong cast.

Being 1976, gave me an opening with 76 Trombones into a medley of Strike up the Band, When the Parade Passes By, I had the whole company in Red and Silver uniforms, all tailored, and the girls had white skirts instead of silver. I had made six pairs of plywood cutouts of soldiers in the same coloured uniforms, hooked on to each girl, so as to make 18 soldiers marching down the centre treads, and with the 8 principals, the stage was filled with moving soldiers. This got the show off to a wonderful start, and this carried through. The show opened on the 29th May. and ran through to the 2nd October. It was a heatwave, we even put outside theatre notices saying "It's cooler inside". The show was a resounding hit. But you will never believe me when I tell you I put on a similar type of show at the Pier Pavilion. I produced the "8 o clock show" with *Roy Lance* starring. He designed the best layout for a flyer, or leaflet as we called it then. I ever had. It was printed in three colours, the result was exceptional. Sensational the publicity, and sensational the show. The cast were a mixture of real established "pros" all talented and eager to do their best, not only on stage, but off, mixed with some young aspiring hopefuls, who turned out to be excellent. We of course, had people asking "What time does the 8 o clock start ?", I thought I had made it easy for them, but no....Having a large stage, I was able to use some large pieces, that I hadn't used at the Arcadia. To make it a little easier for myself, I opened the Pier season on the 6th May, giving me time to gather my thoughts for my own performance, and production of the Arcadia show.

To give you some idea of the artistes involved in both shows, the cast in "Showtime" included *Bobby Dennis, Gwen Overton & Clive Stock, David Andre, Janice Armstrong, Jimmy Webster,*

Silvari & June, Alan Beale, The Showtimers, and The Les Brown Orchestra. While in the "8 o'clock Show" there was *Roy Lance, Vince & Rita Starr, Norma Hughes, Roy Minting, Jill, Judith & Janice Minting, Willie Wyse, Andrea Wardale, Paul Leonard, Albert Tinkler and Arnold Tucker.* Quite a pay roll for Robbie and I. It was a big investment, like the whole of showbusiness.....a gamble.

Despite the heatwave, the business was phenomenal. It proved a belief I always had, :- *Always have good opposition,* in this case it was my own opposition.

To retrogress, on the opening night of <u>our</u> show, we had a terrible storm, the electric power went completely, the flats were in complete darkness. Candles to the fore for the people who had just arrived, and this the first day of the season. Gwen was rushing about, and she had an opening night. Her dear mother and father came to baby sit, so to speak. What a problem, and the known adage "The show must go on" still held sway.
All the guests were kindly and charming and didn't rock the boat. It was pouring with rain, and to quote *Harold Taylor* on an occasion, "I wish I hadn't bloody come" (Harold on a concert once was the last turn on, and everybody had paralysed them, his opening line, described his feelings).

The world seemed against us. We contacted the electricity board, who were to come as soon as possible. Gwen had to get to the theatre, I stayed on until I could wait no longer. I arrived on the Overture and Beginners call, leaving my in-laws with the baby so to speak.

The opening night went without a hitch, but I know Gwen was very apprehensive about the whole predicament. We never wanted to experience such a night again. The whole operation of the flats was like pioneering.

231

Gwen made a tremendous success of the whole enterprise. The people fell under her spell. her kindly and caring attitude was infectious and made everyone happy. The sun shone, the shows had started well, two theatres packed.

On the 31st May, Robbie and I presented the Pier Orchestra at the Pier Head. This was a little theatre right at the end of the Pier. We had morning shows at 11 a.m. and evenings at 8 p.m. Although the public was dwindling through age, for this type of entertainment, there was still the loyal middle aged music lovers, who enjoyed the Palm Court atmosphere. The Sunday Celebrity Concerts were remarkable. We closed the Arcadia on Sundays giving the Pier the whole slice of the cake. *Russ Conway, Semprini, The Beverley Sisters, Margaret Williams, The Male Voice Choirs, John Boulter, Wyn Calvin, The John Morava Orchestra, and we added Ken Goodwin, Freddie Davies, and Roy Hudd* to complete the comedy side of our policy.

The one entertainment that Llandudno lacked, was the Christmas season for Children. On the 27th December for two weeks, we presented "Aladdin and his wonderful lamp" this brought *Roy Minting* in as Widow Twankey, *Calvin Kaye* a dancing and singing violinist, played the Emperor. *Norma Hughes and the family of Mintings. Sally Ford* as the slave of the ring. GWEN was the Genie of the Lamp, and I played Abanazer. Naturally I had the local dancing school of juveniles. It was a very happy time until the end of the second week, when a local man informed the Council, that I had not taken out licences for the children, and they were all sent home, with three shows to go. We all fell apart. The kids who had been so lovely, wept profusely, their unhappiness gave us all heartache. I do hope the man who had caused this tragic finish to a super pantomime, thought about his montrous action. It certainly taught me, I never forgot the licences in subsequent pantos.

The kids and the parents had enjoyed the whole atmosphere of the pantomime, and they were all very annoyed with the outcome. A bitter sweet show brought us into 1977.

Every November at the Park Lane Hotel in those days, there was probably the most popular theatrical function ever. It was the VGS stag night. This was always over subscribed, there was a waiting list of a few hundred each year. Being a member of this famous Golfing Society, I attended the 76 night with its usual hilarity and fun all round. I learned from my good friend and comedian *Barry Johns* that *Bunny Baron,* who presented many summer shows and pantomimes, was asking about me. Bunny didn't like anyone putting on more shows than he did. He was more than annoyed, as my good friend and impresario *Duggie Chapman* had the same number as Bunny, and I had two more. He said to Barry, "Whats that Welsh bastard like ?", he was alluding to yours truly,. Barry said "Well first of all he is not Welsh, and he is a very nice management to work for",. Many artists who worked for me, worked for Bunny as well.
I was just leaving the evening, when from behind a pillar, *Bunny Baron* approached me. "I would like you to come and see me, can we make an appointment ?" This was a bit of a shock, knowing we were competitors, I was very surprised. Bunny had always been alright with me, even when I was with Sandy, he always spoke highly of Gwen and I, and said, you should do more feeding of comedians. Anyway I made a date to see him in his offices at Baker Street. The meeting was very friendly,(he didn't know I knew what he had called me) the nitty gritty of the discussion, was that he would like me to buy him out. He had summers at Hastings, Felixstowe, Lowestoft and Weston-Super-Mare, and pantomimes at Aldershot, Lewisham, and Hastings, plus a large Wardrobe department at Broadstairs. Lisa his wife seemed to be in favour of this. I knew what my answer would be, but as a negotiator, I intimated that I would have to discuss the matter with my partner.

233

Bunny had given a figure for the value of the business (So he thought). I always impressed on my dear Robbie, that we should never go to a meeting together, and be faced with a yes or no answer. We could always keep it all open, by saying, I must discuss this with my partner, I did discuss it all with Robbie pointing out the situation, that we were only buying goodwill. Bunny had tremendous goodwill with the entertainments officers of the various venues. Once Bunny was away, the business could disintegrate. As I was living in London it was easier for me to do the business, as Robbie was in the north. I reported to Bunny, that we were not interested in buying his business, putting my reasons. He understood, and we parted amicably. This was in January, so what was to transpire for the coming year.???

I need not have wondered for long. A call came from the **Bunny Baron office**...would I come to the office, Bunny had thought of an idea for me. We met and he offered me the post of Managing Director of the **Bunny Baron Organisation.** I would have a guaranteed salary, plus a commission. The offer was generous. I stated that I had a duty to my partner, and that I must be allowed to carry on my company of **R.C. Productions.** and the other venues under my control i.e. New Brighton, Cromer and Burnham-on-Sea. It was important that I saw to the productions and opening nights. Luckily my Llandudno operation started well before the Bunny Baron seasons. This all being happily effected, Bunny put a full page advert in "The Stage" informing the profession, that I had taken over as Managing Director. It also gave the names of the staff. **Gordon Holdom** was the General Manager. Gordon I had known for over twenty years. He was a baritone and he sang with **Jean Tyler,** a lovely lady with a good voice, and our paths were inter twined a lot in the after dinner world. We had two persons in the wardrobe at Broadstairs, Syd and Pat, and **John Alton** in publicity. The contract was signed.

It was April 1977 and I was in for a shattering season. Out of the blue, I had the chance to present **Billy Connolly.** He needed a good capacity theatre that was in good repair. So we leased the Astra, formerly the Odeon, in Llandudno. I was given two quad posters, and one advert in the local paper to cover the performance. This was before Billy was anything like the super star we know and love. It was unbelieveable, we only had two weeks notice, and we were sold out. The first half was a group of a head banging cocophony of electric sounds dominated by guitars. They were pretty good. The second half was the "Big Yin". It was a very successful night. I went to the big man and said "Who do I make the cheque out to ?", he said "Bumfreezer and Goosepimple", can you imagine me making out the cheque to such a name. Thats how it was to be, everyone was satisfied.

This experience gave me the idea to put on more concerts at the Astra. I lined up eight Sundays, I gave **Larry Grayson, Leslie Crowther, Harry Worth** two each, **Ken Dodd, Little & Large,** one each. with good supporting casts. Perhaps we were spreading our operation too thin, The Astra had a capacity of 1645 seats, and the Pier Pavilion, 1800. The only artist to fill the Pier Pavilion since the sixties, was **John Hanson,** otherwise the Welsh Conservative Conference, was close to capacity.

The Pier company asked us if we would start our season earlier, as Llandudno was celebrating the Centenary of the Pier. Now we knew that to open on Sunday 1st May would be financial disaster. Robbie and I had a meeting. We recognised that we were very much part of the town, and we both lived in Llandudno. We agreed to open early. I decided to do a "Golden Years of Music Hall" to celebrate the hundred years. Apart from the resident **Roy Lance, Roy Minting and Full Company**. I brought in a guest star each week. Good friends filled the role so perfectly. **Sandy Powell, Bob & Alf Pearson and George Bolton** were the star attractions. . Needless to say, we didn't make any money the first three weeks.

The lovely GEORGE BOLTON.

Bob and Alf were great. Their harmonies were rich and easy on the ear. They kept very much up to date. Bob had the sharpist and funniest wit of all the artists I knew. So sad that he died early, and for years Alf has been without the brother he loved so much. We miss those melodies from out of the sky.

George Bolton was a forceful comic, and his wife Freda had a voice the size of George's. It was a tragedy some years later when George had a major operation, and Gwen and I went around to see him, he lived a couple of miles from us in New Malden. It was a sunny day, and he was in his dressing gown. I saw some sheet music on the table, sixpence a copy. I said "I would like that copy" George said "You can have it, and all that pile there, most of them are out of print" I started to gather the old copies, and George suddenly said "Come to think of it you might as well have the props, I would not have any further use for them" I said "Are you sure ?' Yes was his reply, "As long as I can keep my top hat, frock coat, I might want to do chairman in an Old Tyme Music Hall" There were skips full of his dame costumes, and so I started to load our Estate car with all the props as well as costumes. George stood at the front door, as I walked backward and forward loading the car. He stood there watching his whole life pass before him. As I packed I was full of tears, a wonderful career packed in our transport. The owner watching and mentally saying farewell. **Sandy Powell** our good friend from 1953, was a complete treasure. The public loved him as he appealed to all ages. There was a moment during the season at the Arcadia, when **Bobby Dennis** was ill and could not appear. This was one of those moments when producers have to think on their feet, and act swiftly. Bobby, was never off, he always managed a performance, this time he missed the only appearance in a long distinguished career. I rearranged the show, and as Sandy was closing the show at the Pier Pavilion, I asked him if he would do me a favour and do the spot before the first half finale. Willingly he agreed, and thus we were saved.

Up and down to London and back.
He didn't want any fee, . What a pro.?.

For the Arcadia show, I brought back **Bobby Dennis,** a big hit from
76. to take the place of Gwen and I, I engaged an artist who I had
admired for a long time. He was the most delightful man to
produce and direct. What a performer ?? **Barry Kent,**
singing star from "Mame" and "Camelot" at Drury Lane. He was
superb. *Janice Armstrong, The Ramons, Brian Thomas,*
Francesca Boulter, Val King, Sally Henderson with The Les
Brown Orchestra and the Six Showtimers. Having opened all the
shows in Llandudno successfully, now came the stark reality of a
new career in the Bunny Baron set up. Whereas I had been paying
rent, publicity, artists salaries and staff, but taking whatever the
profits there were, Robbie and I took all the risk. Now I have a
system where you are presented with a guaranteed sum of money
by whatever Council you were working for. There was little risk,
you could cut your cloth accordingly. Getting the 7.23 a.m. from
Llandudno Junction on the Monday morning, arriving at Euston at
11 a.m. Taxi then to Luxborough Street, Baker Street and working
in a strange office until Friday, and then catching the 5 p.m. back
to Llandudno Junction where Gwen would be waiting for me. To
the flats where Gwen had a meal. Off to the Pier to see the artistes,
they wanted to see the guvnor, like the Arcadia on the Saturday
night, then on Sunday supervise the Celebrity Concert, back on
Monday on the 7.23 a.m. and off we go again.
My mother, bless her, would look after me through the week, this
was a difficult job, as she had very bad arthritis. Being a very
determined lady she made sure I was well fed. I had always had a
very keen apetite right from the age of four (After I had my tonsils
and adenoids out) I needed to be nourished to keep up with all the
flying about and the stress. Lisa Baron decided she must look after
Bunny full time, so she went to live in Brighton. *June Miller,* had
been a dancer and was a good friend of my niece *Dallas*
Wareham, who was also a dancer, she came into the office as head
of wardrobe selection and general assistant June was great..

237

She had a wonderful sense of humour. I would be on the phone, and things would not be going well, and as I put the phone down, this little face would peer at me saying "Good ere innit" I would collapse and lose all tension.

I was now in the thick of it, I had to be two headed, I realised I now had bosses on my shoulder. The Municipal Entertainment officers called the shots, each mainline star had to be approved by them. One entertainments director, would ask the tea boy, if they had heard of "Such and Such, what did they think of them.?". Sometimes we could lose a star on the opinion of a junior member of the department. The only advantage was that once Council had agreed a performer, if they did not prove to be successful, or a draw, I could always say "You wanted so and so". This situation happened once, and it was very embarrassing. I was summoned to Felixstowe, when I arrived, I was told that I had to alter the act of **Peter Butterworth.** I was quite horrified, as Peter had been booked before I had taken over. The thought of the humiliation for Peter really upset me. He and I walked along the Pier and I diplomatically got to the nub of the act, and being the lovely artist he was, and the good sense with which he was imbued, we discussed and finalised the changes. All being happily effected, the act was accepted by the Entertainments Director.

With all the tough business men in our profession, including those who would eat their own young,. London was a rough place, where you could be taken for a ride very easily. The big boys kept their foot on the little boys. Being the Baker Street office was more difficult than I thought, and it was lonely, I just wanted Friday to come as soon as possible, so that I could get the train from Euston, back to my girl and North Wales.

There were summer shows at Hastings, Weston-super-Mare, Lowestoft and Felixstowe. The opening night at Lowestoft was tremendous. I stayed the week with the rehearsals.

In charge of thirteen different productions.

Bernie Clifton was the star. He was quite out of this world. Bernie made sure the whole company was involved with all his comedy wheezes. There were numerous props for this show, Bernie invented so much business, that props dominated. His own spots, and especially "The Red Shadow" were solid. He had an exceptional singing voice, and it was exciting to be in his company. The show was an outstanding hit. After the opening night I drove through the night, across the country to Llandudno. The route from east to west in Britain is horrendous.

My compliment of shows were as follows :- Summer shows at the Arcadia Theatre, Pier Pavilion Llandudno, White Rock Pavilion, Hastings, Spa Theatre, Felixstowe, Sparrows Nest, Lowestoft. Floral Pavilion, New Brighton, Pier Pavilion, Cromer. Playhouse, Weston Super Mare. Marine Theatre, Burnham on Sea. Pantomimes at Lewisham, Hastings, Aldershot, Weston-Super-Mare, Arcadia, Llandudno, Hayes, Middx. I later added the Mecca at Grays and Palace Morecambe. It was very stimulating to employ so many artists who were not on star salaries. When you think there were approximately an average of 16 to 20 artists in each venue, I was involved with many friends who happened to be good performers.
After my journey from Lowestoft to Llandudno, I checked on the Celebrity Concert at the Pier, and then instead of getting the train to London, I was off in the car, at 7 a.m. to Weston-Super-Mare. Band call for the opening on the monday night The bill was topped by **Los Zafiros.** The band call was going through without any problems, until Bunny and Lisa Baron arrived. **Jack Martin** was the Entertainments Director.
Los Zafiros were going through their music, and I thought their music was all the same tempo, and in Spanish, I was not happy, nor was Jack Martin. Jack went straight to Bunny and complained about the sameness of the music, Bunny went into a nervous state, and in a depressed mood, said to me "You'll have to sort it" he was now like a man possessed.

I said "I already have in mind how to sort it out", "Go now mate" he said excitedly, Jack came to me, of course I was the new boy, Jack could see I was already to have a word with the "boys".

Going up on to the stage, I managed to stop the rehearsal. They didn't know me from Denis Compton. Quietly I pointed out that the patrons would not accept five slow numbers in succession, and not in Spanish. I suggested two fast numbers, and in English. They agreed, all was well, and they were a great hit that night, and for the season. Bunny had now calmed down, and we went for a drink at lunchtime. I could see that the nervous system, was beginning to pull Bunny down, and his health was very slowly deteriorating. Bunny and I had a good rapport. I must say, he was exceptionally supportive of me. I took my hat off to him, he did not interfere with me in any way. If the roles had been reversed, I am sure I would be making suggestions and generally interfering, especially as it was my firm. But no, Bunny went along with everything I did. I didn't let him know everything, as I realised he would worry, and that would not be good for his health.

Off to Hastings to get the show with great possibilities, open and up and running. *Freddie (Parrot Face) Davies,* I had booked to star and produce. Fred had a flair for production, although he was a comic, he had great taste for nice production scenes with a good selection of appropriate music. Having this successfully accepted by the public, I was able to go back to Llandudno to see to the tremendous programme I had lined up. Having two venues with Sunday Concerts, Two revue type summer shows, and an orchestra at the Pier Theatre, with all the star names that were *really* stars coming to the town, I realised that in Llandudno, we were rightly called "The Entertainment Centre of Wales". North Wales was contributing to this accolade, whereas North Wales was usually forgotten by the Principality.

The Concerts at the Astra Theatre were slow to start, we had a disappointment, inasmuch that **Eddie Large** had an appendicitis, and could not appear. The bill was changed to read **Cannon & Ball.** Now Tommy & Bobby had only been seen in the Clubs. Gwen and I knew of them, as we had worked on the same bill in the "Rub a dub dubs" in South Yorkshire. Our visitors were not familiar with their brilliant comedy. **Michael Barrymore** was in support, but he had not yet become famous. It was a financial downer. It broke even over all, and the Pier Sundays were as good as ever.

Back to Baker Street and the preparations for pantomime for Hastings, Weston Super Mare, Aldershot, and Lewisham. I had negotiated a new venue through Mecca. I did a very good deal for a seven week pantomime. I made one mistake, and that was letting Bunny know I had taken a large cinema, and I was going to produce "Robinson Crusoe" starring **Charlie Drake.** Bunny went spare, Charlie had recently acquired a reputation for being trouble. He had a fall out with British Actor's Equity Association, and had been banned. When I told Bunny I had booked him, and in the bargain I had bought 3000 pieces of crockery, for the famous china smashing scene, he was out of control. He shouted "I'm not coming to see it, I don't want anything to do with it", Lisa said she would see it.

The cinema stage was bare, so we had to bring in our own gantry, a lighting rig. We used cut-outs mainly, and with the skill placing specials in advantageous places, we made some very attractive lighting effects. Robinson Crusoe starred **Charlie Drake,** with the fantastic dame, **Trevor Bannister.** and my particular friend **Valentine Dyall.** Val and I talked cricket most of the time. We had a first class company for a 7 week run.

There was a tentative feeling of apprehension in case Charlie mis-behaved. **Alec Myles** was the producer, and very well he did.

Charlie was wonderful, he did not complain about anything, and he had every right, for the dressing rooms were portakabins, and there was water seaping in everywhere, it never stopped raining. Considering all the drawbacks, we mounted a very good show, but the cinema was too large for the catchment area. I had negotiated a very good guarantee, and a handsome profit ensued.

The Lewisham pantomime was giving Richard a headache, I had put him in as Stage Director, and it was not easy for him. The subject was "Babes in the Wood" with what I called the **Richard Stone** repertory company. **Ian Lavender, Bill Pertwee, Melvyn Hayes and John Gordon.** It mean't that there were two from "Dad's Army" and two from "It Ain't Half Hot Mum" It seemed to be a continual war between the two shows. There were temperaments between these four performers, while **Craig Douglas** and Richard tried to keep the peace. I was very surprised at these talented artistes behaving as they did. Despite all this unease, the show was successful. I used to wait each night for a call from Richard to say that the whole thing had blown up, or that his car had broken down again, and he wanted help.

The two week pantomime at Hastings always seemed to be happy, although we booked the artistes for this one at the last minute, it seemed to be a case of "What's left".We used to find that there were many excellent performers happy to do only two weeks. **Roger Dennett** was the Entertainments Officer at the time, and he was still playing cricket for Hastings, so we used to swap many stories. I never saw him play, but I had it on good authority, that he was more than useful. My rapport with the entertainments officers of the various councils was good, Gwen and I had appeared for many of them. The Aldershot pantomime was difficult to mount. The Princes Hall, was not a theatre as such, it had a very shallow stage. It was a joy to have **John Junkin** starring, not only a versatile man, but a writer to boot.

The Fulcrum Theatre at Slough asked us to do a pantomime.
This 400 seater had all the modern facilities to mount a splendid
production. *Freddie Davies* produced a wonderful show. It had
class and a high standard of performance, and great comedy. The
music chosen was melodious and popular, and very up to date..

Billing has always been a ticklish point with some artists. I believe
Webster Booth used to surreptitiously measure with a ruler, the
size of his name on the posters. I had a problem with Richard
Stone. We had *Aimee MacDonald and Peter Goodwright* in a
show, and both came from the Richard Stone stable. Richard said,
"Of course they must both have their names, sharing top of the bill,
in the same size type." Later it transpired that Aimee, was to be in
bigger type than Peter. I did one of my optical illusion tricks, by
measuring the same space exactly, with a surround, Aimee in
slightly larger type than Peter, so looking at the poster head on,
they looked exactly the same size.

1978 was a settling down year, I knew I had taken on more than
enough, but it was all working out. Richard came in as Production
and Company manager, and this took some of the load off my
shoulders. Casting all the shows took patience, and with the Bunny
Baron office taken the majority of my time, I had to make sure I
was not letting Robbie down in any way, He expected me to have
all the casting done for Llandudno, Cromer and New Brighton.
In March, at Easter, Richard and Kay were married. It was a very
cold and windy day, and we were all bbblown to bbb.......y. I had
an Easter Show in at the Arcadia and during the wedding breakfast,
I kept popping backward and forward from the hotel to the theatre.
I had a speech to make, and it only coincided with an entrance to
the hotel. The wedding was lovely. Kay looked delicious. At the
dance in the evening the wonderful *Reg Dixon* came in and sang
"Confidentially". Reg was a lovely human being, and his warm
and infectious comedy made a special contribution to a very happy
and memorable day.

Barry Kent being such a popular favourite with the Llandudno audience, I had no hesitation in bringing him back for 1978, and the comedy would be in the hands of a very underrated comic, *Frankie Holmes.* together with *Don Reid, Carol & Roger Bryan, Ann Harriman, Jimmie Webster, Lesley Anne Riding, Sally Henderson, The Showtimers and the Les Brown Orchestra* they all made another successful season.

At the Pier Pavilion on Monday nights *Wyn Calvin's Guest Night.* Guests included , *Willie Wyse, Love'n' Stuff, Llewellyn Williams, and Albert Tinkler. Gwen* also played on the Monday night. Tuesday to Saturday *The Clifford Henry Show* with *Sugar & Spice, Janice Armstrong, Richard Naylor and Jackie Allen & Barbara.* The seed of nightly shows was growing in my head, it would flower later.

Stars for our Sunday Concerts included *The Bachelors, Miki & Griff, Beverley Sisters, Semprini, Hinge & Bracket, Edmund Hockridge, Moira Anderson*, The first concert of the season was on the Whit Bank holiday Sunday, for this date we had booked our good friend *Russ Conway.* Unfortunately the doctors had told Russ he must not work for three months. Robbie and I were in a quandary, who could we get to replace him, and at such short notice, and Bank Holiday Sunday at that. We phoned Austin Gleave who had contact with many bands and musicians. He suggested that we book *The Millionaires Orchestra.* Some of the lads were from the *Syd Lawrence Orch.* the Millionaires were probably one of the best in the north. Sunday 28th May 1978 saw "The Millionaires" at the Pier Pavilion, a great feast for those who appreciated big band music. Robbie and I, being musicians were looking forward to this concert. We went into the circle to hear the music, and there was not another soul in sight. The stalls were fair, we had lost about £1200. We loved every minute of the concert. Thats how we were, we loved our work.

July 9 we brought *Hinge & Bracket* to Llandudno for the first time. I had to find special furniture, aspidistras, antimacassars. but it was all worth it, the audience loved them, and there were 1500 bums on seats. On the 10th September I had booked for the first time *The King's Singers,* this was the only date they had available. I suggested to Bernard Kay during their rehearsal, that it would enhance their performance, if they put two microphones into the pit out of sight, so that the bass part of the arrangements would not be lost. He would not countenance this at all. I said that my audience were a bit "Mutt and Jeff", and that it was a large theatre. He was most adamant, and quite objectionable. I threw in, I am paying you. He was quite offensive, he knew best. It all happened as I thought, half way back, our patrons could not hear, so at the interval, they started to leave. I was very disappointed. Artistes sometime never give us credit for knowing our own venues, and audiences.

On the Bank Holiday Sunday on August 27th, we had a triumph. *Little & Large* who could not play the year before, because of the appendicitis, made it up to us, by doing two shows on that night at the Astra, and *Windsor Davies & Don Estelle* came to the Pier Pavilion to do two shows. I must point out, Llandudno is not a twice nightly town, nightly at 8 is the perfect timing. . *Norman Murray* kept phoning up to see if we had sold out both houses, and when I said we had not, he was most upset. He said "this must be for the birds, and we were only helping you out because of Eddie's illness."I said "This is Llandudno, people arrive on Saturday, and if they are attracted to the top of the bill, they will book. don't worry it will work itself out"

Sunday morning, the usual queues at the Pier Pavilion from 10 a.m. went from the box office to the Cenotaph, and stayed there until 12.45 p.m. At the Astra I had sold out the second house, and the first house was filling up. It was marvellous, I ended up with 1300 seats sold for the first house at the Pier and 1800 for the second house.

At the Astra, the first house was 4 short of the full house, and the second house was full at 1645. So on the Bank Holiday in the Queen of the Welsh Resorts, we had six thousand three hundred and eighty six people enjoying a live show. It was an achievement that has never been , or likely to be surpassed. Robbie and I were ecstatic. Llandudno was surely the entertainment capital of Wales. My sincere thanks go to *Little & Large* for their generous and ethical action in making up to me the disappointment of the year before. Real performers are real people.

Russell Gradwell, who I mentioned earlier used to follow me into the bank on some Monday mornings, warning everybody therein, not to get in the queue behind Clive Stock, as you would be ages before you got to the teller. I was putting in two theatre's Sunday night takings, and the Pier Pavilion and Arcadia returns for the friday and saturday. It looked good, but soon most of it was paid out.

Being the Managing Director of the Bunny Baron Organsation, put me, not only as a member of the TMA...Theatrical Management Association, but a member of the negotiating committee. This entailed meetings with British Actor's Equity Association regarding salaries for the forthcoming pantomime season. It was a little new to me, but being a member of Equity from 1943, I was on both sides so to speak. The first series of meetings were very worrying. Equity had threatened to strike all members for the pantomime season. They were in the driving seat, as there were hundreds and thousands of pounds already in the box offices in the theatres in the U.K. The Musicians' Union had always increased their rates regularly, so the increases were borne by the managements without steep and sudden rises. Equity on the other hand had made spasmodic rises. The dancing girls paid the price of the dilatory attitude of their Union. I remember many years ago, when the minimum wage for chorus was eighteen pounds a week of 8 shows, we had 8 girls. Equity suddenly demanded £32 a week.

This meant we had to cut to six girls, this made unemployment even worse. In 1943, as I said before, there were 90% of the profession out of work. Nothing has changed, it is still the same today.

As chairman of our committee, was one *Charles Vance.* Charles was an actor-manager-producer, and really should have been a lawyer. His artistry with words was masterly. Alongside me were *William Dickie (Richard Stone) John Newman (Newpalm) Gilbert Harrison (Triumph) David Kirk and Nat Day. John Barron* was the mouth piece for Equity, and on one meeting *Kenneth Williams* attended. He vaguely acknowledged me, and proceeded to say nothing.

We were all in a state of apprehension as the threat of strike was getting nearer, and we were not sure of the number of dancers we could employ. We had knots in our stomachs, and the feeling was nauseous. If the strike had happened, and all Equity members had withdrawn their labour. The outcome would have been a catastrophe. Thanks to the common sense of that fine actor *John Barron* and the skill of *Charles Vance,* a successful compromise was reached, and we all breathed safely again.

1978 had been very busy, and all the different enterprises had afforded me great experience. *Alan Randall & Roger Kitter* followed the tremendous success of *Bernie Clifton* at Lowestoft. It was not as entertaining as the 1977 season, but the two stars were outstanding. Felixstowe had a few problems, the show starred *Dailey & Wayne and Joan Savage,* but we had a pianist who was sub standard, and I was in the position of "guvnor", I had to sack him. On the way to Felixstowe I had a blow out, the tyre was split completely. I was shattered and when I arrived dear *Joan Savage* had coffee ready for me, and tried to calm me down.

247

A gamble with change every night.

In one of the Felixstowe summer shows, we booked a young very good all round comedian, by the name of **Lenny Henry** He was a big man, and was larger than life, he made an immediate hit, and it was obvious he was to become one of our outstanding comics. He always made you feel welcome whenever you came backstage to see him, and he always called me "Meester Stock". In the show I had a young baritone named **Graham Cole,** a good looking singer, who turned actor, you will know him as Tony Stamp" from television's "The Bill". Graham was tall and easy on the eye, and it was anticipated that he would have a successful future. He also happened to have a very easy personality. I used him in pantomime at Morecambe.

The after dinner scene was beginning to change, and many functions were cutting out the entertainment altogether. The "Master's Song" was declining, lodges were starting to get one of their own members to sing to cut the costs. The cabaret act was being dispensed with. I thought about it seriously, and I decided to take a different approach. With the contact of so many secretaries, when they wanted the "The Ladies Song" I suggested that I sing it, and then after the presentation to the lady President, I should come back and sing a medley, that I had arranged especially for the ladies. This would last about twenty five minutes maximum. I would get a good fee, and they didn't have to pay for a cabaret, this also meant the dancing would be non stop. This became very popular and I was now busier than ever, my popularity with my fellow performers probably changed, as I was cutting the number of engagements available.

We now enter 1979, the Pier Pavilion was my first planning job. I gathered some fine performers to feed my new concept of a different show every night, except Saturdays. I started contracting, and finalised Mondays..*Wyn Calvin, Syd Francis, The Authentics, Ceinwen Roberts, Andy Squires and Jean & Rex Lear.* Tuesdays..*Dai Francis, Jackie Knight, Willie Wyse and the Barcias.*

Now theatre owners.

Wednesdays...*Welsh Serenade with Gari Williams, The Llanddulas Choir and Harpist..Heulwen Haf,* Thursdays..*Variety Memories with Billy (Uke) Scott, Roy Minting, Cody & Oran, Bob Rogers, and starring ANNE ZIEGLER & WEBSTER BOOTH.* Friday nights, "Mr & Mrs" starring *Derek Batey, Gwen Overton & Clive Stock, Jackie Allen & Barbara.* **All married couples.** The Sunday stars were being scheduled to correspond with the different parts of the season. Early...semi classical, late July and August....The flavour of the day. Then back to semi classical for the end of the Sunday season.

I brought Jack Martin up to Llandudno from Weston Super Mare, to show him my shows for changing every night, he was impressed, but he said "We'll never do that in Weston" It was amusing, as the following season, he did exactly that. He changed every night, using *Semprini and John Hanson.*

There was still a lot to prepare, but I had to stop momentarily, as Robbie and I had a rush of blood. In 1976 Gwen and I had a rush of blood, by buying the Flats, and now Robbie and I were making history repeat itself. Out of the blue we bought the Palace Theatre, Morecambe. The usual legal matters were taking up a little time, there was good and bad publicity, implying that Robbie and I were going to leave *Ronnie Coyles,* out of the forthcoming season, Ronne had played 10 seasons at the Palace. The locals were up in arms, we took on board all these groundless rumours, and finally on the 30th March, The Stage newspaper had the headline, *Music Men buy Morecambe Palace.* other headlines were :- *Theatre's curtain of gloom is lifted. Palace promise of Live Shows. Palace sold but show goes on.* This just over a thousand seater was ours. The theatre had had a good track record. *Hedley Claxton* had presented some excellent summer shows there, and although *Sybil Sheldon* had let the building get into a bad state of repair, the whole new operation was a challenge.

So as not to have too much aggravation, and give ourselves more extra tension with all the shows in the pipeline, we let *Ronne Coyles,* perform the season, he had roughed out. I could see by the returns of the past three years, the takings had been reducing every year, and a new approach was inevitable. With all the artistes I had at my disposal, it could be quite an easy transition to up market the show. This would happen in 1980.

In Baker Street, I was planning the summer and some pantomimes for the future. Having contracted Easter at the Arcadia, I suddenly realized I had not booked the top of the bill for the forthcoming summer at the Arcadia. This rattled me, I was usually well on top of things, but on this occasion, I was not like my Boy Scout training, definitely not the motto "Be Prepared". This was a time to assess my life, the whole involvement was probably a little too much, especially being all over the Country. Basically, I was feeling the strain of being parted from Gwen, we had been together all our professional lives, and now in the twilight of our years we were apart, I was unhappy.

Having no star for the Summer at the Arcadia, I felt I was letting Robbie down, so I did something I had never done before, I telephoned *Kenny Earle,* a good pro, artist and agent. He was looking after an act that I had great admiration for *Hope &Keen.* I gave Kenny an ultimatum, I said "Kenny I want Mike and Albie for the summer in Llandudno, I can pay so much, and I want an answer, one way or the other, by 4.30 p.m." It was then 2 p.m. Never had I held a pistol to anyone's head before. It was sheer desperation. The call came at 4.30 p.m. YES, it was O.K. Now the publicity had to be put into place, and with all the other shows over the country, I felt real pressure.
The shows for the Bunny Baron outfit, I quickly cast for the main artists, leaving only a few spots to be filled. Even the stars for the pantomime season had been booked.

The preparation for Hastings, Weston Super Mare, Felixstowe, Lowestoft were completed. The decision had to be made, I either stayed in Baker Street, and became one of the busiest impresarios in London, or I had contentment and happiness, and went to Llandudno to be with my wife, and also my partner Robbie Cleaver.

With Lisa Baron, being the main Director, as Bunny had sadly passed away, I had a discussion. "Would you release me from my contract, I have programmes and casts all under control, I feel that there is not a lot to do" Lisa kindly let me go, and my old friend *Freddie Davies* took over my position. I was off like a shot to North Wales. There was plenty to do. To produce the show with Hope and Keen, and book all the Sunday Concerts.

"Showtime 79" was a lovely show with the sons of *Syd and Max Harrison. (Hope & Keen)* add *Ken Wood, Karan Simmons, Julie Llusion, Alexander Joannou, The Showtimers* and the *Les Brown Orchestra.* A very strong show, to compliment this versatile group of performers, I brought in a good friend, *Barry Daniels.* Barry was a fine baritone, but also a first class impressionist. *Larry Grayson, Roy Lance, Barry Daniels and myself,* were prolific reminiscing fanatics on old film stars from the twenties up and until the sixties. We signed letters and postcards names like :- *Marion Davies, James Dunn, Jed Prouty, Slim Summerville*, and stars of that ilk. The four of us tried hard to out do each other, and a lot of fun was had by all.

The Sundays at the Pier Pavilion included *Russ Conway, Semprini, Bobby Crush, Beverley Sisters, Tammy Jones, Moira Anderson, Miki & Griff, and Frankie Vaughan.* Gwen and I had known Frank in the 60's. When we got together on the first Sunday, Frank said "I am going to give you a great show" and so he did. When he moved his *"V Men"* in with all the equipment, speakers, mics, amplifiers, I thought of my elderly patrons and the sound.

I need not have worried, the balance was the most perfect, and my people thought he was wonderful, and so he was. In the middle of his act, he brought me on stage to talk to him. It was ad lib and real magic. He came to see us twice and gave us two superb evenings and sell outs.

The STAGE newspaper each summer held a party for all the stars of the various resorts. It was usually Blackpool or Yarmouth, but on the 9th August 1979 it was featured at the St. Georges' Hotel, Llandudno. The photographs included *Michael Forte (Charles Forte's brother)* patron of the North Wales Arts. among those attending were *Anne Ziegler, Webster Booth, Mike Hope, Wyn Calvin, Derek Batey, Albie Keen, Billy (Uke) Scott, Alex Munro, Russ Conway, Ivor Emmanuel, Ken Wood, Gwen Overton, Barry Daniels, Julie Llusion, The Minting family, Jackie Allen & Barbara, all the girls, and my partner and I* being responsible for all the artistes in town on that day. It was a great party. There was tremendous prestige for Llandudno in the National press.

One day I strolled into the Arcadia to collect some mail, and I received a letter on the St. George's Hotel, headed notepaper. :-
Dear Mr. Stock.
Last night I came to your show, I thought it was excellent. I come from the U.S.A. and we do not have shows like this. I hope you would come across the water, and present this type of show for us. In the meantime, Good Luck to you and all the artistes,
Signed..............*Walter Slezak.*

Can you imagine my delight, wonderful Walter Slezak in the town, and comes to see my show. I was on to the local newspaper. The answer from the press office, and a young receptionist, was "Who's Walter Slezak ?" I was bubbling, "Have you never heard of Walter Slezak ??" "He made many films as a villain, surely you saw "The Pirate, with *Gene Kelly.*"

252

I eventually managed to get hold of a reporter, but the same reply, no one had heard of Walter Slezak. Telephoning the St. Georges' Hotel, I wanted to know the room number. No one by that name staying, there were two foreign sounding names. It was arranged that a reporter and photographer would meet me in the vestibule of the hotel. When we all arrived, they intimated that the foreign looking gentleman, as I had described, had left the hotel. It was very frustrating, and I was disappointed.

I went to the theatre that night, and told the company, how we had had a letter from Walter Slezak, praising the show. I then, started to read the letter, and as I was reading I caught the eye of **Barry Daniels,** I paused for a moment, and I looked him straight in the face, as he smiled, I said, " You B-----d, You wrote the letter on the hotel paper".. We could all see the joke. Barry had tried to get one over on me with the old time stars, and he really succeeded.

The Palace Theatre, Morecambe starred **Ronne Coyles, Ronnie G. Finch, Jane Harrod, Howard Layton, Irene Stephens, Impact, Simon Browne.** My policy was to use the theatre, and as they had not had Sunday concerts before, I put in Sunday Concerts, these featured **Hope & Keen, Miki & Griff. Moira Anderson, Dai Francis, Russ Conway, Ken Goodwin,** Ken's car broke down, and he got a taxi all the way from Oxford to Morecambe, what a "pro". Talking of "pros" I put **Kitty Gillow** in an old time Music Hall. When my Richard saw this little old lady come through the stage door, he thought his father had lost it, but of course, **Kitty Gillow** when dressed was immaculate, she stormed them. Kitty was one of our foremost Male Impersonators. During that Sunday concert season, **The Houghton Weavers** were outstanding, and they helped to raise the standard, and they stimulated the Sunday habit. The variety in artistes was comprehensive, and we started to have patrons that didn't usually go to the summer show. It was great to see people frequenting the venue.

Trevor Stanford alias RUSS CONWAY.

"I'm looking for a piano, Oh yes I said a piano" Salad Days.
Dorothy Reynolds & Julian Slade.

Russ Conway was probably one of the most consistent and successful entertainers, we ever had in the North West.. His first performance at the Palace Theatre, Morecambe was most interesting. Thinking he would have the audience eating out of his hand, he for some unknown reason lost his way. Russ had a habit of having a few envelopes on the piano, that had "Jokes" written thereon. He started to talk and began to lose the attention of the audience. I was standing at the back, and there were murmurs of "Play" "Stop talking and play". I felt very uneasy and made my way through the auditorium, and through the pass door. I positioned myself behind a black leg (side masking curtain) and quietly said, so Russ could hear. "LOVE STORY", he began to play this tune. There came another blank, so I whispered "Pal Joey", Russ did a lovely selection from "Pal Joey", and after I had, through the tabs, said "All The Things You Are", Russ got on to his usual routine, and built to a standing ovation. I went on at the end to thank him for coming to Morecambe, there were tears for both of us. I remember Russ saying :- "Steady feller" Russ always gave me little heart flutters, as he would suddenly be quite contrary. He gave me a real fright at the Pier, Llandudno one night.

I arrived one Sunday, nearing the interval, only to find his loyal recording lady waiting for me. With anxiety in her voice she said, "Russ is not going on" He is definitely not appearing" The show was coming to the end of the first half. *The Llanddulas Male Voice Choir,* were coming to the end of their programme. Straight way to the dressing room to see the virtuoso, and ostensibly to enquire about his health, Russ greeted me in his usual courteous manner. I steered clear of any thought of not appearing, and entered in to the usual small talk. Russ suddenly talked about the arthritis in his hands. he thought it was through not playing enough. He then, demonstrated with his stiff fingers.

He was only playing regularly twice a week, with alacrity and cunning, I said "I have an idea that might be the solution". he was interested. "It is only a germ of an idea, there is possible mileage, in incorporating the Palace, Morecambe and the Arcadia, Llandudno...two nights at each per week, and this may give you the exercise", "that would be great" Russ said. The question of pianos was going to cause grave problems, as Russ and I had slight variance with pianos. Anyway he was now in a good mood and happy, and as I left him, I beamed "The audience are absolutely ready and waiting for you" he quietly said "Thank you Doctor Stock" he went on and paralysed them. We had a real love-hate relationship, that continued up to his death.

During my last days with the Bunny Baron office, Gwen was looking for a house to suit us, as we were going to sell everything in London, and come to North Wales permanently. With the company of her close friend Irene Allen of the act *Jackie Allen & Barbara,* Irene was BARBARA, they were very close pals. Irene always seemed to know where the good properties were. They came to Llandudno to live in 1978, like so many artistes who came to the Arcadia, they loved North Wales, and made their roots in Llandudno. Irene & Gwen found two possible, suitable houses. I came up to look, and favoured 12 Tan-y-Bryn Road, Rhos on Sea. This was a very large property, standing in a large grassy area surrounded by very large and tall trees. The front lawn was originally a tennis court with ample room around. My first thought, was that it would be a great cricket pitch, there was length for a good run up to bowl. The house contained large tall rooms, 4 reception, 6 bedrooms, 2 bathrooms, 3 toilets. There was the alternative of turning it into a separate flat. We were thinking of this for my mother, so she could be self contained. My mother had lived with us all our married life.

We decided on this large house, it had been built in 1906, and belonged to Sir Arthur Cayley, the Squire of the area at that time.

So on the 16th October, 1979 it was ours. We named the house *"Dilkusha"* as our former residence. I had burned my boats, ties with London severed, and now a resident of North Wales.

After a fine production of "Aladdin" in 79, we produced "Dick Whittington" at the Palace, Morecambe with a popular cast. Having two theatres to ride in sinc, made casting a challenge with trying to bring artists in with a view to the future summer shows in either theatre. Summer show theatres were busy in the holiday period, but did very little to attract audiences in the winter. Richard and Kay were battling with the cold of Morecambe, the theatre was having burst pipes, and generally the theatre was suffering from the lack of maintainance in the past. There was very little we could put in the theatre in such a dreadful winter, the one re-deeming and warming feature, was that in the January, Kay gave birth to our first grandchild. The birth of Kerry Ann was a complete joy to us all. Kerry Ann Jimmy (As I called her) gave Richard and Kay plenty to keep their days occupied.

There were two shows booked for the Palace, during the winter. One was "An Evening with *Mike Harding"* and the other was *Jasper Carrott.* . Owing to the sea coming up to the front of the theatre, sandbags had to be stacked, to keep the water out. *Carrott* , after taking the "Michael" out of the theatre, and everyone in it, mentioned the sandbags. In his strong midland accent he said "Haven't they told them the war is over".

For the Easter show, we brought *Ronne Coyles* to Llandudno and *Frankie Holmes* to Morecambe. This gave Robbie and I a chance to see how their talent registered in another town, with a view to giving them a full season later.

Sundays were now regularly at two theatres in Llandudno, at the Astra Theatre we had *Leslie Crowther, Dickie Henderson, Ken Goodwin, Ted Rogers, Roger De Courcey, Freddie Davies and Harry Worth.* At the Pier :-*Moira Anderson, Miki & Griff, Bobby Crush, Beverley Sisters, Anne Ziegler & Webster Booth,*

So busy with so many artists.

We brought in *Tammy Jones, Ruby Murray* and a golfing pal of mine:- *Thomas Round with Gilbert & Sullivan for all.* Tommy was the Peter Pan of all tenors, and Robbie of course accompanied each programme.

Sundays at Morecambe included *Thomas Round with the Gilbert & Sullivan for all, Moira Anderson, Bobby Crush, Miki & Griff and Tommy Trinder.*

For the Pier Pavilion, Llandudno summer season we featured a new star from "T.V's YOUR 100 BEST HYMNS" the voice of *Valerie Monese, Roy Lance, Sugar & Spice, The Kobaks Family, Liz & Kim,* and starring the one and only *Tommy Trinder,* Tom became a very good friend, we fixed him up with a good flat with a friend of ours, he was very comfortable, he said I had restored his faith in the Grand Order of Water Rats.

His success was legendary. Starting as a juvenile singer in "Casey's Court" a show that started *Charlie Chaplin,* He had held the star spot at the London Palladium longer than any other artiste. Twelve Royal Command performances, The first compere of T.V's Beat the Clock" in Sunday Night at the London Palladium, this man was a regular world beater. A season in Latin Quarter, New York, and also the Desert Sands, Las Vegas. His films included The Bells Go Down, Champagne Charlie and the award winning film "The Foreman Went To France.
Tommy had been the King Rat of the Grand Order of Water Rats..three times. In 1975 he was honoured in the Birthday Honours List with the C.B.E. Past President of the Lords Taverners, and of course Director and Chairman of the Fulham Football Club. It was a joy to have him in Llandudno.

Tom, as I called him, had a very long career in the world of entertainment. So there were many stories about his exploits.

When Trinder, performing in a West End night club, introduced himself one night, with **Orson Welles** in the audience, "Good evening. If it's laughter you're after then Trinder's the name....you lucky people !" "Well why don't you change it ?", growled **Welles** with menace in his voice. As quick as a flash, Trinder came back, "Is that a proposal of marriage ?". Tommy Trinder was the epitome of your typical cockney comic. He was a great favourite with the Royal Family, havin appeared beforethem on many occasion. The great story, that has been repeated time and time again, was the time when Tom appeared before the Duke and Duchess of York. When next Tom appeared before them, after he had attained majoe stardom, and the Duke had become King George the Sixth, the King said to Tom at the end of the show , "well Tommy, you've climbed high in your profession, since last we met. " Trinder's reply was the classic: "If you don't mind me saying so sir, you haven't done so badly yourself !". Tom was born in 1909, the son of a Tram driver, and left us in 1989 at 80.

Robbie and I were bringing some "tried and true" performers to the "Naples of the North". They were very much the flavour for the visitors that came to North Wales. The discerning middle aged public, who frequented our hotels, were good old solid supporters of Variety and Music Hall.

Right through the gambit of entertainment, there was always the discernment of quality and skill of the performer, North Wales would not accept the mediocre.

At the Arcadia, I did a policy that had only been a dream when I had spoken to Russ Conway that night in the dressing room. "Showtime 1980" had **Russ Conway** on Mondays and Tuesdays.

Dai Francis on Wednesdays and Thursdays, and **Derek Batey** with his "Mr & Mrs" on Fridays and Saturdays, with a full supporting show and **Barry Johns** as host.

At Morecambe *"Tonight at 7.30" John Hanson* on Mondays and Tuesdays, **Russ Conway** on Wednesdays and Thursdays, and **Dai Francis** on Fridays and Saturdays with full supporting cast and **Ronne Coyles** as host of each programme. Our son Richard had a full and busy programme to look after. The laugh was that **John Hanson** used to meet **Russ Conway** on the way down the M6 while Russ was on the way up. It all dove tailed and the seasons were happy and successful. Russ was very taken with Richard and his family. For some unknown reason he called the baby Kerry..."Perkins", we never understood why, but he was very helpful to Richard.

With Russ, the question of pianos was always a bone of contention. He very kindly brought his own Steinway to the Arcadia for the season, and it was up to us to take really good care of this excellent instrument. Halfway through the season, Russ asked me to come underneath the stage, as he thought the whole theatre was on a slope, and there were some imaginary stalagmites in the basement. This was all fantasy. I convinced him that there were no problems. He reluctantly accepted this, though I wondered what the next figment of his imagination would be.

Through being so busy I did not have much time for cricket or social get togethers. One Sunday morning at the new house, we had a coffee and drinks party, Gwen, Robbie and I enjoyed it very much with our loyal artists, it was nice to have a social gathering, and chat about the business, in the comfort of our own home. **Webster Booth, Leslie Booth** as he was known to us, was sitting in a large armchair, with me sitting on the arm, we sang together, the Wilfred Sanderson classic.....................

From :-Anne Ziegler & Webster Booth to John Inman.

As I sit here, remembering you
The scented dusk, like blessing falls,
The Flowers lie dreaming in the dew,
and sun gleams red on old red walls. On eves like this it used to
be, That life was full and love was new, but now there's nothing
left for me ,But to sit here,   remembering you.

Oh what a wonderful voice Leslie Booth had. He was one of our
leading tenors in the days of Heddle Nash, Walter Widdop and
Walter Midgley. His singing of the traditional ballads and the
operatic arias, was so delightful, that I listen to him regularly on
my tapes. It was a tragedy when he passed away with terminal
Alzheima's. I was privileged to know him. As I write, this is 2002,
Anne Ziegler is still alive, and lives here, in Llandudno.

One of my quick notions, was on learning **John Inman,** who had
shot to the top of the popularity parade, was to go to Blackpool for
the summer season. He had made a tremendous hit in T.V's "Are
You Being Served". I telephoned **Bill Roberton,** an old friend of
mine, who was looking after John, and suggested he do some
Sunday Concerts for us at the Pier. Blackpool being just two hours
away, I felt it would be ideal for John to pop down the M6 on a
Sunday. Bill thought it would be a good idea, but said "John
hasn't got an act". Not wanting to teach my grandmother to suck
eggs, I quietly said to Bill. "He <u>must</u> have an act" you have got a
very hot property television star, and he **must** have an act" I made
it a bit difficult for him, by telling him of the restrictions, about
Sundays, no props, no wigs, no cross patter or dancing.
My suggestion was that he could host the whole programme, do
short introductions, and intimated the "camp" he could have with
the Male Voice Choir. He said he would talk to John about it, and
come back. John had thought about it, and back came the idea that
he had two spots of about 6 minutes each. When John arrived to
do the rehearsal, he told me he had another spot to make three all
together.

The clever way out that John had contrived was to have an actor in the audience, who was very good indeed, he heckled him through his performance, and they did a double act from stage to auditorium. The Chief Constable could not object to that. John was absolutely sensational, the actor in the stalls was **Raymond Bowers**, a very experienced performer. It is always a nice feeling when you book an artist that you like and that you believe in. The public forget that **John Inman** was a very well established straight character actor, I saw him in 1972 at Blackpool, playing a 90 year old father-in-law of **Jack Douglas** in the "Love Nest". The versatility of John's talent, made him one of the country's best Dames in pantomime, his "Mother Goose" being probably one of the greatest of all time. John was our King Rat in 1993, and left his personal mark on the year.

On the 12th February, 1981 **Freddie (Parrot Face) Davies** organized a cruise on the Fred Olsen ship "Blenheim". this was called the "*The Showboat Cruise with the Grand Order of Water Rats*" SAIL TO THE SUN WITH THE STARS" The show included **Dickie Henderson, Sandy Powell, Freddie Davies, The Bachelors, Gwen Overton & Clive Stock Peter Goodwright, Alan Freeman, Harry Stanley (Music Hall Lecture). Louis Valentine** (A remarkable artist) **and Pat Dodd,** our versatile accompanist. Five per cent of the fares were given to the GOWR charity. The ship called at Madeira, Lanzarote, Tenerife and Gran Canaria. It was for 13 days. The whole experience was a laugh. Sandy Powell could never find his cabin, he was not a very good sailor, we would often find him strolling along the wrong deck looking for his cabin. Kay, his wife had to keep close to him. Kay joined him in the famous ventriloquist doll double. **Dickie Henderson, Gwen and I and Pat Dodd,** danced up the streets in Santa Cruz, it was a relaxing holiday, we only did two shows. **Dec Clusky** challenged me to a table tennis match, and his brother **Con Clusky,** roared with laughter as I took him apart. Apart from being my partner, Gwen was on board as a Lady Ratling.

Each night there was a different type of show, *Alan Freeman* did a "Pop Pickers" night, apart from his fantastic impersonations. *Peter Goodwright* with his wife Norma, arranged a Sunday service of worship, and *Louis Valentine,* taught passengers how to paint. The last night of the cruise, was a Music Hall. Sandy had been saved for this night. He had not been well, and many people came to see the show because *Sandy Powell* was topping the bill, and because he looked so poorly, they thought that this might be the last performance they would ever see. It was a great night, and when Sandy walked on to a terrific ovation, you could see 20 years drop of his life. What a magical performance. Freddie was congratulated on putting together such a wonderful cruise for us Water Rats.

"Showtime 81" continued with the formula of two night change. Monday and Tuesday nights *Moira Anderson,* Tuesday and Wednesday nights *Ivor Emmanuel,* and Friday and Saturdays, *Bobby Dennis & Frankie Holmes* with them a resident show including *The Twain Brothers, Sapphire, Kenny Barnes, Jackie Marks, The Showtimers and the Les Brown Orchestra.* To say it was a very strong show was an understatement, but it was overloaded financially, and I had made a big mistake. It was becoming very obvious that the number of visitors to the resorts of the U.K. were decreasing, and quickly. I wanted to take the show off at the end of June, and start again with a revised line up. Robbie would not hear of this, we had always been successful, and he didn't want to admit defeat. We asked the two main stars to take a cut, Ivor agreed, but not Moira, so we struggled along with a loss. If it hadn't been for the addition of *Kenneth McKellar, Ray Alan & Lord Charles, Ken Goodwin, Roger de Courcey, Dickie Henderson*, and *Billy Dainty* to our regular stars at the Pier on Sunday nights, we would not have broken even. I learned my lesson.

Those of you that know Llandudno, will remember that between
the Great Orme and the little Orme, there is a long sweeping bay. It
has often be called "The Naples of the North". On the front next to
the Arcadia Theatre, the Aberconwy Borough Council, built a 1.7
million pound conference complex. This was to be opened in the
October by Prince Charles and Princess Diana. Their first
engagement after their honeymoon. Advertisements, for a General
Manager, were being inserted into the local press together with the
Stage & Television Today, our profession's National newspaper.
Two local Councillors were hoping I would be interested in
becoming the General Manager of this prestigious Centre. I
thought very seriously about the proposition, I asked Gwen, what
she thought about the challenge. Her feeling was that whatever she
said, I would make up my own mind. With her usual wisdom, she
said "You have been your own boss for so long, how will you put
up with a Director above you, and others giving you orders ?" My
daughter-in-law, Kay said "Go for it Dad" This position was to
run the new building AND the Arcadia Theatre. On reflection I
had learned that the visitors were receding, and I realized that
risking my own money could come to grief, especially after the
season we were experiencing. I told the Councillors, I would wish
to be considered.

The rigmarole of all the forms and procedures that go with Council
business commenced. I filled in so many forms and finally there
was a short list of six to be considered. The candidates had come
from all over the U.K. We all were interviewed, and when we
were sitting outside the Council Chamber, awaiting the verdict, the
Town Clerk came out to tell us that none of us would be
considered. The post would be reviewed and regraded, and would
be advertised at a later date. My friends' the Councillors, told me,
that I had the best interview, and that I walked it, they were going
to readvertise   the post.

The Councillors expected me to try again, and were most upset when I said "I am not trying for it again, if I wasn't wanted the first time, I certainly wouldn't try again". I was still very busy with the day to day duties with the weekly show and the Sundays, and the Morecambe operation. There was no time to meditate on the new building, although the builders were nearly finished, and there was a joining section with the Arcadia that made the whole complex nearly ready for occupation.

The Council began new contacts, advertising and published more information regarding the regrading, and of course, the new salary. Three or four Councillors now came to me to try and change my mind about re-applying. They pointed out that the job attracted security, a pension, holidays with pay. and 36 hours a week, and other benefits. I had wanted this job all along. The Conference side of things would need concentration, but the Arcadia was my baby, and a continuous love affair I had with the venue.

The short list this time was down to four. I was last to arrive at the Council Chamber, only to find that an old friend *Gilbert Harrison* was a candidate. We were very pleased to see each other, apart from our theatrical connection, we had been at the Green Room Lodge at meetings and Ladies Nights. My heart sank. To be really honest, I considered him to be far more qualified for the post than me. With resignation in my being, I went into the Chamber to a full Council attendance, about 42 members in all. The interview seemed interminable. One main question was "How will you manage to accept that there is some one who has superiority over you" this was a hard one to answer, I thought and said "Well two heads are better that one" They wanted to know if my partner, Robbie, would be happy if I was accepted by the Aberconwy Borough Council. I had talked with Robbie, and he was thinking of retiring, so he was very amenable. The interview seemed to go on forever, finally I left the Council Chamber and I joined the other candidates.

We sat outside, and it was enjoyable having a chat with *Gilbert Harrison*. We spoke the same language, we were theatre people. Eventually the Town Clerk came out and said a few words to each of us, Gilbert and I were 3rd and 4th. Gilbert was told in a very amiable way, that they would be getting in touch with him. I thought he had got the job, and I could not fault that choice. I was left on my own to wait. Two Councillors eventually came out and ushered me in. There were smiles on most of the faces of the Councillors. I was informed that I had come through the interviews, and that they offered me the engagement of *General Manager of the Canolfan Aberconwy Centre*. I was to do my best to make it viable, and manage the *Arcadia Theatre* to be an integral part of the Leisure complex. Naturally, I was very pleased with myself, and quite oblivious to what was in store for me. Firstly, I knew nothing about Local Government procedure. This was to bug me as I started the job. The building was sparse and cold looking. At the back of the building there were large machines controlling Gas and Electricty, each pipe with a different colour. I used to spend time in this control room. My staff called them "My Babies", where is the Boss ? "Oh he is with his babies" Local Government was an eye opener. It was completely incompatible with entertainment.

Now I had secured the job, I had to find time, surreptitiously, to plan the summer show for Robbie, i.e. "Showtime 82". There was no way he could mount the whole show and the publicity on his own. It was a position that had to be handled with care, as now I was employed by the Council, I was not allowed to engage in any outside occupation. There was no way I could let Robbie flounder on his own, he would only contact me to arrange everything, as I knew the ropes. Very quietly, I cast the whole show.

A strange new life.

"I do it the Company way" How to succeed in business without really trying.   Frank Loesser.

The rules laid down were to hamper decisions to organize and book artistes for live entertainment. The Council had no idea of show business, why should they. Robbie and I had presented and paid for every show at the Arcadia, and also the Pier Pavilion. This was going to be a tremendous up hill struggle. The forms alone were immeasurable. As far as staffing was concerned, and their duties, these were governed by the Green book and the Purple book. These books were created by Local Government and the Union. Until we had the whole operation under way, and we knew what was required, it was difficult to engage personnel.

To start there was a receptionist come typist, the stage manager from the Arcadia, and me. The building was to be opened at the beginning of October. There was a lot of activity from the Chief Executive and the chief officers. Prince Charles had given a directive to the effect, that the disabled should be given a prominent position, this we did. The building afforded a very large car lift, to carry all the wheel chairs to the first floor The Parks department surpassed themselves, the floral arrangements were tremendous. Our multi-purpose large conference hall, with the skill of the artistic gardener, was divided in two, so as to give an intimate atmosphere. They let me have my way in putting on a Cabaret Ball in the evening, to celebrate the Royal opening.

We were very slowly receiving technical appliances for the big exhibitions and conferences, I always remember large solid pieces, from eight feet by four feet, reducing to eight feet by one foot. These were for the exhibitions to house all the goodies to sell etc., the first was the Wales Craft Fair, to be ready for the beginning of January 1982.

The great day of the opening arrived, the Mayor and Mayoress Councillor Tom and his daughter. With the Prince arriving, the officials were jigging about, the local Council was jumpy.

The Chief Executive gave me a script, for me to hide and use the new radio mike, It was to describe where the Royals were, and when they were leaving Prestatyn, and all the great receptions, they were receiving along the way. I went through these five pages, the quality radio mike was a great success. Having finished, I went on to other duties. No sooner had I reached my office, I was instructed to do the whole speech again. His Royal Highness had been held up at Rhyl and would be delayed, so I had to fill in. The same people were still in the Hall as at the beginning of the morning. So mentally being a good "pro", I made a precis of the speech. never have I found anything so difficult. as cutting down the original text, as I went along.

The moment arrived, and so did the Prince. There were speeches and introductions, and the unveiling of the plaque. The Royal couple mingled with the crowd, especially with the disabled. Princess Diana was very shy, and the look lowering her eyes, was very noticeable. Her conversation was non-existent, but she looked very glamorous. I managed to have a word with Prince Charles, but it seemed very difficult to extract any verbal contact. from his beautiful wife. There were minimal refreshments, and the Royal party left us to further their Tour of the Principality, and the Local Government Officers quickly evacuated to leave yours truly alone. It was 3 p.m. in the afternoon. I made a check of the building to see all exit doors were fastened securely. I was completely by myself, alone. The bars were all locked up, and the catering staff were to be back around 7 p.m. The catering department was run by a private consortium. Sitting alone, I reflected on the mornings operation, and suddenly it hit me. I had arranged a cabaret dance for the eveing to commence at 7.30 p.m. I went to the main ballroom to see what state it was in, and then went behind into the bar (Luckily I had keys to every door in the building.) As Jimmy "Snozzle" Durante would have said, "Its a catastastroke". *There was nothing ready, no beer in the bar, no spirits, no soft drinks.*

What was I to do...my experience of pipes and beer setting up, was
very limited. I went to the basement, for I knew the stocks, if there
were any, would be kept there, and with the aid of the car lift, I
loaded up crates of bottled beer, all the soft drinks I could see,
bottles of spirits. The physical effort was exhausting. I was fifty
five years of age, and I was working like a navvy, I got to my
office and fell into my chair. Gwen arrived, and said "Come on,
you have to receive the guests at 7.30, and its ten past seven now"
Quickly I put on my dress suit, still perspiring, and went to the top
ot the stairs leading to the grand hall, and received all the V.I.P's.
It was a sort of a "Welcome to my building" type of a greeting. My
boss, and Director of Leisure was **Peter Hall.** he was alright, he
had a lot of commercial training, and was not indoctrinated with
the Local Government syndrome. He liked the old days of variety,
and we used to recall old comics. But that's another story, let us
come to the evening in question. It was a pleasant atmosphere
because I knew 90% of the guest list, the members of the public
knew me better than the members of the Council. I was still on hot
bricks, and remained that way until I hosted the cabaret. When my
artists took over the entertainment. That was the first time I relaxed
the whole day. The cabaret was a triumph. I had Councillors
coming up to me saying "These artists are excellent, where did you
get them ?." With satisfsaction I said "Well ! if you had come to
the Arcadia over the last few years, you would have seen them".
They had never had any idea of what artistes had entertained the
visitors who stimulated the town's economy. The worst example I
had, was the day I took a list of all the stars I had booked for the
Sunday Concerts, to a middle aged clerk, to type. She read
through the list from the top to the bottom, and said "These are a
lot better now that we are doing it" The "we" made me enraged,
the list was of all the artists I had used for the last three years. I
knew then that I would never belong to this local government
circus. It was a doctrine created to stifle any individual talent, or
commercial entreprenurial skills.

It was several months before we had anything like a viable staff. Peter Hall and I were too honest, we didn't want to have staff idle, although there were times when everyone was working at 3 a.m. in the morning setting up conferences physically. Once staff levels were set, it was almost impossible to add to it. The year of 1982 was a trial time for the running of the Conference centre. Next door in the Arcadia, Robbie (with my help,) had Ronne Coyles heading the summer show. The object of the exercise was to maximise income and, as was drummed into me, that I should be "The custodian of the ratepayers money"

Apart from the Wales Craft Fair, The squash courts were coming along very well, we introduced *Pop Mobility, Weight Watchers, Discos, Meetings, Badminton, Carpet Bowls, Table Tennis, Concerts* and many other odd projects. Meeting an enterprising man from the Midlands, together we had a *Roller Disco* night for the youngsters weekly. This was a success as well as a financial profit. It kept the youngsters off the street, and politically, show the ratepayers, that we were doing something for the town and the youth. Having made a decent profit on this attraction, it was all brought to an end. The Fire authority, complained that it was a fire risk. The youngsters would be trapped trying to get out of the building, if there was a fire. They would only have 3 minutes to vacate the building. It was very difficult speaking to the Fire Chief. It was quite alright for me to have a concert on the first floor, for elderly people, but not the Junior Roller Disco. I pointed out that the elderly people with sticks and wheel chairs would take much longer to clear the hall, and get out to the street. "Would you give me a chance to prove to you that the Roller Disco would evacuate in under three minutes. ? Instead of any warning, would you press the fire bell at your choice of time, so that we would not have any prior warning to know what night you were going to pick for us to discharge the contents of the building. ?" They would not give us the opportunity to prove our point. The Roller Disco came to and end and many teenagers were very fed up.

Conferences and exhibitions started to become regular bookings. In 1982 it was estimated, that one delegate to a conference, at that time, was worth £42 a head to the town's economy. The accommodation in the hotels, for a town of our size, had more beds than any other town dealing with conferences. Many well known politicians came to the Canolfan. When the Welsh Conservative party came, I remember having a long conversation with Margaret Thatcher. The "Iron Lady" was most charming, and we talked about some M.P's that I knew personally. The P.M. gave me a lot of information about friends, I had not seen for years, a very delightful lady. Neil Kinnock was a regular visitor. Mr. Kinnock had a good sense of humour.

Family wise Richard & Kay had a second daughter, Laura Michelle was born on the 21st April, 1982. Gwen and I now had two grandchildren. The birth was difficult, but a lovely looking girl emerged to join an equally beautiful Kerry. Gwen and I were thrilled. If the business at Morecambe had not been up to the success of Llandudno, the production of these two girls more than made up for it.

Robbie and I assessed the situation, and we sold the Palace Theatre, Morecambe in the spring. Brian Walker bought the venue with a view to making it a multi purpose entertainment centre. He stated that Richard would be kept on as manager.
This did not last long, after six months Walker gave Richard the push. The family were now in dire straits, they could not sell their property, so out of work they stayed in Morecambe hoping to sell. It was well over two and half years before they sold, and the four of them came back to Llandudno to our "big house" and used the flat in Tan-y-Bryn. in 1985. It was fortuitous that we had plenty of room. It was wonderful having the family all under the same roof. Serious cricket began with Craig, Richard and I started to coach this very talented youngster, not yet in his teens.

It was now a task to get a summer season for the Arcadia Theatre in 1983. Peter Hall left this entirely to me. One of the big problems was the "Estimates". the Council did not have any yardstick to go on, as the figures of the past, were the property of Robbie and I.

There was a highlight to come for 1983. Our old friend *Howard Keel* was to do a National tour. The tour of the north was to finish on the Sunday at Stockport, he then had a night off, and opened in Croydon on the Tuesday. I telephoned *Derek Block* who was organizing the tour, and I intimated to him, that I would like Howard to come to us on the Monday night. He was not impressed with this. I explained who I was, and that we were together in "Oklahoma" at Drury Lane, and all the smaltz. If he could not fit it in, I would understand. Derek phoned to California and Howard said "Yes of course". What a wonderful feeling for Gwen and I to see our old friend, who was so successful in "Dallas" on television. The publicity was duly circularised. We gutted the Arcadia stage for all of the rigs that Howard carried with his show, we hardly recognized the old stage area. The lighting specials were added to our existing rig and we were ready for a packed house, and a sell out, an outstanding performance. The town was a buzz with the thought of the big American in our small community.

Needless to say, Gwen and I were thrilled to be with "Harry", Howard Keel. It was a night of pure nostalgia, and as *Tommy Trinder* would have said **"Junno's & "Jeever's"**, <u>Junno</u> what happened to so and so, and <u>Jeever</u> hear from so and so. This financial success went into the winter figures, and with the added success of *Barbara Dickson, Keeley Ford* and some popular band concerts, I, personally proved Will Catlin wrong. Do not close for seven months in the winter. This was a lucky period for me. The estimates were done for the following year.

The officers, *in their wisdom,* wanted to increase the anticipated profit. My advice to them, and I tried to explain, "show business cannot be guaranteed" I did suggest a reduction in the estimate, but the fianancial department "paid me no mind" and we were very short of the target for the next winter. The summer season starring **Ken Goodwin** was a real profit maker. We had made a nett profit of around £35,000. Needless to say, we never saw any of this to maintain or make repairs to the theatre. Being a "Custodian of the ratepayers money" pleased the Councillors.

During my personal reign at the Arcadia, on Friday nights, not a very popular night usually, we would have as many as nineteen coaches booked in the show. On the last night of the season, I would give the six best couriers a bottle of whisky for their support during the 20 week season. On the Ken Goodwin show, we once again had the coach party support, and I gave six bottles of whisky to the drivers. I was not supposed to do this. I was called into the Chief Executive's office, it reminded me of being called to the Headmaster, I was forcibly told that I had no authority to give gifts to coach drivers. Smack handies....My response was..."If you do not let me do this gifting, then we shall lose business next year" and this is what happened. No gift, no support. The coaches started to leave the theatre, and found other venues to visit the next summer. It was very frustrating. It proved my point that Local Government was not compatible with commercial entertainment.

The security of the building was the biggest headache I had to endure. It was a system where all the doors on a circuit had to be tightly secured to effect the alarm board being working correctly. It happened as many as three times a night that the alarms went off, and I was the key holder. The fire service would ring me and off I would go to the Canolfan in the dead of night. I had to wait for the Police to arrive before I would go into the building, in case there was an undesirable within.

I was very fed up with this intrusion into my sleep. Gwen was very annoyed with the disturbance. In the first few months, I had performed many hours overtime, and as a senior officer, no payment was to acrue, it was time and a half, hours off in lieu. It was not long before I was owed three and a half months leave of absence. This of course, I never received.

The whole operation and the local government syndrome was getting to me. I had slight dizzy spells, and for no reason I would cry. **Ken Goodwin,** unbeknown to me, went to Peter Hall, and intimated that unless I was to get away, he would have an officer away with a nervous breakdown. Ken had had similar experiences with nerves, and could see the signs. Gwen telephoned our lovely friends, Ralph and Rene Hearsum, who had a bungalow at Lyme Regis, and they agreed very readily to have me visit for a while. When I arrived, the sun was shining, and it was Wimbledon fortnight, and so I relaxed. Rene, really kept me fed and watered. After a week I began to feel more tranquil. The second week, I went off to see my fellow performers in summer shows a long the south coast. I met up with **Russ Conway** again, and many other pros, including my old friend **Bill Maynard.** After three weeks, I returned to duty refreshed and more able to deal with the pragmatic consequences of the complex dealings that made the Canolfan a busy place. The biggest problem with the whole operation, was that it was really out of our hands, the Catering. It was sub standard. The Catering manager had a separate office and personnel. These were casual, as the amount of catering was very spasmodic and did not have any consistency. One big conference we serviced and required a full four course meal, went dreadfully wrong. The delegates, after the main course, came at me with fists raised on one hand, and a plate of burnt potatoes, in the other. I thought I was going to be manhandled. I tried to find the catering manager, but he had locked himself in his office, and no one could get to him. The bad reputation stayed with us for a long time.

I had scheduled Sunday concerts in the Arcadia now, we had some old favourites ....*Miki & Griff, Edmund Hockridge, Moira Anderson, Roger de Courcey, Paul Shane, Bobby Crush, The Houghton Weavers, Ray Alan with Lord Charles, Ken Dodd, Frankie Howerd, The Beverley Sisters, and Leo Sayer.* A good line up. I used to go on and compere, to save the Council extra cash, and keep my hand in. I was happy with this as Councillors came to the show, and commented favourably on my performance, to the effect, "You haven't lost it then ?", but of course this didn't last long. Officers and Councillors would telephone for me, on a thursday afternoon, only to be told, "that I was on the show Sunday night, I was having time off in lieu, and was not available" I was immediately told not to compere the shows any more, as I was needed in the office. Once more saving money was not important, anything to stop me stimulating my job.

My staff criticised me for, as they told it, I was featherbedding my artists. My assistant manager, had a down on performers, he was an ex guardsman and policeman. I quietly breathed into his ear, that my artists would always be on time, and would never let us down. he would probably have more trouble with the staff, than the theatre folk. This turned out to be true. The assistant manager, was very eager to become friends with *Ken Dodd* when he came to the theatre, it felt good to be seen with this incredible star.

In 1985, I brought *Freddie Davies* in to produce and present the summer show "Showtime 85" This starred *Peter Goodwright and Tammy Jones.* this was a good show, and did reasonable business. This played Monday Tuesday Wednesday. *Derek Batey* with his "Mr & Mrs", on thursdays, *Wales in Music & Song* on Fridays, and we put the local theatre club in on Saturdays with *"Move Over Mrs Markham.* For the Sundays we added *Danny La Rue, Michael Barrymore, Little & Large and Vince Hill & Roy Walker.*

In February on the thirteenth to be precise, Kay gave birth to Craig Daniel. Gwen and I had a grandson. The heir to the Stock family. A bonnie lad to carry on the name. We were so thrilled for Richard, and for us to have Kerry, Laura and now Craig, we were over the moon. His progress will be marked as we go along.

For the first time in my life, I was now to be in the office from 9 a.m. to 5 or 5.30 p.m. The keys were handed to an assistant, who took all the emergency calls, and saved me getting out of bed through the night. The hours were now static, and we got on with the mundane business of meetings, memos and letters. When first confronted by a memo, I started to answer it straight away. I was promptly told not to do this. I should put the memo or letter in the pending tray, and leave it for a few days. I would then find the questions therein would have answered themselves. It was quite amazing, it actually happened, the position rectified itself, and no answer was necessary. In business I had always answered questions straight away.

Business with the Council, never seemed to have any urgency. As I had contracts to negotiate, I contacted the legal department about a certain contract, one morning, only to be told that they had not been able to get hold of the person involved. The legal officer said that he would telephone the following morning. I said, "What is wrong with trying this afternoon, there are at least three hours left before close of play". That was the situation. It was to take a lot of time to get ready to go home at five o clock.

In 1986 Freddie split the summer season up even more *Roger De Courcey* starred with *Billy Burden* for the early part of the season and *The Krankies, The Great Soprendo* did the Mondays and tuesdays for the second part of the season, The *Charlie Williams Laughter show"* covered the Wednesday and Thursdays for the whole season. *Friday Night is a musical night"* with those brilliant pianists *Anckorn & Dolovich.*

The Llandudno Theatre Club presented *"Shut your Eyes and think of England"* The season was not very successful, Fred Davies, completely overspent on the wrong attractions. He had asked my advice on certain artists, and I given those he ought not to have booked, but there are not many people who take advice very readily. The season made a loss, and I was very upset for him. The experience taught me that the habits of the general public were changing, and I had enjoyed the best of the business.

The meetings were an education, and I had to sit in the full Council in case there was a query on the Canolfan and Entertainment. One momentous meeting caused me to be bewildered. The Councillors spent around 45 minutes discussing Mrs Jones' allottment. An important point of financial policy took ten minutes to discuss, without real attention to detail. It was a real education, and I was not impressed.

The Canolfan Aberconwy, despite the frustrations and lack of stimulation for enterprise I had in mind, the whole operation was up and running. I was missing the "round of applause" at the end of the day. The one thing about live entertaining, you know immediately whether you were successful or not, by the reception of at the end of the performance. . I went to a Council meeting for an upgrade. They usually made their mind up in half an hour, and it was normally negative. I went into the Council chamber for the usual "Why do you think you should be re-graded ??" Answer :- "Because I am a specialist in entertainment, and the usual Council employee, does not have that qualification" I left the chamber, and waited two hours, only to be told, I had not been successful.

This news did not make me very contented, it was spoiling all the good things that were being successful in a difficult enterprise.

On the 23rd July, 1987 my dear friend Harold Robinson Cleaver, dear "Robbie" passed away. This was a bereavement for the whole of my family. He had been like a second father to me, and we gelled perfectly. At the funeral, I had the uneviable task of delivering the Eulogy. It nearly broke my heart. After I had spoken about Robbie's outstanding career, as one of the best theatre organists of our time, and with the aid of that super organist *William Davies,* who had arrived from London just in time, I sang a farewell. This sad and difficult farewell, was to bring a change in my career.

Ronald Smith, who had been the Musical Director for the St. Cecilia Singers of Chester, you remember the "Magic of Ivor Novello", well he telephoned me, and asked if he could make an appointment to see me in my office with Joan McGill. It was pointed out to me that Joan was a Director of Ruthin Castle and the Welsh Medieval Banquet. We made a convenient time, and I met this charming lady from Ruthin. "Could I help her to find someone to takeover the banquet as the host ?", was her request.
Ronald had told her that I had an agency, and would probably know someone who could fit the role.

It transpired that *Bernard Woolford,* who had been the Court Steward for nearly twenty years, had a difference of opinion with the management. Because the Ladies of the Court had not backed him up in the contretemps, Bernard had given in his notice. He thought that because of his successful record, the Directors would not accept him leaving. Well they did. They needed a replacement. Putting on my thinking cap, I arranged that an actor. *Alex Ward,* and *David Paul,* a magician with a good line in patter, should go to the banquet and see what was required. Gwen and I went with them. Looking at the whole evening, I realized that neither of these two, would cope with the function. Apart from being the host, you had to produce the whole show, and produce rotas.

277

It was not only the running of the girls and the food, but you had to be on top of the guests, and be prepared for the hecklers and different nationalities. After the banquet, I said to Mrs McGill, that my candidates were unsuitable, and I would find other people with the right qualifications. **Ronald Smith,** unbeknown to me, had said to her that I was the one who could really fit the bill. Joan asked me, if I would take the job. My reply was that I had a secure post as General Manager of the Entertainment complex in Llandudno, with a pension, I was sixty one years of age, and near retirement, and I thought not. We parted very amicably. I liked this lady, she was charming, with a friendly personality. I would now look for more performers to play the Court Steward in the Original Welsh Medieval Banquet, that had a thirty year history. The position of Court Steward was a very difficult post to fill. An actor could deliver the traditional part, this was scripted, but eighty per cent of the show was spontaneous, and you needed a quick comedy brain for any spontaneous handling of all situations that would arise. My thinking cap was on. The telephone went, it was this nice lady. Ronald Smith had been talking to her again, she asked me would I reconsider taking the post, when I said "No" again, Joan said "Could I bring my brother to see you, and maybe you might change your mind. We arranged for Terry Warburton and his wife, plus Joan to come to the house for a discussion. I agreed to this, I felt nothing would be lost in having a real discussion.

A meeting was arranged at my home. In the meantime, I was thinking would this change of employment, really suit me, and how long would the contract be in duration. It was a gamble, I had some experience now of catering, I had always controlled artists in my shows, and performing after all was my first love.

I kept a very open mind, and as I have always advocated **"Keep all the balls in the air"**

A brand new career in North Wales.
"They stare at the Castle and ponder"   *Camelot.*
Alan Jay Lerner. Frederick Loewe.

At the meeting we had Freda and Terry Warburton and Joan McGill, the three directors of Ruthin Castle, together with Ronald Smith and his wife Pauline. Ronald played the spinnet at the Medieval banquet. Dear Gwen made coffee and goodies for the assembled company. They talked about everything but the banquet, so Terry and I went into another room to talk. He wanted me, even though he only knew of me by reputation. The subject of money came up, and I pointed out my security with the Council. Tentatively, I said I would need such and such a figure to even consider it. I had made sure I asked for a lot more than I was getting with Aberconwy. Inwardly I thought I had asked too much, and had blown it. Terry immediately without a pause added another thousand pounds. Would I accept the position. I promised him I would consider the offer, and I would contact him in a few days. I liked this family. Freda and Terry were charming. Freda had been a stage dancer, so we jelled immediately. They all left in good heart, it had been the most pleasant of discussions, nothing like the meetings I was used to.

Naturally Gwen and I discussed the stuation. I was sixty one years of age, and the Council would say "Goodbye" in four years. I went to **Peter Hall,** and asked for a pay rise and up grade. When he said No, I asked him if he could ask the Chief Executive, if he could sanction a rise. He would not ask.

So my mind was made up. I had an offer I couldn't refuse. I would be going back in front of the public doing what I did best.

Gwen and I had a holiday booked with Vicki and Ken Goodwin in the October. I contacted the Warburton family and said "Yes". I arranged for my solicitor to draw up a contract, all was agreed, and I would start on the 1st November, 1987. I had experienced six years with the Council. I honestly feel that those six years were a great experience, and I would not have been without the learning of complicated local government administration for anything.

So Gwen and I went off to Spain, for what had been a regular two week rest with our dear friends *Vicki & Ken Goodwin.*

I would like to point out at this juncture, that when we became friendly years before, Vicki (Laine as she was before marrying Ken) made costumes for our shows at the Arcadia. She also ran a floorshow called *"The New Pennies"* and through my agency, I booked her in the after dinner world. Ken we met around the early 80's. He was unhappy with his agent, and asked me if I would look after him. With all I had on, I didn't feel I could do him justice, but Ken is an unusual man, he doesn't trust people, owing to experiencing some dirty tricks. I was happy if he was, so I started to find engagements. In the July of 1987 Ken underwent a traumatic cancer operation. It was major, and if he had not been fit, he kept himself very fit with walking and running and swimming, he would not have come through the dreadful ordeal. The clever surgeon had very successfully cleared everything, and although there would be tests and visits back for check ups, it seemed that all was well. He had lost a lot of weight and he wasn't looking his usual self, but slowly he came back to a full recovery.

Ken and Vicki had a lovely villa in the Costa Blanca, and a separate guest suite. They were very kind letting us spent a fortnight each time, in the sun. We played tennis every day, and with the constant sunshine, we felt rested and well.

On the picturesque mountain of Aldea de las Cuevas, there were many styles of villas. A very attractive two bedroomed property came on to the market, and we decided to buy. Vicki and Ken were so thrilled that we would be there with them. Ken, who is very tall, and at that time very strong, picked me up, and nearly crushed me with the excitement of our purchase. We kept the villa for eight years, but had to sell. We were only getting out to Spain for two visits of two weeks at a time, and this was a luxury, that was of no real benefit. We were so lucky we were able to stay with Vicki and Ken in their guest suite, after we had sold the property..

The Welsh Medieval Banquet.
"What merriment is the King, pursuing tonight" Camelot.
Alan Jay Lerner. Frederick Loewe.
On the 1st of November 1987, I started my duties at Ruthin Castle.
Ken Dodd found out that I was changing jobs, and when he found I
was to be the new Court Steward at the Welsh Medieval Banquet,
he named me the **Court Sherriff,** so I kept his title.

There was a awkward situation at the banquet, as Hugh Roberts
had been holding the fort for three months, and here was this
Englishman coming in to take over the whole operation. He was
not at all pleased, and to be honest I could not blame him. The
whole atmosphere was like being on eggshells. There were some
ladies who were Welsh Nationalists, and were not prone to be
friendly. I made progress in a short time, as I was getting many
laughs and the show was getting tremendous standing ovations at
the end of the evening.

The first change I made, was to get a cassette of all the singing in
the programme, produced, not only to show the excellence of the
voices, but to realize some income for the Castle and the Girls. My
friend **Gordon Lorenz,** produced the tape on one Sunday in
Manchester. It was a first class result and it sold like "hot cakes". I
altered the running order, so that we finished on a high, instead of
down as it had been doing. When I wrote my own version of the
famous "Bedgelert" legend and put it to the music of "God Bless
The Prince of Wales", the very Welsh ladies started to come to my
way of thinking, and tolerated this Englishman. I knew that it was
momentary, so I began auditions for new girls who could sing and
serve. I found some very good voices and nice people With
rehearsal, I started to get them all to move as one, and walk like
professionals, with movements in unison.

The whole show was now looking professional, and even the girls
were feeling good about themselves.

The show was really spot on, and I was finding more laughs every show with suitable ad libs to the Americans. I was really enjoying myself, except for the journey there and back, driving in the summer was fine, but in the winter on the narrow roads with the car lights coming at you, was no fun.

On the domestic front my mother was far from a hundred per cent, and started to go down hill. Gwen was so caring in looking after her, but it soon became too much for her to manage, Mother was not the best of patients, but in the end, she gave up.
Into a residential care home, which she was not very keen about, and she made it known to me, that my father would never have let her go into a home. Struggling on, she finally gave up on the 23rd of May, 1989.

It was very traumatic for us all when she left us. A lady who had been the driving force when we were children. Dorothy Stock, had a facility for always being right. She would often say, "I don't know anything about your profession, but I would have thought....." she would then give her thoughts on the subject under discussion, and she would be absolutely right. As she got older her forecasts were not quite so accurate, like us all.

My mother was a tower of strength through our lifetime, and although she was not in favour of my marriage, she soon became very close to Gwen, and there was a strong affinity between them. Her passing for me, her first born, left a space. I had now become the eldest of all the Stock family, I didn't have anyone to report the happenings of our family to.

In August 1989 Gwen and I went to Spain to stay with Vicki and Ken, in the middle of the holiday, we had a telephone call from Cec my brother in law, to say that my dear sister had been taken into the John Radcliffe hospital in Oxford for a triple by-pass heart operation.

Gwen and I were absolutely bowled over, we could not imagine anything like that happening to Beryl. We could not do anything about it, and made contact as soon as we returned. It transpired that she had a thirteen hour operation, and everything was alright. In her usual way, when we saw her, the comedy was flowing and she came out with all the lewd and funny remarks, we had come to expect of her. Her sense of humour was one of her foremost attributes. Having been placed on instructions for diet and other medical do's and don'ts, she adhered to all the rules of dealing with a by-pass. She was great, and her health improved to her former strength. Beryl and I and Cec and Gwen are very close, so much so, that only three weeks after we were married, Beryl and Cec were married. Cec is like a blood brother, we were in the choir together, we were at school together, and we played cricket and football together. He has always been part of the family, and mother treated him like a son. Mother of course passing on in the May, never had the heartache of Beryl's operation. Mother was always very involved with all family problems and celebratory occasions.

How she would have loved to have celebrated our party on the 17th March, 1993 when I celebrated 50 years in show business. Gwen and I were going out for a meal with Richard and Kay. I was ready early, and for some unknown reason Gwen seemed to be lagging behind. The table had been booked, and we had to go and pick the two of them up. I called up to Gwen "Come on its time we were going" and she came back "I am just coming, I won't be a moment" as I walked up the hall, the door bell went. I opened the door, "Bang" there were loads of people, my dear sister and Cec, my brother and Jill, *Jess Yates* and Serena, *Roy Lance* and Irene in wheel chair and many more, bringing up the rear was Kay and Richard, Kerry, Laura and Craig. Richard had organized everything, he marshalled the cars up the road, and would not let any one out, until he gave the order. He had arranged the whole party to celebrate my 50 years, in showbusiness.

283

Letters had been sent from many people in London, *William Franklyn, Ted Cast, Joe Church and Pat,* and *Russ Conway* telephoned. *Freddie Davies and Vanessa* made a late entrance, they had travelled miles. I was of course, in tears, and no matter how I tried to quell the liquid, I carried on in water falls. Gwen of course, had organized the food. *Beryl Travers* the cake expert, had produced a cake in the shape of a Showboat, being my first show, and Richard had made a red book to assist him in presenting a "This is your Life" programme narration. He had somehow found access to old scorebooks, and there was a photostat of the 208 partnership with *Hugh Goldie* at Stoke D'Abernon, and other press cuttings, there were many speeches that Richard had organized, my brother in law, my brother, Fred. The last speech was completely spontaneous. *Jess Yates,* asked if he might say a few words, Gwen and I had known him for many years, he talked about the long time he had followed our careers, and he was most emotional talking about how much love there was in our family, probably because there was so much wrangle with *Paula Yates,* who turned out to be *Hughie Green's* daughter. For me, my son had given me so much happiness, that I cried all night.

Back at Ruthin Castle, I shouldered on with the dodgy atmosphere, of the Welsh-English egg shells that existed. It was very hard to comprehend that if England were playing Finland, as happened on one occasion, my Welsh colleagues were supporting Finland, it seemed quite hard to understand. The one happy note, was that the Warburton family gave me carte blanche to run the banquet without any interference. The guests were 90% American during the summer, and a very different kettle of fish from October to March. In November and December it became very hairy. It could be Hen Parties, Drunken people from Wrexham and Liverpool, Japanese and the odd American isolated in the middle. In 1990 we had one hundred and ninety five banquets, with an average of over ninety one guests per night.

The Ruthin Castle Medieval banquet was the place you should go to, when visitng North Wales. The reputation was famous in the U.S.A.

Hope & Keen would often play the Grand in Llandudno, and would stay the night. One lunch time they asked me what I was doing, they having worked for me at the Arcadia when I was the Impresario, and now back performing. A precis of my duties as Court Sherriff was forthcoming, and I intimated that I was finding it difficult to find one liners and put downs. Mike then gave me a super one liner, I stored in the head for future reference. It was a pure coincidence, but, on that saturday night, I had two hen parties, 68 ladies ???, in all. One sprig from Wrexham 26 in the party, 20 from Hope Street in Liverpool to my right, and one sprig of Americans in the middle. There was a cacophony immediately the entertainment started. They had had plenty of mead and wine, and the women were vociferous.

One Liverpudlian, was at me right from the beginning of the evening. His accent was so thick, the Americans were bemused, as they could not understand a word he was saying. Well into the programme the noise was straining the eardrums, I was having a hard time, I eventually said "On the left we have natives from the North East of the Principality, the ladies are from hell, and here on our right, visitors from Hope Street, Liverpool (The gag that Mike Hope had told me, clicked in)

My Lords and Ladies, you know Liverpool, thats the place where the Supermarkets have a "steal by date". A huge laugh, and as it subsided, I could hear murmurings "We're not thieves, we pay our tax, what an insult", and the whole twenty went out of the banqueting room. I then, introduced the harpist, and more or less followed on the back of the irate table, and as I was going to go out after them, my herald Hugh, held me back.

285

It could realy be uncomfortable.

Hugh said "I shouldn't go out there, tempers are frayed, and they are very angry". I carried on with the show, and I was pleased to get to the finale.

Leaving the banqueting hall, I was met firstly, by a blonde lady with her fists raised and shouting "I demand a public apology, and I want to see the owner of the hotel" others joined in, with "We pay our taxes, you have insulted Liverpool". The whole ambience was chaotic. The fellow that had been giving me such stick, came at me,, and said "How dare I suggest that they were thieves, and why Liverpool ?" I came back at him "You were at me all night, and as soon as I come back at you, you can't take it. If your party had come from Cornwall, it would be Supermarkets in Cornwall, I am glad my team beat you last week end, I have supported Arsenal since 1936.". The whole mood changed, here was a football supporter, and we started to have quite an amicable chat, although the ladies were not very friendly.

Another time I had a rough looking bloke, having a call out session with me, and all of a sudden a lady from the end of the top table, ran down the side of the sprig, and poured wine all over this loud mouth, not feeling excited about the demonstration of wine tasting he immediately rose and gave chase. The lady in question was staying at the hotel and went straight through to the other end of the building, she had completely lost the wine sodden punter, who was so frustrated he came running back into the banquet, and as I turned to introduce the harpist, he hit me full in the chest and sent me back somersaulting over a table, so that I landed on my side, on my head, on the stone floor. I was in shock and I called out "This is the finish, I am not doing any more, Good night everyone" I was taken upstairs and given a large brandy. My head was throbbing where I had hit the deck, and I was trembling with the shock. I was reassured by the guests, that if I wanted a witness, they would be prepared to give evidence. Evidently, so many people went to reception the next morning to see if I was alright.

Gwen and I, a few days later, took a flight from Manchester to
Spain, and next to me were a couple who had been in that night,
and went through it all over again. These incidents were very rare,
the Americans were charming , and involved themselves in good
humour and general fun. They were an absolute joy to entertain.
The rapport I had with the blue rinse large American ladies, was
enjoyable, they fed me with one liners that came out of the back of
my head, and of course being completely, ad-lib, the girls were in
hysterics, the first lady Beryl, once she exploded, she couldn't
stop, and so the guests joined in and the happiness permeated
through the banqueting hall. If I hadn't had a night of laughter,
then I felt I had failed, but that never happened, only in the winter
we kept a straight programme, because of the drunks.

The banquets were going very well, and we were very close to all
the couriers who came with their parties from the U.S.A.
On April 20th 1996, I presented the *"Festival 1996"* show for
charity. This was for the Province of North Wales, There are many
masonic homes all over England and Wales for poor and distressed
people who are less fortunate than ourselves. There was no time
for any rehearsal, so everything was gone through in the morning
of the saturday, the show was at 3 p.m. I had some good "pros"
*Jackie Allen & Barbara, Mike Seeley, Stuart McDonald and
Shaw Thing* together with a good choir, and the top of the bill was
Russ Conway. Although there was a lack of rehearsal, and the
amateurs did their best. The show was a triumph. At the finale the
Provincial Grand Master came on stage to thank me and give Russ
Conway, a cheque for £1,000 for his own Cancer Charity. This was
a great surprise for Russ as he had come up from Eastbourne for
expenses. These are the delights of our business, spontaneous acts
of generosity.
Gwen and I were going to move from our lovely large home to a
smaller abode, the big house was now too much for Gwen to
manage, and we were rattling around, just the two of us.

Happiness and sadness.

The Turkish man who was buying our home was pushing us to complete by the end of August, this was far too early, we had found a lovely chalet bungalow, but we couldn't get in before the 1st November. We agreed the completion date.

We now had to find a flat for September and October. Our home was packed up, Pickfords removed everything from the house, it took two complete days. Seven filing cabinets of music, costumes, press cuttings, clothes Video recordings of our shows, tapes, trophies, the abundance of framed photographs from our star friends, and all the memorabilia, as well as all our clothes.

On the 26th October 1996 there was the greatest tragedy of our lives. During the night the depository at Pickfords, Hoole Bridge, Chester, went up in flames. 300 people had lost all their possessions, 18 houses were gutted, cars in the street just melted. The morning brought scenes of utter devastation. It was a horror. Nothing was left of the warehouse but charred remains, twisted metal, bent steel girders and steam rising from the remains for several days. It was a disaster. On the Friday morning we couldn't prove we existed with an established name and standing in show business. Well dear reader, with all my reference books and programmes gone, to write this autobiography has been a difficult labour. My love and thanks to friends in Australia, New Zealand and America who have sent me programmes and press cuttings to help replace so much.

The press made a big display of it, The local press featured the headline "50 years of memories lost in fire" Gwen and I with the help of close friends, went out as though nothing had happened, and got together a new home. We were shattered but not undaunted, we supported each other when we were depressed, and came out of the whole horrendous tragedy, stronger and ready to enjoy our new home. Two fabulous pairs of neighbours each side, we had never had neighbours before, and all was ready for another phase in our joyous life.

In 1997, fifty years after his momentous year ***Denis Compton*** passed away, he was 78. Of all the greatest cricketers, he is the one who stands out above the rest, I was very upset, but very proud of the skill he had given me. I digress, back to the original Welsh Medieval Banquet. There was a slight atmosphere between the Hotel and the Mediaevil banquet. The reception staff, were very unhelpful to our operation. There seemed to be a "them and us" situation. It was strange, the management never came down to see us at the banquet,and I suppose as long as they didn't have any complaints. They left me to get on with it. The antagonism between the "beds" and the "banquet" was uncomfortable.

This eventually seemed to subside and the two sections became amicable. It was difficult to make all the participants realize we needed each other.

On Tuesday August 27th, 1991. The Grand Order of Water Rats had a very special ceremony. There was to be a new rat, initiated, and a special lunch to be held in the Hilton. The new rat was ***Bob Hope.*** I was so pleased I could get down to be part of this wonderful occasion, for this was one of those moments you will never forget. I had a chat with the great man, and he was so interested in Ruthin Castle. While we were talking, he called over to his lovely wife Dolores, and said "Hey Dahl, this guy entertains in a Medieval Cassell". A great day.

I had a Herald by the name of Mike Dunseath. For two years he watched me, and I wanted him to take over, when I felt that I had had enough. I liked Mike. He was a gentleman, and in his costume he looked magnificent, he was stately and regal, and had a commanding presence, He was the opposite of me, I was a comedy busy body, getting amongst the punters with gags and singing character songs. In 1999, I thought it was time to let Mike take over.

So I left on the understanding, I would come back when Mike took his holidays, or had to see his family in the south. Joan his wife shared the position of spinet player with Ronald Smith, When Mike went away, Joan went with him, so I would be pleased to come back and have the stimulus of performing once again. While I was back in July of 2001 and Joan and Mike were in Holland, I had a telephone call from Joan. Mike had been involved in a car accident, and had been killed. The shock to me was devastating, so I could imagine how Joan was feeling, her call was to the point, she was quite marvellous. Through this tragedy I had to carry on, until I could find a replacement. It was my job to audition new candidates, and be impartial, because of finance and other considerations. One candidate, who auditioned was Campbell Finnie. He came in before the banquet and started the first speech. He said "I can't do it, I've lost my bottle, and left. This was a blow to me, as he looked tremendous in his costume. He was tall, with curly hair, a lovely voice, he had some local operatic amateur experience, and he should have been absolutely right. I suggested he came back again, for further auditions.

I had arranged four candidates for audition, I knew who the best choice would be, but he was too expensive. They were all different in their own way. They soon found it was not quite so easy, they auditioned in front of the punters, so they could get the feel of the atmosphere. I stood on the side in case they got into difficulties. They all had a proper audition and so a director of Ruthin Castle chose from the list of candidates, and I took my leave.

This was the first time I had not been engaged, and to be able to have some leisure. Not to do that journey to Ruthin each night was a great relief.

What was I going to do ?, write the autobiography was one full time task, and that would bring back some memories and nostalgia.

The time has come for saying "Goodbye".
All Dreams must end, Off comes the make up" Bells are Ringing.
Adolph Green & Betty Comden. Jule Styne.

After well over sixty years in show business, I was now unemployed. What was I going to do now ?. In 1992 and 93 I had presented the *"Ken Goodwin Show"* in a church, much to the chagrin of the local council. They intimated that I had taken business away from the New Theatre. The two years had run over nineteen weeks each season. The thought of doing that all over again, especially as I was a one man band, would necessitate tension and stress. It was now time for writing this book, and taking life a little easier.

Luckily I enjoyed reasonable good health. I had sustained Hypertension since 1963. and I was now diabetic, this required strict diet. Testing my blood on the little machine regularly, was a bit of a bind, but generally I was within bounds of the margins set by the figures that were laid down by my excellent G.P. *Dr. Geoffrey King* was my doctor, and I had great faith in this gifted medico.

It was fortuitous that I stopped playing cricket at seventy, as I had problems with the stiffening of the middle finger of the right hand. Two very painful injections brought no improvement, and the locking persisted. Then the ring finger on the left hand locked and would not straighten up. An operation was performed by a hand surgeon so that the tendon was cut (not nice), and hey presto ! the finger eased and returned to normal. Without any further treatment, as though in sympathy, the finger on the right hand became normal, as if by a miracle.

It was now a time, when through age and illness we were losing our friends. There were some of seventy years plus, and a few who were taken before their time. No matter how you are prepared for this pain, you are never in control of your emotions, and I unashamedly admit, that Gwen and I find it very hard to keep back our tears at such times.

Farewell dear friends.

Past King Rat *Joe Church* proposed me in to the Grand Order of Water Rats. *Frankie Vaughan* gave a tribute luncheon at the Savoy, for dear Joe. It was magical. You witnessed then the affection and love, that one rat had for the other. It was a room full of happiness shared by so many members. Joe passed away soon after, and brother rat *Peter Goodwright* wrote the following :-

In lodge there is an empty chair with collar draped upon.
It means that death has hovered near-a Brother Rat has gone.
Relieved of pain and illness-all earthly cares will cease –
Past King Rat Joe Church – may your spirit rest in peace.

In Variety's golden days-as every pro will know,
The hardest spot to get a laugh was known as F.C.O.
"First Comic On" – when the audience is cold.
Needs a very special talent-if you've got it, its like gold.

Past King Rat Joe had got it-he made people laugh and roar,
They'd been on trains and buses only half an hour before.
But with plank of wood and gags, Joe melted down reserve,
And another show was started with expertise and verve.

From the Grand in Clapham-to the Met in Edgware Road,
March booked all the theatres and the pace never slowed.
And so to the Palladium with standards even higher,
With Joe Church as your comic-the laughs would be sure fire.

And not just theatre-radio-too-and television shows,
Joe had success in all of these, as everybody knows
Touring, cruising, travelling-you need help with all that.
And behind the scenes, his luck was in-he had the lovely Pat.

A life time spent with laughter-it's been up as well as down,
That often seems to be your lot, if you choose to be a clown.
But your legacy is that laughter-and though we're sad you go.
A warm smile wraps our memories, because we loved, Joe.

Another farewell.

Joe Church appeared at the London Palladium more times than any other comedian. A feat that still holds sway today. My North Wales memory of him, was in the sixties, when the Pier Pavilion and the Arcadia theatres played football against Hotpoint. He was great I remember that.

Frankie Vaughan, a very close friend for over forty years passed on. Our profession was, to say the least-"Gutted". Here was not only a wonderful artist, but a gentleman and an ambassador. He received the O.B.E. in 1970 for his fundraising for boy's clubs. The first pop star ever to receive such an award. He was King Rat twice, and was a prime example, of artists who dedicate their lives to charitable works. Before his death, he was honoured with the C.B.E. Gwen and I loved him. He never had a big head, he just loved his wife Stella, his family and all his brother rats. When Gwen and I were doing clubs in Sheffield we stayed in the same house as his father. Mr. Abelson was very kind to us, and we talked endlessly about Frank. In a strange city, we were grateful for his help......."Life father, like son".

In February, 1994 a very sad blow to Llandudno, was the complete gutting of the Pier Pavilion through fire. This listed 2000 seater building had served North Wales as the largest auditorium, for well over 115 years. It had been host to *Caruso, Gigli, Campoli, The Halle Orchestra, Sir John Barbirolli, Dr Malcolm Sargent, Anna Pavlova, Ivor Novello's "Dancing Years", Sir Thomas Beecham, Sir Adrian Boult, Sir Henry Wood, Paul Robeson, Richard Tauber, Tetrazini Petula Clark, Rawicz & Landauer, Arthur Askey, Vic Oliver, Lloyd George, Stanley Baldwin, Neville Chamberlain, Winston Churchill, Harold MacMillan, Edward Heath and many others.* These wonderful people contributed to elegance and charm, and were International Celebrities.

Under our banner, we presented ....*Semprini, The Beverley Sisters, Donald Peers, Russ Conway, David Hughes, Moira Anderson, Edmund Hockridge, Sandy Powell, Frankie Vaughan, John Inman, Kenneth McKellar, Ken Goodwin, Wyn Calvin, Gwen Overton & Clive Stock, Bob & Alf Pearson, George Bolton, Ken Dodd, Leslie Crowther, Charlie Chester, and Ted Ray.* Ted called the Pier Pavilion, "An aircraft Hanger with lights" Ted had many comical sayings, he called me "The Singing Armpit". It was sad, as the real concert hall of North Wales, had gone, leaving the public with sadness and memories.

My dear partner, **Robbie Cleaver** was so much at home at the Pier Pavilion with his own Hammond Organ securely in the pit, so that he could accompany all the concerts from the fifties to the beginning of the eighties. Gwen and I would drive from Clacton across country to find Robbie waiting for us, to accompany our act. Very often we would try out something new and he would be with us all the way.

The Arcadia Theatre was now alone, from five vibrant and successful theatres, it stood as the last bastion of "Live" entertainment. It was not long before a new theatre was built. The Arcadia was now closed and derelict, it was closed for environmental reasons, amongst others of a dangerous nature. In the October, **Howard Keel,** returned to Llandudno and the new theatre. It was a joyous moment to reunite with him and his lovely wife, Judith. Howard had become a member of the Grand Order of Water Rats, and he prized this Order highly. It was another bond with Britain, that was so important to him. The press went to town with the reunion, and the photographs were a plenty. There were memories to recall. It was pure nostalgia, and plenty of "Junnos & Jeevers".

We were enjoying nostalgia, and all the memories of people who were very close to us, came flooding back. This gives you a very warm feeling, you know what I mean, dear reader.

In April, 1998 I was thrilled to get a letter from the Arsenal Football Club, signed by *Arsene Wenger.* As a supporter since 1936, he called me "Clive Stock, No 1 Arsenal Fan" he realised I was having a pretty hard time in North Wales with all the Manchester United and Liverpool fans in the area, he said "The Gunners will make every effort to bring trophies to Highbury."

More friends leaving the world behind. As the Irving Berlin lyric goes, brought the passing of *Jack Milroy,* this was particularly painful to Gwen and I. Most of our happy times in Scotland were spent with Jack. He was a real funny man, his humour was infectious, and apart from that, he was a nice man. In the periods in the Gaiety Theatre, Ayr, he created the famous characters of "Francie & Josie" those two Scottish teddy boys. His Josie at the offset was *Glen Michael,* a straight actor who had success in the film "The Blue Lamp". I don't think Jack realised how big these two characters were to become. In the sixties *Rikki Fulton* became Josie, and the magic of these two together, forged the partnership into the fore front of well loved double acts. They were Scotland's Morecambe & Wise. Jack's death was a great loss to Scotland's world of entertainment.

On the 23rd September, 1999, Gwen and I celebrated our 50th wedding anniversary. I decided that we should have a really good dinner and entertainment for our family and friends. Gwen was against it, she didn't want any fuss or celebration. Looking back I suppose, I always did what I wanted to, and I learned it is better to get on with it yourself. So I arranged everything, more or less, without Gwen knowing. My dear *Beryl Travers and her son Simon,* were in charge of the cake. My thoughts for the cake were to recount the showbusiness of our career.

A large square cake was the order of the day, this would include the theatres, the shows, the partnership with Robbie, and various stars who featured in our lives. The lovely Travers pair had their work cut out. It would entail a lot of titling. The work on this edible edifice would take some time, so due notice was given. Invitations and the selection of individuals were sent out to the 90 guests. This would be a production. I recorded on C.D. all the incidentals i.e. Fanfares, tunes for informal toasts, congratulations and family music. Everything recorded in strict order with a full script, which was in the hands of my dear son.. .Richard. He would use his excellent Disco equipment. My dear friends from the south *Ralph & Rene Hearsum* would be with us, and Ralph would don his red coat to do the toastmastering duties. My super sister Beryl acquiesced to my request to propose the toast to the guests, which she excelled herself in, seducing the crowd into the palm of her hand. While Past King Rat *Wyn Calvin. M.B.E.* found exactly the right balance between comedy and the serious recall of our careers, finishing with a touch of "The Merry Widow" the three of us did together. The mood was ready for the cabaret, and when I tell you there were six acts, and the show was completed in just under 30 minutes, you would be astounded. *Ian Garry* of "Hello Dolly" fame, opened with the news number from "Gyspy" he wrote new lyrics to incorporate secrets about us, the amount of work he had put into this parody was worth it, as he received an ovation, which he so richly deserved. *Vicki Goodwin* compered the programme. *Stuart McDonald* followed with his bagpipes, tenor sax, Flute and powerful singing voice to the accompaniment of micro disc tapes, that seemed to have found a different order. The lovely tenor voice of *Bob Roberts,* my colleague from the medieval banquet, sang a Novello favourite for us all, and *Shaw Thing* a beautifully polished singing duo, sang from the "Phantom of the Opera". *Ken Goodwin* closed with a nice tight spot. It was now time for dancing.

Richard with his expert music kept the floor full all the time. It was a wonderful night to celebrate 50 glorious years of our married life together. In my goodnight speech, I brought the ladies from Ruthin Castle to sing the "Goodnight" we always sang at the banquet, then Auld Lang Syne to follow.

Unbeknown to me, Gwen had written a new lyric to the tune of "I must have done something good" from the Sound of Music. She sang this, and the tears flowed, we were both uncontrollable. These tears ended one of the best nights of our life together. The younger members of our family were knocked out with the evening, and were so engrossed, they were swept up with not only the atmosphere of love and affection, but they appreciated how such an evening was presented, using a lot of experience, and tried and true bits of business only demonstrated in our profession..
Only a few weeks after this marvellous family evening, when the grandchildren were still talking about it, and the joy for all, the joy was followed by sadness. ***Roland Jones*** passed away. He was involved in a head on car crash with a school coach. Roland was my deputy when running the Aberconwy Centre and Arcadia Theatre. We had a good rapport and worked well together as a team. He was better at the Local Government syndrome than I. I was beginning to learn about the so called wisdom of the Council. I would say we had an amicable partnership. It was so sad to see his passing at the age of sixty six after just retiring, he retired after having a stroke. He was a workaholic and enjoyed his job.

In my so called retirement, I was seeing to the dates of ***Ken Goodwin.*** This entailed booking cruises and concerts. It was difficult with Ken living in Spain. The policy was to get him over to the U.K. for spells of bookings, so that it made his book, as we call it, viable. Luckily dates seemed to coincide, and his bookings were fairly consistent. It was easy to recommend Ken, as his material was clean and never offensive, he had universal appeal with his clean gags and ukulele playing.

We had a good relationship and we were close friends. With a long association with his wife, Vicki, the partnership was very important to us. It was a friendship we guarded with great affection. One of our most important dates, is a tri-weekly meeting for coffee, with *Jackie Allen & Barbara, Annette & Ian Garry.* This is six "pros" having fun. We keep ourselves, and anyone around in stitches. Laughter is the tonic for everyone, it is amazing that we never discuss the same subject twice. We are three couples, completely different, but with one common denominator. We love showbusiness, love our families, and love each other. These meetings we all look forward to, as we have such close camaraderie.

It was now time to get down to this autobiography, the difficulty would be finding suitable photographs and press cuttings for inclusion. The terrible fire had taken all the photographs and memorabilia that would have been of interest to you, dear reader.

It is now March, 2003. It seemed unbelieveable that it was exactly sixty years ago I started in West End musicals, and also thirty years since joining the Water Rats. Both these achievements have afforded me great happiness, and status in my chosen career.

The chequered experiences of joy and sorrow were very self evident. Our very good friend Russell Gradwell died after a gradual illness. Gwen and I were very broken up, and Val, his wife, was very brave during the whole bereavement. We were there for her. As I said aforementioned, you are never ready to cope with a passing. The one obituary that I had been waiting for was the passing of *Mary Ellis.* The whole profession was anticipating this sad occasion. She was known as the world's oldest living actress, and she died at the age of 105. My memories of her in "Arc de Triomphe" were golden, I was very lucky to have been on the same stage as her. The sheer talent of both singer and actress made Mary the outstanding leading lady of the 20th century.

Likewise in the same week, another colleague of mine from the "Merry Widow...*Diana Gould ..Lady Menuhin* reached the grand age of 90. She married Yehudi in 1947 and gave up her dancing career with much regret. Yehudi Menuhin died in 1999.

It seems so strange to me, that all these people I am recalling, you dear reader, I am sure may never have heard of. I can only assure you, that they were artists of great talent, and I, being an emotional person, feel the loss very deeply.

The worst was yet to come. My family was not prepared for a death that rocked us all. It happened on the fourth of March..... My brother Brian, dropped dead in the street in Wolverhampton. He had just been into the jewellers to collect a clock, and came out and that was it, so sudden. My sister and I were stunned and paralysed. None of the family could come to terms with this awful tragedy.

Brian had dedicated his life to the community. He had been a very active Conservative in Bristol, Norwich, Wolverhampton South West and Hampstead, where we grew up. His positions had been varied from Ward Chairman, Treasurer, Vice Chairman Europe, to Chairman and President. He was also President of his Rotary Club, and went on to have divisional titles.

The suddenness of his death seemed so unfair. He was the youngest of the three of us, and we could not comprehend why he should leave us so suddenly. The funeral was on the 13th March, and like so many families, it was one of the only times, the whole family were together. Our son, Richard had the chance to be with his cousins. Victor Lyon, Brian's closest friend of 66 years read a eulogy, and with great difficulty, I spoke off the cuff. It was the hardest speech I have ever made. I broke down from time to time. My dear sister, who had been so close to Brian, especially when children on evacuation, read a verse that she felt was appropriate.

Beryl, barely made the finish. Gwen and I were utterly distraught. His wife, Jill, and son Nicholas have the arduous task of sorting out all the affairs of my brother, and then the coming to terms with his absence.

The words of The Reverend O.T. Jones come to mind, as he often told us....*"You are only sure of the moment"*, how right he was. Although the pain is receding, we constantly think of Brian, and all the fun and affection we had as children These memories will stay with us forever.

May he rest in peace, and may we try to live up to the many ideals he tried to live by, and succeeded in carrying out, throughout his life.

Life was becoming much easier, and I was not controlled by the clock, except for the speaking engagements I carried out. I was asked to address several institutions, giving my fee to the Water Rats. From being busy every minute for seven days a week, to a leisurely day to day slowing down. The family are always in my thoughts, I could now have time for them, they were meaning everything to me, and with us all being in close proximity, it was a joy to see them at regular intervals.

My Grand children give me great joy. Kerry Ann, is a very clever lady, a "whizz", with computers, and a huge amount of intelligence. From Bangor University she gained a Degree, and now holds down a very exacting job in a Technical College, Her department takes advantage of her computer skills.

Laura, who is now Laura Michelle Lawrence, is the artistic one. Her singing voice is very attractive, she writes poetry, and is a great follower of the Arts. Her very easy and lovable nature, make her a favourite with all her friends, and her excellent husband, Dale.

The latest generation.

The three great grandchildren, are growing into little people. They are becoming "personalities". A very quick assessment of these three loving and interesting children, would make me believe they are entirely different from each other. Jordan, is the eldest, and has a big beam on his face, most of the time. He is loving and kindly, and a very happy boy. Calista, is a very intelligent child, well ahead of her age group, strong willed, and seems as though, there is nobody who will pull the wool over her eyes, or put on her. Jadzea, the youngest is a completely happy child, who smiles for a living. Without being biased in anyway, my offspring are a very good looking set of people.

How lucky we are to have a loving son, and his equally loving and talented wife, Kay. These two together set a loving atmosphere for their children. They must take great credit for the way they have brought up their family. My sincere thanks to Kay and Kerry for the help they have given me with the computer, to enable me to publish this book. My wife and I adore them all.

So dear reader, it was now a case of "Been there, done that etc.," The grand daughters were settled with their children, Auntie Sis, at ninety nine years of age, so cementing five generations.

The continuing of my life would be through my son and his son, Craig, who would not only keep the name perpetuating, but his whole character and talent would reproduce the main part of my experiences, my career would have an extension, and he would continue where I leave off..

What of the future ?

***"This my friend is only the beginning". The Roar of the
Greasepaint, The Smell of the Crowd. Newley & Bricusse.***
Craig's cricketing prowess included :- Scoring 137 not out in the
under fifteens, Youngest North Walian... 50 in senior cricket.
Voted top junior at the sports awards in the borough. In 1998
capped for Wales under 13's. 1999 picked as a leg spinner for
Wales against Gloucestershire and scored 104. At the age of 16
was capped for the West of England, scoring his maiden century.
He played regularly for Denbighshire under 19's. In 2002 was
capped for Glamorgan under 17's then selected for North Wales
under 21's. Craig has scored 1000 runs, and taken 50 wickets in
each of the last four seasons. His football talent has been suggested
to Everton, and he played rugby for North Wales.

The brilliance of Craig, can be traced back to his time in the "Big
House", when at the age of around six, he faced some fast bowling
on a suspect lawn. He had to play to the offside all the time. We
pitched the wicket close to the bank on the leg side, and made him
play to the off. He had to hit the ball through gaps marked by
stumps at regular intervals, and there were inducements of money
for shots played through the covers for four. At that age the pace
of the bowling, made sure that when he started playing serious
cricket, fast bowlers had no fears for him, with shots of class, he
would despatch the ball effortless to the boundary.
Add to these sporting attributes, his acclaimed performance in his
public school's production of "West Side Story" and the singing
lead in "The Forbidden Planet". My career over ?????. It has only
just begun.---Craig will now carry on where I left off. If he has half
the enjoyment and success as we have had, then his life will be one
of tremendous stimulus and happiness.

The whole STOCK family wishes Craig...Iechyd Da, Hir-oes for
his time now in New Zealand. "Go for it ! Craigles"

A few days before he left. Craig set a new Rydal School record, by scoring 118 and 118 not out in two consecutive innings, back to back. Will that record be beaten, I doubt it. He is now in Wellington, New Zealand, having the life of "Ol Reilly".

May I, dear reader, thank you for travelling with me through my sixty years in show business, and this journey through nostalgia.

Of all the highlights during my life, and what little success I have, is all due to :- "Walking through life with you dear Gwen, has been the greatest pleasure of all".

The complete happiness and love that has been given to me by my darling wife, has made my whole existence perfect. May God bless her...... always.

As I come to the finale, or as we say in the business, "Who goes best time". I think of the words I used to sing in Cochran's "Tough at the Top" written by Sir Alan Herbert. Say it all :-

> *This is not the end, it is but a beginning.*
> *When the fight is lost, there's a fight worth winning.*
> *Nothing is wasted, nothing is in vain.*
> *The seas roll over, but the rocks remain.*
> *They can break man's happiness, but not man's will.*
> *Little lamps of liberty, will smoulder still.*
> *Till the trumpets sound and we break the chain,*
> *And the wings of the spirit ride the free air, again.*

SLOW CURTAIN.

HIGHLIGHTS. of CLIVE STOCK

1938. Selected to go to Lords with a possibility of playing County Cricket for Middlesex.

1940. Won the London Junior table tennis championship. then played for England.

1941 joined insurance brokers in Lloyds as junior broker.

1942. presented concerts for the Red Cross.

1943 Appeared for IVOR NOVELLO in the West End where I started to learn the rudiments of acting, lighting and production. 43/44 5 West End Musicals in 20 months. Joined the RAF

1945 Singapore and shows with Kenneth Williams, Stanley Baxter, Peter Nichols, John Schlesinger, Peter Vaughan.

1947 Representing Royal Air Force against the Army at cricket, scored 133 my highest batting score.

1948 Appeared in the original "Oklahoma" at Drury Lane, and met my beloved Gwen Overton (the first British leading lady of the show)

1949 Married Gwen and originated two roles in C.B. COCHRAN'S last musical "Tough at the Top" renewed from 1944, association with Wendy Toye. Appeared in live television pantomime with Jack

Hulbert. Film part in the film "The Small Back Room" by Nigel Balchin, directed by Michael Powell.

1951 Starred in the original production of "Brigadoon" in Australia and New Zealand. Played Grade A tennis and created Brigadoon cricket team.

1952 Played cricket against RAY LINDWALL & KEITH MILLER and scored 60, and then played the comedy lead in "Brigadoon" in New Zealand.

1953 Created double act with Gwen Overton in summer show for Sandy Powell. The act being established for 37 years. Played minor counties cricket with Sussex.

1954 featured at The Gaiety Theatre, Ayr for the first time. and then to Torquay for pantomime for Salberg.

1955 The tragic fire at the Gaiety Theatre, Ayr, Gwen calls fire brigade, Booked for the Edinburgh Festival at the Gaiety Leith for three weeks, went on for 15 weeks.

1956 Our son Richard was born. Double act was split, so did series on television for 13 weeks, A.T.V's Treasure Chest. impressions of old time stars.

1960 Became Director of The Theatrical Profession Service with Jack Train, Michael Powell and Sir Tom O'Brien.

1962 Three seasons at the Arcadia Theatre, Llandudno.

1964 Played County Cricket for Caernarvon.

1965 starred in cabaret on board the "Queen Elizabeth" and "Queen Mary" with Rawicz and Landauer. Continued career in the after dinner world in London. More summer shows Eastbourne, Clacton.

1969 Became partner with Robinson Cleaver and devised and produced "Showtime" for 12 years.

1973 Became member of the Grand Order of Water Rats. Captain of Llandudno Cricket Club.

1975 Elected Chairman of the Concert Artistes' Association.

1976 Gwen and I back in the Arcadia, also took on the 2000 seater Pier Pavilion, Llandudno.

1977 Became Managing Director of the Bunny Baron Organisation, so with my six theatres added to Bunny's seven, Now responsible for the productions in 13 theatres.

1978 My partner and I buy the Palace Theatre, Morecambe.

1981 Became the first manager of the Aberconwy Conference Centre together with the Arcadia Theatre for the County Council.

1987 Returned to performing as the Court Sherriff (a designation that Ken Dodd was responsible for) in a

13th Century Castle as host and producer of the original Welsh Medieval Banquet.

1989 Appointed Senior Grand Warden of the province of Surrey. Elected President of the Rotary Club of Llandudno. Elected President of the Llandudno Cricket Club.

1990 Became manager of KEN GOODWIN.

1996. Fire in Chester...lost ALL possessions

1998 Appointed Senior Grand Warden of North Wales.

2001 Resigned from Ruthin Castle

2002/3 Booking KEN GOODWIN in cabaret and cruises, booking cabaret in the Llandudno hotels including personal after dinner speaking.

Been married nearly 54 years, although they said it wouldn't last

Major highlight A wonderful son and daughter in law.

3 Grand children and 3 GREAT Grandchildren.

In the year 2003. 76 not out.

ACKNOWLEDGEMENTS.

My sincere thanks to all who have helped me to compile facts and figures, after the heartbreaking fire in 1996.
Diolch yn fawr.

Special and grateful thanks to all our friends in Australia and New Zealand. United States of America,   who sent Press Cuttings.

Personal thanks for all practical help to :-

ALAN BARHAM   PETER HEPPLE.
JUDITH PHILLIPS.   DOUG McKENZIE.
KAY STOCK. KERRY STOCK. LINDA CECIL.
GWENDA WILKIN. MAURICE WEINTROUB.
HUGH GOLDIE. NORTH WALES WEEKLY.
PATRICK NEWLEY.   JIM KENNEDY.
THE ENTIRE WARBURTON FAMILY.
ROY HUDD and TOMMY EYTON JONES